Blake
Thompson
5/27/17

Met @ New River
Gorge Canyon Rim
Visitor Center

When Gauley Ran Blood

Rock D. Foster

HEB, 12:1-2

A Civil War Novel
by Rock Foster

For book orders contact:
Rock Foster
4401 Route 31
Somerset, PA 15501

E-mail: rock@lhtot.com
Homepage:
http://www.lhtot.com/~rock/

First Printing August 1999
Second Printing April 2002
Third Printing September 2005
Fourth Printing December 2009

Library of Congress Catalog Card Number: 99-90744

ISBN-13   978-0-9673546-0-6
ISBN-10   0-9673546-0-9

Printed in the United States of America
Chelsea, MI

Dedication

This book is dedicated to the author and finisher of my faith, Jesus Christ, and to my wife and lifemate, Joan Elaine Miller Foster, who came into my world to love, support and assist me according to His script. These two have stood beside me in spite of my many faults (and edits). May the success of this endeavor be credited to these who deserve it and to whom I am forever indebted.

To Chris and Becky Hughes, my great-grandparents, who will set me straight when they pick me up on the ferry that crosses the Crystal Sea.

To Sergeant Issac Prottman Hughes, 36th Virginia Infantry, Confederate States of America, who has crossed that ferry and will not have died in vain.

To my family who insists to this day that everything is relative.

Acknowledgements

Thanks to historians that have kept the flame burning; Terry Lowery, Tim McKinney, David Phillips, Gary Walker, Ruth Cornell, Bonita Bell, Carol Bell, Shirley Grose, and Virginia Fletcher, whose work I sincerely appreciate.

Thanks to my niece, Cindy Murphy Morris, who pricked my ancestral conscienceness which inspired this project.

Thanks to my friend, Donald (Greg) Gregory, who kindled my interest in hillbilly history.

Special thanks to my primary editors:

Dr. Ed Brandner	Sally Martin
Elaine Foster	Tim McKinney
Jean Wells Foster	Dr. Bill Ramsey
Rev. Kerry Johnson	Russell Richter
Charles Martin	

Thanks to my many supplemental editors, contributors and friends who encouraged me to "go on with it."

Karen Abdiroglu	Phyllis Mrosco
Flora Backus	Dale Ramsey
Marie Hughes	Dr. Richard Seecof
Annie Johnson	Debra Weible
Bill Metzger	Margaret Young
Candise Miller	David Zielinskie
Joseph Miller	

When Gauley Ran Blood
by Rock Foster

Table of Contents

When Gauley Ran Blood
by Rock Foster

Maps

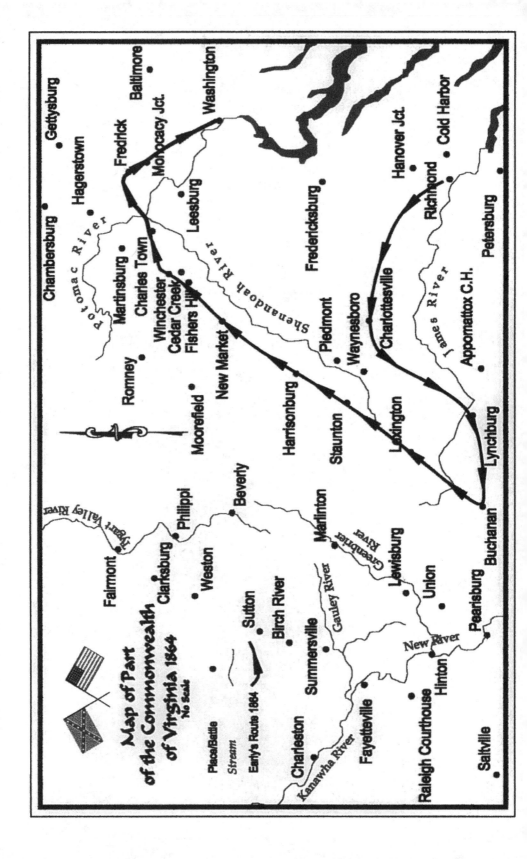

Map of Part of the Commonwealth of Virginia 1864
No Scale

Place/Battle
Stream
Early's Route 1864

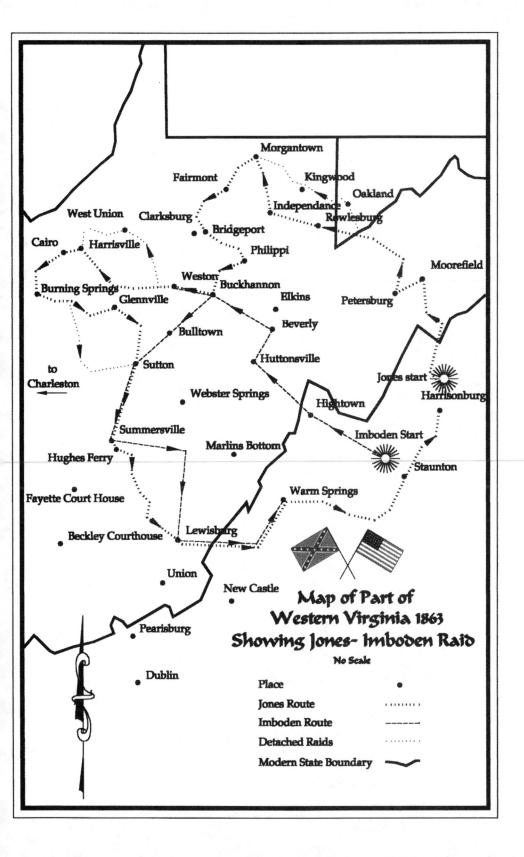

Map of Part of
Western Virginia 1863
Showing Jones- Imboden Raid

No Scale

Place	●
Jones Route	....
Imboden Route	– – – –
Detached Raids	. . . . . .
Modern State Boundary	⌐‾⌐

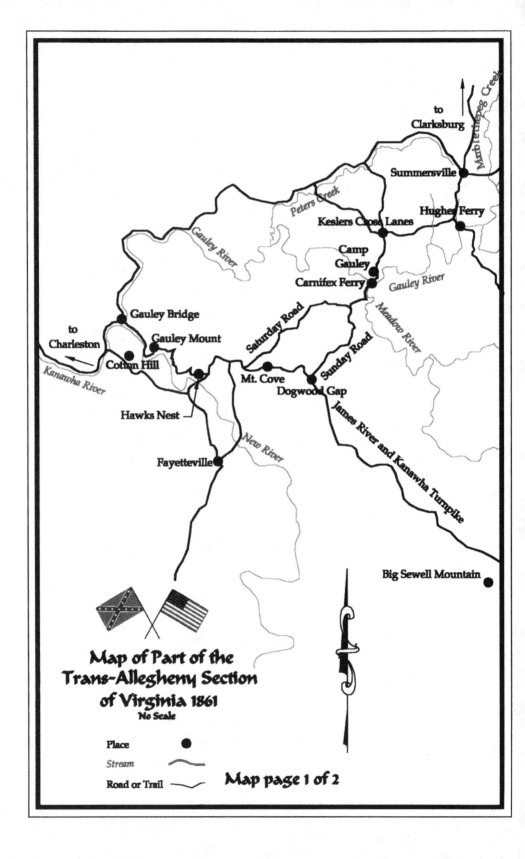

Map of Part of the
Trans-Allegheny Section
of Virginia 1861
No Scale

Place ●

Stream

Road or Trail

Map page 1 of 2

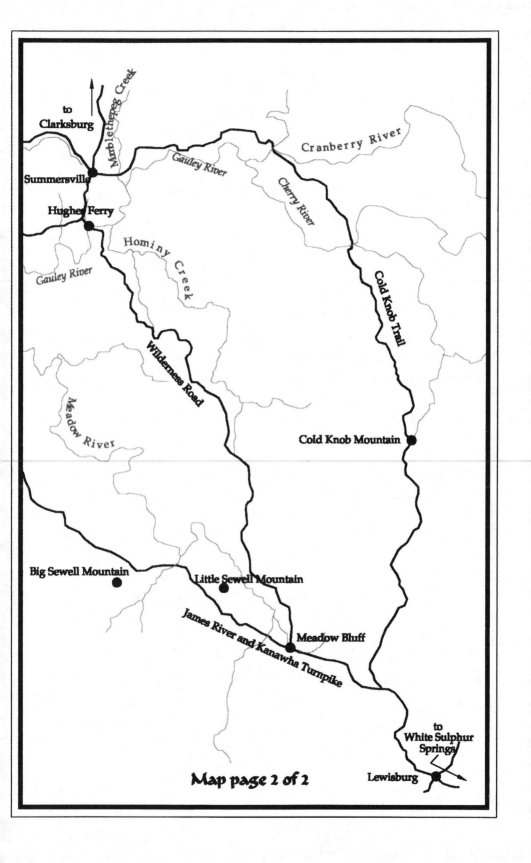

Map page 2 of 2

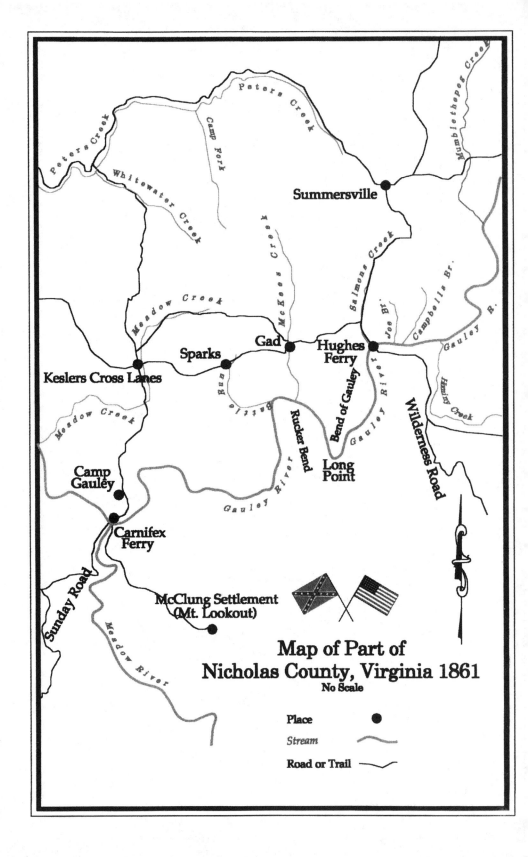

Map of Part of
Nicholas County, Virginia 1861
No Scale

Place ●

Stream

Road or Trail

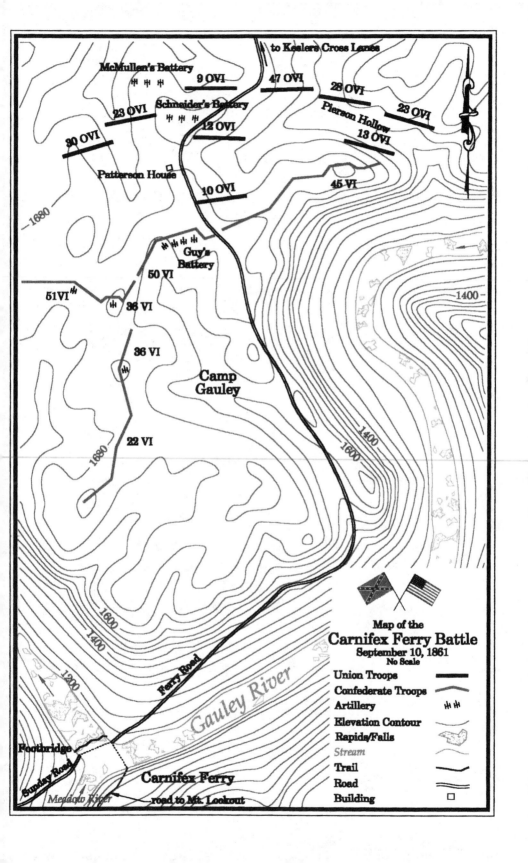

Map of the
Carnifex Ferry Battle
September 10, 1861
No Scale

Union Troops	
Confederate Troops	
Artillery	⚞⚞
Elevation Contour	
Rapids/Falls	
Stream	
Trail	
Road	
Building	□

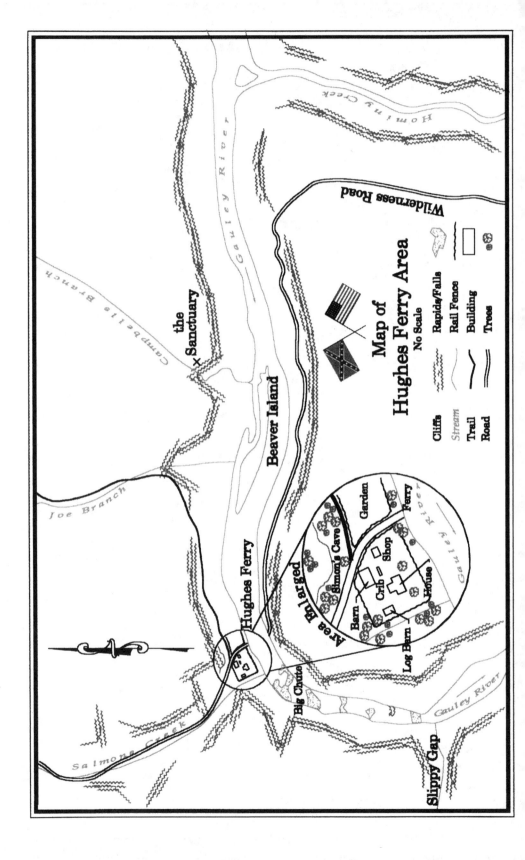

Map of
Hughes Ferry Area
No Scale

Cliffs
Stream
Trail
Road

Rapids/Falls
Rail Fence
Building
Trees

Wilderness Road

Hominy Creek

Gauley River

Campbells Branch

the
× Sanctuary

Beaver Island

Joe Branch

Hughes Ferry

Area Enlarged

Big Chute

Salmone Creek

Slippy Gap

Gauley River

Barn

Simon's Cave

Garden

Ferry

Log Barn

Crib
Shop

House

Gauley River

Preface

At mid life, I discovered a two hundred year old family heritage and quickly became consumed with the pursuit of the study of my ancestry. I had contracted the infamous "history bug".

While I was in pursuit of genealogical information at my Aunt Margaret's home, my cousin Becky asked if I had heard the story of the meeting of our great-grandmother and her namesake, Rebecca Jane Hughes Hughes, and our great-grandfather, Christopher Columbus Hughes. She informed me that Aunt Margaret had first hand information on the subject in that she had lived with her Grandma Becky for the first thirteen years of her life. I was fascinated as she explained how the couple had met during the Civil War on the family run ferry that crossed Gauley River near Summersville, Virginia, (now West Virginia).

Becky was a young mountain girl and Chris was a Confederate soldier in the 22nd Virginia Infantry Regiment. As they became acquainted, the relationship blossomed. During a trip across the Gauley on the ferry, Chris asked Becky if she would wait for him to the end of the war. She agreed, and after years of patiently waiting, he returned to her having participated in some of the most deadly battles of the conflict. They were married on November 29, 1866.

As I continued to study Chris' life, faith, family, the activity of his regiment, and incidents at Hughes Ferry during the Civil War, I realized that this was a story that had to be shared with others. My unorthodox presentation of fact and fiction is for the entertainment of the reader.

If you study the Civil War you soon discover the methods used at that time to record history. These records were often in the form of letters, personal diaries, written or telegram orders, and battle accounts recorded by participants. I have utilized or created these same forms so that you might experience the mode of communication during that period of time.

Before you discount what you read as fiction, maybe you should first consider the facts. I encourage you to check out the bibliography and to dive into the river of history for yourself. You may come away dripping with astonishment.

When Gauley Ran Blood

The battleground was left to the memories of the men who had fought and died there. The fields were plowed with furrows created by cannon balls. The seed that was sown was the dry crusted blood of brave soldiers both North and South. It would take four more long years before the harvest of peace would come to the nation. A new state would be born, but the price of bearing this offspring of the war would be the tears of those mourning their lost.

Chapter 1
A Bridge with A Soul

Rebecca sat on the porch in her rocker on an unusually warm day in early November 1919. Her mind was prone to wander but for now she was only recounting the events of the day. It had been a quiet but good visit at the gravesite. It seemed like an appropriate time to visit an old soldier's grave even if he was a hero of another war. Armistice Day he called it. Celebrating peace in the "Big War." Her Chris had once met Woodrow Wilson, the one that started the holiday, long before he was President when he was just a child in Staunton. That was a long time ago, 1864.

The new tombstone was a nice addition to Chris' gravesite. The old C.C.H. chiseled out on the footstone six years earlier at his death looked patriotic, but the new marble stone, though small, stood distinctly in the churchyard. Its backdrop was a harvested cornfield. They had placed a small Rebel flag on a pole above the rounded lettered slab. Rebecca had laundered his tattered chestnut uniform and best white shirt and had placed them atop the stone as if he had entered the grave for a mere change of clothes. She had kept them since their marriage in 1866. After nearly fifty years together, she longed for him to fill them again, just one more time.

His hat was missing ... no... there was no hat. He had worn his hat for years after the war until it was just a rag. He finally lost it to a brush pile fire at Dave and Gussie's when it was swept from his head by a pine bough right into the glowing coals as he was adding to the heap. Their daughter Gussie insisted on buying him a new one. He would forget his loss at times and point at the non-existent bullet hole in his new hat when he reminisced about the war. He and John Halstead, one of his old captains, would talk way into the night, winning every battle to the glory of the Confederacy and the 22nd

1

When Gauley Ran Blood

Virginia Infantry ... even the ones they lost.

Others had been at the grave before they arrived. There were fresh flowers with not one wilted leaf. Who would remember an old soldier this long after his death? He'd been dead over five years.

"Mum, 'bout time to go?" her son Dick said. "Lizzie and the kids need to get back to the house. She's not up to par today, needs her rest. Could you take some of the kids this evening? The little ones always vex her so. She loves them but she just can't keep up with them. I think it's Harry's and Anna's turn."

Rebecca just smiled and Dick helped her into the wagon loaded with his pregnant wife and six children. The forty-minute ride home across Gad Hill had been made many times by the family going to and from church. The tree-covered hills were gray with an occasional flash of lingering red leaves on the sugar maples. The occasional breeze held wisps of cold fall air that drew the children together in the wagon for warmth. Rebecca could feel her grandchildren edge against her rear hanging from the back of the small wagon seat when they huddled. Just like her kids used to do when she and Chris carted them to church. When the breeze passed they would go back to their places along the sides of the wagon. The Methodist Episcopal Church South they called it, after the church split. She and Chris had some of their best talks traveling to and from church. They loved to talk. The ride provided them the opportunity without too many distractions.

Dick and family, minus Harry and Anna, got off the wagon at the farm at the top of the hill on the land Chris and Rebecca had given them. Rebecca lived on up the road about a half-mile in the old home place she and Chris had built many years earlier. Harry, who had just turned nine, jumped into the seat beside his grandmother anxious to get to drive the wagon.

Dick shouted as Harry whipped the reigns against the horse's back, "Harry, don't forget to fix those rails behind the shed. Anna, do what your Grandma Becky says. I'll be up in the morning to get you."

As the wagon rounded the curve she could see Chris' features in her grandson's face. She longed for her mate. She quickly swept a tear from the corner of her eye as Anna maneuvered into the wagon seat.

When Gauley Ran Blood

She clung to her Granny's dress to keep from bouncing from the seat. Little Anna, a thousand questions ...but entertaining like her grandpa had been. It was mid afternoon when they arrived home. Time for Anna to burn up some energy.

Anna stuck out her feet and bent her head back toward the ground and then pulled her feet quickly beneath her and drew up her head as she twirled beneath the rope swing which hung from a branch in the sugar maple. As she pulled in her limbs she could feel the air moving faster and faster around her with her dress flapping wildly as she spun like a bobbin being loaded with thread. First clockwise then counterclockwise she would go until at last the swing would stop its rhythmic rotation and with a final back and forth wobble attempt to unseat its occupant.

Anna stood up from the seat to be met with the swirling that continued in her head so she promptly plopped back toward the board seat. As she grabbed for the rope that suspended the seat, her hands slid along the lines and she felt the burn of the rope into her small fingers.

"Granny, Grann-eee" whined Anna as she ran for the old lady in the rocker on the porch of the unpainted and graying house.

"What have you done, child?" asked Rebecca.

"My hands are a burning, Granny," cried Anna.

"Let me see 'em, girl." Rebecca said as she softly took her granddaughter's little hands and gently rubbed her coarse wrinkled hand across her palms and then blew on them.

"There now that'll make 'em better." Rebecca blew on the hands as she set Anna on her lap.

"We'll rub bacon on 'em if the sting don't stop. That takes the burn away for sure. How did you do this to yourself, anyway?"

"That old rope on the tree swing, Granny."

There beneath the sugar maple was suspended the same heavy hemp rope that had once danced along the Gauley trailing the ferry. After the steel bridge was built across Gauley River in 1903 there was no work for the ferry. The flatboat had sunk into the sand and Rebecca's brother Virgil, who was the last ferryman to operate it, gave Chris the rope because he asked for it. He brought the towrope to the farm to

3

keep somebody from taking it. It had hung in the shop for years until Harry and his older brother Christopher had asked permission to make a swing from part of it. While Chris was alive he never wanted the rope cut. Rebecca never asked but she thought she knew why. She let her grandsons build their swing after Chris had passed away. Might as well get some use from it, she thought.

"Bout time that old ferry rope stopped causin' me grief!" Rebecca spoke under her breath as she continued to console little Anna.

"What's a ferry, Grandma Becky?" asked Anna.

"Its a boat with a rope attached that people used to get across the Gauley," replied Rebecca.

"Zat da same as a bridge?"

"Well, a ferry is a bridge with a soul, girl. A bridge stays put and a ferry moves back and forth from bank to bank by the ferryman a-pullin' on the rope. He puts his soul into it. That rope on your swing is one of the last ropes used at the ferry before the bridge was built. I used to help your Grandpa Chris and Uncle Virgil and even my dad afore Chris and I were married. I've burned my hands many times on ropes like that, just like your burn."

She looked at her wrinkled but soft white hands as she rubbed Anna's and remembered the day they were as hard and callused as any roustabout's from tugging on the ferry towline. Many times as a young girl she had pulled a wagon and four-horse team across the Gauley River on her dad's ferry. She had done it a time or two when the Gauley was in the low brush. When the raging Gauley was in high tide not even the strongest of men would dare attempt passing even an empty flatboat without a horse and towline.

Times were hard then, especially during the war.

She was much too old now to be complaining but Becky, as they called her back then, knew her youth had been taken from her. She had been forced because of the times in 1861-65 to grow-up fast and smart. She had not been given privilege because of her beauty, although she was handsome for a woman, but because she handled herself with true respect. Her father and mother had both drummed it into her head. You must make people respect you. Their message had not been

4

directed as much to her but at her five brothers. Becky had been taught right was right and wrong was wrong.

She had heard Madison Hughes, her father, say it a thousand times, " To have any respect you gotta make a man respect ya."

He lived this credo. Whether building a new flatboat or serving passengers on the ferry he always demanded respect, and usually got it.

Becky helped her father at the ferry during her early teens and during the war while her brothers fought or hid. She gained knowledge most women of her day did not possess. She was born with a keen mind and her father helped her develop business savvy. This is where Becky learned her debating skills. She could banter the legs off a piano stool.

People of all types traveled the Wilderness Road between Summersville and the James River and Kanawha Turnpike heading for Fayette Courthouse, Lewisburg or Meadow Bluff. When they got to the Gauley it was a ride on Hughes Ferry or a long walk up stream to Brocks Ferry at the mouth of Mumblethepeg Creek or downstream to Carnifex Ferry at the mouth of Meadow River. Not many were willing to go that far out of their way and had to pay the price or barter their way across.

Had it not been for Becky during the war, the ferry would have had to fold. She helped her dad like a son. Her four older brothers had moved from home. She and her younger brother Issac Prottman Hughes, Prott, they called him, were the only children left at home. Prott joined the Confederate Army early in the war and had spent little time at home and naturally couldn't help very much. Her father had been a workhorse in his youth but middle age had not treated him well. It wasn't that he was ill or even that old but his back often went out and that left him as helpless as a newborn deer. Her mother, Mirriam, who was several years older than her spouse, was not physically able because of her age to do the heavy work required at the ferry. When she wasn't delivering babies for women in the community, she spent most of her time keeping house and working in the family's vegetable garden, especially during the summer. The ferry required only moderate strength most of the time but when a "Gauley washer" came through, passing rains from the Yew Mountains to the east, a large Belgian horse would struggle to tow a loaded ferry across the current of the coffee brown torrent.

As Rebecca rocked in her chair with Anna's head on her bosom she closed her eyes and faded into a half sleep. An old favorite poem ran through her head again and again. It was her most loved poem written by the English poet Thomas Dunn English during his travels in America. She had committed *Brown Waters of Gauley* to memory years earlier. It, like the river, was fresh in her mind:

> *The waters of Gauley,*
> > *Wild waters and brown,*
> *Through the hill-bounded valley,*
> > *Sweep onward and down;*
> *Over rocks, over shallows,*
> > *Through shaded ravines,*
> *Where the beautiful hallows*
> > *Wild, varying scenes;*
> *Where the tulip-tree scatters*
> > *Its blossoms in Spring,*
> *And the bank swallow spatters*
> > *With foam its swift wing;*
> *Where the dun deer is stooping*
> > *To drink from the spray,*
> *And the fish eagle swooping*
> > *Bears down on his prey-*
> *Brown waters of Gauley,*
> > *That sweep past the shore-*
> *Dark waters of Gauley*
> > *That move evermore.*
> *Brown waters of Gauley,*
> > *At eve on your tide,*
> *My log canoe slowly*
> > *And careless I guide.*
> *The world and its troubles*
> > *I leave on the shore,*

When Gauley Ran Blood

I seek the wild torrent
And shout to its roar.
The pike glides before me
In impulse of fear,
In dread of the motion
That speaks of the spear-
Dread lord of these waters
He fears lest I be
A robber rapacious
And cruel as he.
He is off to his eddy,
In wait for his prey,
He is off to his ambush
And there let him stay.
Brown waters of Gauley,
Impatient ye glide,
To seek the Kanawha,
And mix with its tide-
Past hillside and meadow,
Past cliff and morass,
Receiving the tribute
Of streams as ye pass.
Ye heed not the being
Who floats on your breast,
Too earnest your hurry,
Too fierce your unrest.
His, his is a duty
As plain as your own;
But he feels a dullness
Ye never have known.
Be pauses in action,
He faints and gives o'er;
Brown waters of Gauley,
Ye move evermore.
Brown waters of Gauley,

When Gauley Ran Blood

My fingers I lave.
In the foam that lies scattered
Upon your brown wave.
From sunlight to shadow,
To shadow more dark,
'Neath the low bending birches
I guide my rude bark. Through the shallows
whose brawling
Falls full on my ear.
Through the sharp, mossy masses,
My vessel I steer.
What care I for honors
The world might bestow-
What care I for gold
With its glare and its glow,
The world and its troubles
I leave on the shore
Of the waters of Gauley,
That move evermore.

As majestic and serene as any of God's wonders Gauley could turn ugly. It's not that the river was always that mean for at times in early fall you could walk across it at almost any shoal. The water would be as clear as a looking glass. When floods passed through it created mayhem. It was the huge rocks and boulders in the river and the virtually horizontal white and gray sandstone cliffs forming the river basin that posed the greatest obstacles. The cliffs ran for miles on both sides of the river. Where there weren't rocks and boulders of barn size proportions there were lengthy eddys of deep flowing water. The rocks and boulders, in conjunction with the raging water, created formidable rapids and deathly falls. These were not soon forgotten by the family and friends of their unwary victims.

There were few gaps in the cliffs where you could safely pass through that coincided with a crossing point on the river. The gaps that existed were filled with the most hateful laurel and rhododendron patches. A man dared not enter them without a lantern for fear of not passing through in a day.

Hughes Ferry was one of those rare places where a low gap met a somewhat docile stretch of river. It was located in a small eddy at the mouth of Salmons Creek that flowed into the Gauley from the north. The high cliffs that defined the Gauley basin followed up the Salmons Creek's valley on both sides until they disappeared into the hillsides. The creek followed the "V" shape of the valley and provided enough level bottom to pass a poorly constructed road adjacent the stream toward Summersville some three miles distance. The road meandered at a steep grade with the stream to the river bottom. At that point it leveled through the green narrow fertile bottomland to the north abutment of the ferry. A trail branched just before the ferry and ran upstream along side of the river.

The south landing was located just below a long yellow-brown sand bar. The road took a sharp left as it passed over tree roots and rocks and traveled along the base of the cliffs for several hundred feet. It then gradually made its way up the tree and laurel covered hillside through a series of breaks in the great boulders that replaced the sheer rock faces at this location. Fiddler ferns grew there as high as a man's chest.

The south road forked a short distance from the ferry with one path going on up Gauley for a half-mile to the mouth of Hominy Creek that flowed in from the south. The other fork known as the Wilderness Road made it's way south along the divide between the Gauley and Hominy Creek. It passed up and down the hills and valleys eventually reaching Meadow Bluff some miles away.

The Gauley narrowed at the ferry to a stones-throw width. On the north shore a path led upstream along the river. A narrow belt of rich farmland wormed its way between the path and the river up to the mouth of the Joe Branch. Becky's family had farmed this property for years raising corn, cane and vegetable crops.

The mouth of the Joe Branch was a fisherman's delight for catfish, bluegill, trout and suckers. This was the family's mainstay during hard times. Suckers were ugly, but an empty stomach didn't mind kissing them. Beaver Island, covered with large sycamores, willows, papaw and driftwood, extended upstream from this confluence; and paralleled a long deep eddy that stretched on up the river to the mouth of Hominy Creek across the river.

The five-cent fee for a man's passage across the river could be traded for everything from a plump hen to a small pig. A four-horse team and wagon could fetch seventy cents or a sack of cracked corn or flour. On one occasion Becky became the owner of a sway-backed mare named Maude.

Becky always started at high stakes with her trades. Depending upon her family's need at the time and often the needs of the customers she would adjust her demands as necessary. Many times she passed people and even teams without charge because times were hard and neighbors or weary and worn out travelers just didn't have the fare or something for a trade. The only part of Becky bigger than her gift of gab was her heart. A family in distress could crumble her hard crust. Becky was always helping out her friends and neighbors because she knew it was right and that they too would be there if her family needed aid.

Becky made it a point to dress as shabbily as possible and often wore an old hat of her father's over her auburn hair. When she didn't have a gray cotton dress on she wore a pair of her brother Prott's linen trousers. She was wise to the things that could happen to a young attractive woman absent of her protective siblings. She had her admirers. She cleaned up well but for work at the ferry she became as homely as a molting duck. There was a young woman inside that body. Nature would not let her forget it however much she desired to hide it. She wondered sometimes what it would be like to have a man. At times she could almost feel the touch of a strong hand against her face.

Anna shook Becky's head by her cheeks with her hands as she interrupted Becky's thoughts, "Are you asleep, Granny? Somefin's wrong cause I been talkin' to you and you just staring at that old swing."

"Granny's O.K. honey, just thinking. How 'bout some supper?"

When Gauley Ran Blood

Anna jumped from her lap and started toward the front door. Becky stood from the rocker. The bible she had been reading earlier had become lost in her dress. It fell to the porch floor and out flew a newspaper clipping. It was from the *The Nicholas Chronicle*, Summersville, West Virginia, and was dated January 9, 1913;

Christopher Columbus Hughes

The subject of this sketch, Christopher Columbus Hughes, was born in Roanoke County, Virginia, February 1836. He died January 5th, 1913, living to be nearly 77 years old. "Uncle Chris" had been in good health, for one of his age, until a week before his death when he was stricken with pneumonia.

He was a member of the M. E. Church, South, for 40 years, and lived an exemplary Christian life. In early life he was united in marriage to Rebecca J. Hughes. To this union were born seven children, all of whom with his aged wife are left to mourn the loss of a kind husband and father.

During the dark days of '61-'65, he cast his lot with the boys in gray where he served until the close of the War. The writer has heard him spoken of by his old comrades as a true man, a good comrade and a brave soldier.

May we keep green his memory and emulate his example. To the bereaved friends and relatives, we extend our heartfelt sympathies.

> *"The muffled drum's sad roll has beat*
> *The soldier's last tattoo;*
> *We'll meet no more on life's parade,*
> *That brave and fallen few.*

11

When Gauley Ran Blood

On fame's eternal camping ground,
Their silent tents are spread;
And glory guards with solemn round
The bivouac of the dead.

A Friend

Becky was never really sure of who had placed the tribute. Perhaps written by his dear friend, Captain John Halstead, or one of the Nicholas Blues or Mountain Cove Guards who had also served beside him in the 22nd Virginia. It could have been one of the Mountain Rifles of McCauseland's 36th. They knew her Christopher and the pain of that time. She could never forget how she had met her life's companion in a struggling time. There was love in her bosom but there was evil in the hearts of men. What a time it was . . . how could she ever forget?

Chapter 2
Business as Usual

It was August of 1861. It had been an unusually rainy year but today the sun shined intermittently through the white puffy clouds. There was heavy dew on the green grass that sparkled in the warm sun. Becky tied off the ferry to the metal ring in the large scaly sycamore tree that stood near the north ferry landing. She removed the heavy board railing that resembled a section of a corral fence from the front of the ferry and hung it on its storage posts to the left side of the road path.

The driver lashed out at his brown and cream colored oxen with a poplar sapling whip and yelled in a deep raspy voice, "Get up. Get up now! Get up!"

The oxen sprang awkwardly from their sleeplike state and jerked across the end of the ferry flatboat and onto the landing and then into the soft shallow mud with their burden in tow. The oxen grunted as they came under the weight of the load. There were a dozen sacks of fresh ground corn on that wagon, now minus one. Last year's corn was nearly all gone and this wagonload was of great value. The new crop would be ripe in about a month so the man was anxious to sell the balance of his crop. He was most likely headed for the Union army garrisoned at Summersville.

"Thank ye, Sir," spurted Becky as the man lashed out again at his animals and continued up Salmons Creek toward Nicholas Court House or Summersville as most people now days called it.

She had seen the man before but this time he appeared to be different . . .to be upset. He had told her how the sesechs, or those that supported the secession of the South from the Union, had taken one of his cows for food and promised to pay him fifty dollars the same day. It had been two weeks and he had not seen

13

them since. They had all but stolen his cow in the name of the Confederacy. Accounts like this were becoming more and more prevalent each day. It was difficult for the sesechs to provide for their army. Weapons were hard enough to supply, but daily food requirements of an entire army in such a God forsaken backwoods as this were impossible. Many campaigns were fought with provisions taken from the land. Interpreted into layman's terms this meant the army would take and plunder as much as possible from the local populous. These things were taken from the mountain people of western Virginia who broke their backs raising fruits, vegetables, grains and livestock attempting to eek out a meager subsistence. Union forces who were usually better supplied by their army also took their share of plunder.

The war in western Virginia was in full swing below Gauley Bridge where the Gauley and New Rivers formed the Kanawha. Armies were new at this game, but they worked hard at developing efficient methods of killing each other and most anyone else who got into their way.

Federal troops from Ohio had driven the Rebs, who were waiting for reinforcements and proper supplies, back into the mountains. The war was growing ever closer to the ferry, and troops under General George McClellan and General R. E. Lee were about to fight battles that would decide whether the North or South would have military rule over the Trans-Allegheny section of Virginia. One of the Wheeling, Virginia, papers was editorializing about a new state to be formed of citizens of western Virginia who were loyal to the Union. They were going to call it the state of Kanawha.

Everyone knew of the Federal troops in Summersville. Rumors were circulating that General Floyd's Confederate troops had crossed Gauley downstream at Carnifex Ferry and were encamped on a mountaintop near the Henry Patterson farm. Thank goodness only scouts from the troops had been seen at the ferry to this point. Some of them could be a real nuisance. They were always in a hurry to get their reports back to their various armies and didn't have time to waste on idle chatter. When they realized the ferryman was in reality a woman they sometimes pushed friendship beyond Becky's comfort zone. She could however take her part.

Becky walked back to the faded gray wooden ferry and placed one foot on the front of it and with a high step jumped to the plank that served as a walkway along the edge of the flatboat. She could make out the outline of a large catfish swimming in the shadow of the flatboat and thought what a fine supper he would make. She bounced her hand along the top of the side railing as she walked the thirty feet to the rear of the boat. There she attempted to lift a sack of grain, but to no avail. She had bargained the grain from the man she had just carried over the Gauley. It was her first full sack. Usually a half to third bushel was the bartered price.

People were in a hurry these days. They didn't want to be delayed by a ferryman's bargaining on the roads that were perpetually visited by bands of bushwhackers. Becky had used this as maybe an unfair enticement for the man to settle. In the end, the man now knew what those friendly to the cause of the South were capable of, let alone the ruthless bushwhackers that sometimes called themselves scouts or government agents. They wore no colors of allegiance, but their own, and at an unwary moment, they would shoot you and leave you for dead to take your possessions. There was evil in the hearts of men. Little did Becky know how her life and the lives of her family and friends would be affected by this rebellion. It seemed that no one could escape the evil vortex. Their lives had been hard, but placid, to this point. Strange things were about to happen in their mountainous Eden. By the end of this Sunday, a chain of events would begin that would impact the remainder of their lives. Normally, the family would have attended church and then come home for a fine lunch, but now there were no services. There was nothing to come home from. People argued so much. It often came to blows. Christian people were acting like heathens. There was evil in the hearts of men. People looked for fault in everyone, but themselves.

Becky grabbed the top of the grain sack that had been gathered like a ponytail and tied with a short length of twine. She dragged the sack to the end of the ferry along the plank and with a hard tug brought the sack over the edge of the ferry and into the rut that had been formed by the recently unloaded wagon. She pulled the load up the rut to the end of the railing and yanked it to the side clear of the road. As she started to roll the sack onto a horse sled they used for moving items on the farm, a voice from up the path which paralleled the road called, "Need some hep, Beck?"

The voice startled Becky as she looked up to see her father making his way down the sandy grass lined path which led from the house. She only glanced a fraction of a second, but her break in concentration under such a burden caused her feet to slip in the fresh mud and she found herself lying on her stomach in the mire. The only thing that saved her face was the ponytail of the sack she had been pushing on.

"Father!" cried Becky, " You scared the life right outa me!"

Becky did not want to show it, but she also was overly aware of people who traveled the roads. The ferry had been spared to this time, but at that moment powerful men were making their plans.

"I told you this morning I was going to recaulk that corner seam in the flatboat afore it gets to leakin any worse," said Madison, as he stretched a piece of hemp between his hands with an outward motion. "Why girl, you're jumpy as a hop toad. I think you need some time. Why don't you go visit Amanda, she always is a tonic for your spirit."

"Well, Dad, there's too much to do around here. I can't go takin off. "

"Get out!" barked Madison. "Don't you think I can handle this place? I was here a long time afore you. Need I remind you that I built this ferry? Why, your brothers and me cut and sawed up the very trees this ferry is made from. Why, if I can make it I can surely tend it? Why its business as usual for me. Go. You might want to clean up a bit afore you go." He raised his eyebrows jokingly and chuckled.

Enough had been said and Becky admittedly had not seen Amanda Ramsey but one time since her marriage to Nicholas. She was a dear friend and distant relative and Becky was anxious to hear about married life. Becky caught her thoughts and rephrased it in her head ...she meant about how they were getting along.

First, time for her weekly bath. It was a cool day for bathing, but the sun came out periodically and heated things up.

When Gauley Ran Blood

She normally bathed on Saturday for church the next day, but with the advent of the war and the suspension of services, she sometimes waited the extra day. Besides, she often swam some during the week and often didn't feel a need for cleaning up. She missed her friends at church. That is where she had met Amanda. Yep, she missed church and that good feeling she always had after the circuit preacher gave his message. She didn't know if there would even be a revival service that fall. Her church always had good revivals, but with the congregation split over the secession issue, who knew?

"I'll be at the Big Chute bathing if you need me before I go," stated Becky as she rose from the end of the ferry with a small flat stone in her hand. She used the stone that resembled the end of an egg turner to scrape some of the mud from her clothing.

"Maude threw a shoe yesterday so I'll be a walking to Cross Lanes to see Amanda and may be late getting home," said Becky as she started up the path to the house for a clean dress and drawers and to bid her mother good-bye.

"Careful bout snakes at the Point," he cautioned her. "Heard that rattlers are bad this year. Steward killed a big one in the crack. Said it almost got 'im. Seven rattles and a button. Big around as your fist." Madison knew that Becky's nearly six-mile walk would take her near the Long Point of the Bend of Gauley River.

"Keep a snake stick close by." Madison had taught her to "feel" her way with a walking stick when traveling through rocks or high grass in hot snaky weather. "Better them strike a stick than yourn leg. You are my only girl and I don't want to lose ya."

She was headed for the Big Chute. The Big Chute was just that. Amid house size boulders and a nearly deafening roar almost the entire Gauley was strained between two large blocks of sandstone. The water backed a short distance from the top of the falls before it jumped eight feet to the bottom. The resulting crash was like calamity meeting catastrophe. Whitewater met whitewater. There was a nice pool below the falls that was bordered on one side by large randomly placed boulders and on the other side by a yellow-brown sandy beach. The surrounded pool was a nice private place for a late summer swim.

17

When Gauley Ran Blood

The lower end of the hole was trimmed by another massive rock that towered 20 feet above the pool. Where the rock met the water an overhang jutted out several feet into the pool. The concave roof of the overhang provided a submerged room that acted as an air pocket beneath the water. A swimmer could dive into the pool above the falls and ride the chute plunging into the foaming liquid below. After a short swim to the edge of this rock, you could walk with your hands over your head pressed against the bottom of the rock to the air pocket. The swimmer would then emerge into the pocket and stay indefinitely by holding a small ledge that ran along the side of the rock. Periodically the air supply would be refreshed by a lapping of the waves against the side and bottom of the overhang. She and her brothers had spent many summertime hours as children swimming and playing at the Big Chute.

Becky slid out of her muddy clothes, dabbed them repeatedly in the water's edge and rubbed them between her hands to remove the dirt. The water, tainted by the cloudy mud, slowly moved downstream and disappeared into the current. She spread her clothes out on a large stone to dry while she dropped into the water above the falls. As she had done hundreds of times in the past she swam for the falls. As she felt the pull of the falls she stopped swimming, took a final gulp of air and let the water pull her over the falls into the soft torrent below. She surfaced and swam immediately to the sandy beach. She had a long walk ahead of her to Amanda's house and regardless of how good the water felt she had to hurry with her bath. Standing in knee deep water with her back to the shore she swept her hair with her hands to the back of her head and dalloped a handful of very fine sandy mud against her arm and shoulder and rubbed. With a splash of water to remove the old, she would place a new layer of the muddy sand and rub. She was about to repeat the process again when she heard a high pitched cracking sound above the drone of the river.

"Daddy, is that you?" asked Becky as she waded to her neck in the water to hide her nakedness. Only the splash of the river answered.

When Gauley Ran Blood

"Who's there?" she paused and listened intently. With one hand across her chest she used her other one to shield her eyes from the glimmering sun as she looked toward the bank.

"Who's out there?" she repeated. A grip of fear seized Becky.

Then she heard a continuing snap followed by a sound that reminded her of a sack of feed being tossed on the ground followed by a deep guttural "Ohoo...ooo!"

With that sound she was into the river and swimming like a fish for the other side. She knew someone or something was right behind her. She had the presence of mind to consider the submerged room below the pool, but she was well into the river and the current was pushing her toward the opposite side. If she could only get to the boulders on the other side, she could make good her escape. With her last two strokes she inhaled mouthfuls of water and began coughing as she exited the water. She darted behind the closest rock and she thought she only heard her own splash. She rounded the second huge boulder and clung tightly to it so as if to hide herself by blending into it. As much as she wanted to be quiet and hide, she couldn't help herself and coughed repeatedly blowing a fine spray against the rock. She painted a picture of a cough on the rock as she walked by blowing her spray against it. She began running again and came to the place where her clothing was left. She slid through her clean brown dress and pulled it down over her hips. With an eye over her shoulder, she picked up her still wet laundered clothing and shoes and took to flight again back up the river toward the ferry.

The closer she got to the ferry the more reservations she had about what had just happened. Why had the ghost given up its prey? What had she really heard? Were all the stories about the bushwhackers making her delusional? What if her dad thought there was something out there? Would he let her travel to Amanda's? Becky by now had convinced herself that nothing was there. After all, she was 18 years old; she had no time for children's fantasies. It was only in her head. She rounded the corner of the house and at that moment a huge form engulfed her. Becky struggled for her breath!

"Dad...dy!" Becky spoke in a broken tongue. "Oh... Daddy."

"Needed more hemp for the boat. I thought you were goin to Amanda's?"

Becky thought on her feet, "I had to bring my clothes back to the house."

"Are you feeling alright? You're white as a sheet. Looks like you still have a little mud on your neck."

"Fine Daddy, but I gotta go. Love you. Tell mother I will be late," uttered Becky as she threw her clothes across the line that was stretched from the two posts that held up the roof of the porch. In the blink of an eye she took off around the other corner of the house. She was on her way to Amanda's.

From the ferry she could head downstream to the Slippy Gap, a hollow which provided a break in the cliffs, and then up to the top and out along the ridge known as the Bend of Gauley. The Bend of Gauley was a two-mile long ridge that was situated interior of a giant bend in the river. The Gauley, nearly flowing south below the ferry, made an almost 180 degree turn back to the north at this bend.

The Long Point was a 250-foot high sandstone cliff that stood at the vertex of the bend in the river at the end of the ridge. The river could be viewed nearly a mile in both the northwest and northeast directions from this "long point." This huckleberry bush covered stage provided a breathtaking view of the cascading river below. The view was as if you were on a bird's wing observing the green tree covered "U" shape of the Gauley River valley below. The high gray and white cliffs intermittently breaking through the emerald colored trees was truly a treasure to behold. It was Becky's favorite view. The road to Gad was a more direct route to her destination by horse but she always went to the Long Point when she was walking anywhere near it.

It was a tiring climb but the walk along the heavily forested ridge top was much easier than the up and down over and around nearly impassable river route. It was also faster. She paused to enjoy the view from the top of the cliff only long enough to glean a half dozen handfuls of the finest marble size huckleberries into her scarf. When she left the top of the Long Point, it was magic how she entered a laurel hidden, leaf covered natural ramp a short walk from the end of the abyss and a few seconds later emerged from the base of the cliffs. Interior of the Long Point was a maze of cracks and crevices, sloping rock falls, ledges and boulders. Knowing the direct route took one only a minute to traverse the zigzag passage. For the unfamiliar that had to check out each crack and crevice for a passage it could take 15-20 minutes to get through. From the exterior it appeared as a solid massive sandstone formation with a small crack showing here and there.

During the warmer months there was always the ever-present threat of the yellow and black timber rattlesnakes. The Long Point was well known as a breeding ground for nesting rattlers. The smaller reddish-brown colored copperheads that dotted the riverbanks below were not as numerous in the Long Point as their also poisonous cousin. Becky hated snakes.

Today, as Madison had reminded her, before she entered the Long Point she picked up a dead limb that resembled Moses' staff. She really didn't feel the potential for snakes was that high but she saw no reason to take an unnecessary risk. Besides, Becky hated snakes.

She held the limb in front of her and felt the ground as she made her way through the cliffs. Some places were lit and she could see. Others were dark, so she used the probe ahead of her hoping to attract the deadly fangs away from her legs or other vital body parts. That was just in case...

It was easy going until she hit the bottom of the Long Point. Then she heard it and froze on the spot! The unmistakable sound of rattlers! She could see and hear them so they didn't have to strike the limb. Two, maybe three, big ones perched on a narrow head-high ledge were catching the recurrent sun through a break in the forest, compliments of a fallen tree. Her path sloped down past the ledge. Had they not sounded so that she could hear and then see them, they could have easily struck her in the head or neck. God was certainly with her today.

What was she to do? Her guide stick began to shake uncontrollably. Becky's heart pounded in her chest as she slowly backed away from the ledge. As she rounded a crevice back into the darkness to retrace her steps to the top, she felt the stick jerk in her hands. The tug nearly caused her to spill her huckleberries from her scarf that was also clasped in her hand. The rod had been pulled between two rocks that trapped it. A small knot on the rod was caught and slid the pole from Becky's hands onto the dark floor of the passageway. As she groped the floor of the crevice for the stick, the rattling sound came much closer but from a different direction.

Becky finally contacted her weapon and stood up into the light to be greeted directly in the face by one of her predators coiled between a crack in the rock. Her immediate response was to shield her face with her hand and in so doing met the snake with a scarf full of huckleberries. As she attempted to free the dangling serpent from the scarf clutched in her hand, she made an upswing at it with her staff. Her blow freed the snake from her scarf but the rod went with it. The snake and rod flew toward the ledge containing the stirred-up vipers. They struck with vengeance. First the snake and then the rod. Becky at full panic dove past the ledge containing the snakes as if diving into a pool in the Gauley. She stirred the leaves as she hurriedly cleared the final opening in the cliffs. She dusted her dress, grasped her lifesaving huckleberries and continued her hike as though nothing had happened, just business as usual. Her bouncing heart and dry mouth told a different tale.

From the base of the cliffs she would travel back down through the pine and laurel along a narrow, boulder lined path to the Gauley again. She loved the song the river played as it slapped its water against the rocks and pools of a thousand sizes generating a never ending roaring crescendo. With the sound of the Gauley ever present, she would make her way to the run that came from the hollow which held the community of Sparks.

The path now followed along the nearly dry streambed and the sounds of the Gauley faded as she continued up the valley past a half dozen small cabins and houses with their little barns, outbuildings and pasture fields. Right to the head of the hollow she marched as her path intersected a well-defined road that led from Gad to Cross Lanes. As she crossed the rolling hills and finally entered the wide valley, she could see the intersecting roads at Cross Lanes and, on the overlooking hillside, Zoar Chapel. The

When Gauley Ran Blood

Meadow Creek valley consisted mostly of small farmhouses and numerous fields that were now nearing harvest. Her friend lived in a small cabin just over the hill from the church. The road to the south led to Carnifex Ferry. The road to the north went up Meadow Creek and eventually looped back to Gad. A short distance up this road a fork led down Whitewater Branch to Peters Creek.

Becky arrived at the cabin and knocked on the door and yelled, "Amanda? Amanda? It's Becky."

There was no response. She tried several times, but to her disappointment, no one came. The six-mile jaunt had tired her, and she sat down on the porch for a brief rest before she started back to the house. It was mid afternoon and she would have plenty of time to get back before dark. She placed her scarf that contained the berries beside her as she lay back on the porch and looked up at the blue sky. When the sun shone through the clouds the heat felt good on her face. The tired girl dozed for an instant but thought this is no way for a lady to act and raised up with a jerk. Becky looked down the lane that snaked its way to the house through a labyrinth of fresh tree stumps and could see the figure of a woman carrying something in her arms. Yes - it was Amanda's form. Becky ran toward the figure. Amanda was crying as Becky hugged her.

"Easy, Beck, the baby!" Amanda scolded between the sobs.

"Baby!" exclaimed Becky. "Has it been that long since I visited? Why it seems like you were just married."

It was at that point Becky looked at Amanda's tear swollen eyes and realized from her countenance that her friend was at the brink of total despair. She knew she would have to approach her friend compassionately. Becky's heart took over.

"May I see your child?"

"His name is William Hance Ramsey, Hance like his dad's, Nicholas Hance." Amanda exhaled and slowly passed the precious blanket clad lad to Becky and immediately commenced to weep again.

"His father is gone! Went to his dad's two days ago and hasn't returned. He said he would be back that evening. I just know something terrible has happened. He has fallen from a rock and drowned, or a rattler got him. He has never done this before. My brother and his friends are out looking for Nick now. I just know something bad has happened."

"Now, you don't know that. Just quit talking that way. Come, I think this boy needs fed. Let's go into the house and you can tell me all about married life. I mean... about how things are going. I can hardly wait. I have a thousand questions," soothed Becky as she tried to distract and console her young friend while holding back her own tears.

Becky knew of the human animals that were preying upon the unaware traveler but dared not hint of it to Amanda. The cold fear that grew from her thoughts could not be revealed to her friend at any cost. She had to be strong.

Amanda told Becky that on one trip down to the main road she had seen blue uniformed soldiers milling around in the Meadow Creek bottom. Her Nick, who like his dad, Riley, was opposed to secession, was a loyal Unionist.

"They wouldn't have any reason to hurt Nick, " she told Becky.

The two women talked continuously through the afternoon hours with Amanda pausing frequently to pull back the lace curtains from the front window and peer down the lane to check for Nick's arrival. It rained intermittently, and Amanda placed a small copper kettle near the table to catch the drip from a roof leak. Their conversation was interrupted only by a brief time during which they took turns praying and asking God to safely return Nick to his waiting family. The couple enjoyed a supper meal of pumpkin and fried mush with fresh huckleberries. Amanda fed Hance before putting him to bed and the girls continued their visit. The shadows were growing long when the sun was not behind a cloud. Becky knew her friend needed her desperately and decided to spend the night; besides, she was anxious to see Nick again. Her folks would be worried, but she could leave first thing in the morning and be back to the ferry by way of the road from Cross Lanes to Gad to Salmons Creek by early light. This was something she had to do, and they would understand. She wasn't a child.

As Amanda lit the oil lamp and placed it on a small table by the door, a knock sounded from the door that startled her and caused her to appear to run in place. Becky grabbed for a piece of firewood by the hearth. They were calmed by the sound of Amanda's brother's voice.

"Anybody home? Mandy girl, you in there?"

Amanda opened the door and her brother, who was in a hurry to get home himself, did not come in but informed her that the men had given up for the day and were going to resume their search in the morning. No sign of Nick was found he told her. What he didn't tell her was that an army of Confederates had moved in on the Patterson farm just above the river at Carnifex Ferry. He knew she was worried enough. In a wink he was off to his home and family.

The young women talked until the clock had chimed 12 and they made their way to the heavy straw tick in the small loft of the house for the night. Becky lay with her eyes closed but only dozed a few minutes during the night. She tended to Hance twice catching him just as he began to cry. Amanda appeared to sleep through the child's crying obviously exhausted from two days of worry for the safety of her spouse.

Before first light that Monday morning Becky was about starting a fire and fixing breakfast. It was damp and the heat of the fire felt good that morning. She used a piece of wood to push the water kettle suspended from the pot iron into the flames. A quick trip outside to the edge of the house and a shoo of her hand yielded three hens' eggs. The chickens, disgruntled having been disrupted from their sleep in their earthened nests built beneath the house, flew in all directions cackling as they went causing no little disturbance. The ruckus awakened both Amanda and Hance. Hance aired his Ramsey lungs and all were fully awake by the time Amanda arose and put him to her breast.

"Want to sell one of them chickens?" a deep gravelly voice spoke to Becky.

She turned to see a bearded man with a large belly in a blue uniform approaching the house. He was carrying a rifle across the top of his shoulders like an ox yoke. Becky had never seen a soldier before and was quite taken by the attractive uniform and flash of gold on the leather billed kepi hat.

"They're not for sale mister," spewed Becky as she started for the door of the house.

"W-e-l-l in that case I guess I'll have to just procure one in the name of the Union Army of the United States Government," the man stated boldly as he leaned his gun on the last stump closest the house. He then began to stalk one of the hens that had positioned herself near a square rock that was used as a foundation pillar for one corner of the house.

"Keep away from my chickens!" cried Amanda as she closed the door behind Becky and dropped the heavy crossbeam across the door to lock it.

The man made no further comments but continued to pursue his prey beneath the elevated floor of the house. The fearful women could see the dark outline of the soldier through the cracks in the floorboards as he crawled on his hands and knees attempting to catch an unwary chicken. All the chickens cackled each time he missed one. This continued for several minutes until the man removed his jacket, threw it like a net atop one of the hens and carefully gathered it around the feathery captive.

"Got-ya!" chuckled the man as he crawled toward the edge of the house.

"Hum..." hummed Becky. "We'll see about that."

She quickly grabbed a towel and picked up the water kettle that had started boiling in the stone fireplace. Her head bobbed back and forth as she located the now white shirted intruder between the cracks in the boards. The man, still on all fours, paused to duck his head beneath the end foundation log. Becky looked at Amanda and then down at the floor. Amanda nodded her head in the affirmative and Becky poured the steaming liquid on a crack in the floor just above the Union soldier. He bellowed like a hound dog caught in a bear's jaws as he scuttled from beneath the house dropping his coat and reaching for his butt crack which protruded above the back of his wool trousers and through his long johns.

"That ain't no way to treat a private of the Union Army of the United States Government!" shouted the man as he commenced to tuck his blouse back into his pants. "I'll have recourse and you can bet on that!"

The chicken had bounced about in the man's coat until it had wedged itself in the sleeve at the cuff. It looked like a giant blue eel with a red head jumping from a pool of dark wool as it struggled jumping up and down to finally free itself. In its last jump, it obviously strained its bowels and blew a white and green starburst pattern atop the man's coat as it exited the trap. The girls peered through the window and could not help but chuckle in spite of the threat.

The soldier, realizing that he had had enough and needed to regroup for the time being, grabbed his coat and rifle and retreated down the lane toward the main road grumbling something about the Union Army of the United States Government. It was just business as usual with the Union Army of the United Sates Government. The girls laughed until they cried.

Becky fried salt bacon and eggs in a large iron skillet over the fire. She placed a cup full of corn meal in the remaining boiling water and made a day's supply of mush. She wanted Amanda to have a good meal before she had to leave for home, but Amanda only stirred her plate to make it look as if she had eaten. She didn't want to hurt Becky's feelings for the effort put forth. They shared the dishes and then Becky kissed her friend and little Hance and started home.

"Don't worry. Nick will be home soon. You'll see."

When Gauley Ran Blood

Chapter 3
Crossed Lanes

Becky thought to herself as she turned the corner at the end of the lane and started down the main road toward home. The dust in the road had turned to mud and there were large mudholes in places that looked like creamed coffee. She walked at the edge of the tall grass to miss them. She had so many questions. Where did that soldier come from? What if he comes back for vengeance against Amanda? Where is Nicholas? Why hasn't he come home? Is there something Amanda is not telling me? Why was the world becoming so complex? Why did there have to be war? She was tired and that helped her anxiety soar.

"Stop or be shot. Give the sign," came a voice from nowhere. "What say ye?"

She was dumbfounded. What should she do? Who was speaking to her? Was it the soldier?

The voice sounded again, "Give the sign. Can you give the sign?"

"I don't' know who you are or where you are or what kind of a sign you want me to give. I do know I don't like this type of sport," answered Becky.

A man in a blue uniform with a rifle emerged from behind a blind of corn stalks placed in the field beside the roadway. A light fog also helped to blur his form.

"Why I bet you're a sesech, missy," spoke the soldier. "You a sesech spy sent to scout our camp from those Rebs at Carnifex. We hardly get here, and you start spying us out."

Becky could tell by the sound of the man's voice he was not fooling as she originally suspected. His clothes looked wet and soiled. His face was wind burnt and his eyes were wrinkled from lack of sleep. He squinted constantly. His uniform was nearly identical to the soldier who had interrupted her breakfast. What had she done now?

"You will have to come with me, madam. See what the colonel wants to do with you. We don't take kindly to sesech spies," spoke the soldier as he pointed his rifle down the road suggesting she walk ahead of him.

Becky paused, turned and spoke, "I am not a spy. My name is Rebecca Jane Hughes. I have just left my friend's house after spending the night. I am on my way home to Hughes Ferry. What right do you have to tell me where to go? Where are you taking me? Did that soldier tell you we did something to him? Who is the colonel?" She assumed he was a superior officer.

"What soldier are you taking about? Did you hurt or kill one of our men? You'll pay with your life if you did!" said the man as he grabbed her arm and shoved her in front of him. "Just keep walking and don't talk, the colonel will get the truth out of you. He knows how to handle prisoners. He may even let us have a little fun with you."

She stumbled forward and threw her head up to keep from falling. She slid in the light mud in the road and came to a stop. Then she saw it. A Union military camp had moved into the cane field just below Zoar Church and west of the Vaughn residence at the road intersection. Many of the soldiers lined the road from the crossroads up the hill toward the church. She couldn't believe her eyes. There must have been 500 blue clad soldiers scurrying about their little gnat smokes cooking or warming themselves. Their weapons were stacked like fire tripods in little clusters through the grounds. A half dozen wagons could be seen, and at least two dozen horses and mules were tied to pickets and fence rails. Smoke from their breakfast fires congregated in a massive cloud that stopped and spread the width of the valley as if a glass pane had been placed in the sky to keep it from rising further into the fog that was slowly lifting. Zoar Church stood on the hill above the scene as though a casual observer. The Vaughn and Campbell homes were surrounded in a sea of blue Union uniforms. Becky knew both families and thought of running and seeking refuge at their doors. No, she might bring reproach from the soldiers against them. She would deal with her circumstances. She had done nothing wrong.

As the couple entered the camp and walked up the road toward the church, many of the soldiers stood from their crouched cooking postures and stared at Becky and her escort. Soldiers, who had been filling their canteens at the Vaughn well, ran behind the house and store to the rail fence to view the young girl. One soldier asked if at the point of a rifle was the only way he could get a girl. Another one jeered at Becky that he would like a turn. For an instant she and her guard became allies and walked together with stolid faces as if to disprove their implied guilt.

Many of the soldiers were pitiful. They were sprawled on rubber blankets along side the road and in the edges of the fields in their wet uniforms. The stench from four days of marching was sickening. Some of the men were so tired they were asleep sitting up Indian fashion in front of their fires that had gone out. Many were trying to dry their jackets by holding them over the fires. Fence rails served as fuel for the fires, but the previous night's showers dampened them so that they would hardly burn. They would squash coffee beans with a rock inside of their kerchief and place it in tin cups of boiled water and then drink the brew. Some of the fires had little iron frying pans with legs, called "spiders," setting atop coals set to one side of them. The men were cooking large ground up crackers called "hardtack" in what smelled like beef fat. They used this as gravy with their beef. Green corn from the fields was consumed in mass quantities. Those who were eating did not look to be overly enjoying their breakfast although they ate ravenously.

As they neared the church, Becky's companion told her to stop as he spoke with a man with a number of stripes on the top of his sleeve. That man entered the church and returned in short order and told the soldier that the Colonel would see him now. The soldier motioned with his hand toward the door, and Becky walked up the steps and through the door into a room where men were eating breakfast. A distinguished looking man sat in a caned chair near the pulpit. He had a long dark beard and receding hairline. He looked up as she entered and their eyes met. She immediately dropped her head. Her hair dropped in front of her face. She

31

wanted to hide. She was embarrassed in front of him and the group and could only stare at the floor. She had never been one to parade in front of men before.

"Colonel Tyler, I found this woman trying to get through our lines this morning. I believe she is a sesech spy and may have killed some of our boys," sputtered the soldier. "She ain't friendly at all."

"Good work, Private, you may continue with your breakfast now," commented the colonel.

"I'll see what she knows. It's early. We haven't hung one spy today," he said in jest.

"I wasn't having breakfast sir, I was on picket duty," replied the soldier.

"Who replaced you, Private?" questioned the colonel, as he stood to his feet obviously angered.

"No one, sir, I thought you would want to interrogate the spy since we have been looking for Rebs so long," stated the subordinate.

"You didn't leave your post, Private? Tell me you didn't expose us unguarded to the enemy?" implored the colonel. "Return to your post immediately, and at your first instance, tell your captain I seek an audience with him. What is your name, Private?"

"Private Hoople, sir," responded the humiliated guard.

Colonel Tyler shook his head, sat back down and pushed his plate away in disgust "You're dismissed. How do they expect you to run an outfit with greenhorns? We would be lucky to make it through this war with good soldiers in our ranks let alone these ignorant farmboys. Captain Berk, see to it that additional pickets on horseback are sent out further. See to it immediately!"

"Yes sir, Colonel Tyler," said the officer as he exited past Becky in a blur.

During this time Becky looked up and saw Nicholas Ramsey seated backward on a chair that had been placed to one side of the group. He was not in a uniform, nor was he eating like the other men. He saw Becky and nodded his head obviously not about to speak during the reprimand of the private. Becky felt relieved that Nick was alive. She didn't know if he was a captive also. She did know that God had answered her prayer. At that moment, she thought it strange that she would find him, of all places, in a church. Just like God to do that. On another note, she wanted to ask Nick why he was treating Amanda in such a way? How could he leave her and Hance alone? Gambling or cavorting, no doubt. Why, they were just married.

She didn't know Nick had been on a scouting patrol for the past two days with Colonel Tyler to the Peters Creek and Twenty-mile Creek areas west of Summersville looking for General Floyd's Confederate army. They had just returned to Cross Lanes the night before. Nick wanted to return home, while most of the men were starting breakfast, but the colonel asked if he would take a scouting party toward Carnifex Ferry before he went home, since he was familiar with the area. They had not had cooked food for over four days, only hard tack and jerky. Most of their supply wagons were still behind them and had not arrived at the camp yet.

Some of the soldiers foraged the countryside for a change of diet. Many of the men were totally exhausted and only wanted to crawl into a ball and sleep. They had been on the go for nearly 48 hours straight with little time for rest, let alone cooking.

"And just what business do you have in this area this time of day, Miss?" queried the colonel.

She pushed her hair to the side of her head to address him. Her mouth was dry and she could hardly speak. She tried to lick her lips but only tasted dry skin. All she could do was force an exaggerated swallow. The man in charge was perceptive of her problem and instructed the other officers to pour her a cup of coffee from the iron pot setting on a bench near the center of the room.

Nick stood to his feet and spoke on behalf of the young woman. "Colonel Tyler, I know this woman. Her name is Becky Hughes. She is acquainted with my wife. She is not a spy. I assure you sir. Her family runs the Hughes' Ferry on the Wilderness Road below Summersville."

Nick then addressed Becky, "Hello Becky. It is good to see you again. Are you alright?"

Becky nodded yes with her head as she took another drink of cold coffee. It didn't taste bad at all. Coffee was hard to get now. She had not had any for several months. The thought of this being her last cup entered her head. She had heard stories of the American Revolution from her grandfather Jeremiah O'dell about horrible interrogations of prisoners. Were they going to burn her face with a hot poker or drag her from behind a horse? She felt that was an extreme punishment for scalding a thieving soldier. If she was going to get it, she now wished she had done more to the fat scoundrel.

"And what were you doing in this part of the county at this hour?" questioned Colonel Tyler. "It would seem you are some distance from home. Have you been in communication with any Confederate troops?"

Becky swallowed and spoke, "I am Rebecca Jane Hughes. I have just left my friend's house after spending the night. I am on my way home to Hughes Ferry. I am not a spy, whatever that might be. I don't know anything about any troops. A soldier came to the house this morning and we run him off. I don't think he was happy about that. He was going to take Amanda's chickens."

She then turned and addressed Nick., "Amanda is sick to death with worry about you! Where have you been? Don't you care about your wife and baby? You can't just take off!"

Nick was about to respond in his defense when he was interrupted.

"It appears we have a bit of a mistake here, madam. I am so sorry if we have inconvenienced you this day. Mr. Ramsey has been at our aid the past few days sharing his knowledge of the local area. Mr. Ramsey, you will see to it that Miss Hughes gets home safely. Take horses so that you won't be gone long. I trust we will not have to come after you. We need your services later this morning. Please take care. There are reports of Confederate troops in this area. Outside pickets have been spotted near Carnifex. Madam, you should not be travelling alone these days. These are perilous times. Good day, madam, we have important work to do today. You will excuse us?" spoke the Colonel earnestly.

Now she thought her inquisitor was quite the gentleman. He wasn't bad looking either, for an older man, in his noble uniform with its sky blue trousers and dark blue blouse with a white shirt. She felt more comfortable and took another gulp. Then she simply stated, "Certainly, Sir."

Nick grinned and started toward the door. He took Becky softly by the arm. She wondered what his hurry was as she brushed her hair with her hand to the back of shoulder and tugged to straighten her dress. She placed the coffee tin on a back bench and made a final glance and smile at the colonel as they approached the door. They exited and walked down the steps from the church.

At once he began, "You've seen Amanda? Are she and the baby alright?"

"They are fine. She is so worried that something horrible has happened to you. Her brothers have been looking for you and couldn't find hide nor hair of you. You disappeared!"

Nick continued, " I stopped at dad's three days ago and he had the runs. The army needed someone familiar with the area. Dad and I agreed I could do as good a job as him. I have been with the colonel as a guide. I thought it was going to be for just one day. I didn't know it was going to be for this long. I came here to the camp and volunteered to show them how to go up Meadow Creek and over the hill to Peters Creek. When we got there, I started home. The colonel stopped me and said it was best if I stayed with them for a few days. He said he didn't want me getting any ideas about telling the sesech about their troop movements. I have practically been a prisoner myself. The colonel said as soon as I take them to Carnifex I can go home."

The two walked down the road through the camp and again Becky turned the heads of many of the men. This time she floated down the road. No comments were made in light of her now civilian escort. There was the sound of a rifle shot in the far distance that made the whole camp flinch at the same time. Most thought it was probably one of their men shooting game for breakfast, even though it was forbidden near camp.

They walked to the area of the camp where the quartermaster had temporarily set up his tent and Nick asked for two horses. The quartermaster queried under what authority he was requisitioning horses. Nick replied that the colonel had directed him to show safe passage for the lady.

When Gauley Ran Blood

Becky was beginning to feel embarrassed that so much attention was being shown her. In a womanly sense she somewhat enjoyed the mannerly way that she was being treated. This had never happened before. She had always had to take her own part, especially with five brothers. She thought she liked this.

"The last four fresh horses just went out with pickets on them. The rest are pretty well tuckered-out. Sorry I can't help you," said the quartermaster as he lifted his kepi and scratched his balding head.

Nick scanned the field and eyed a group of mules tied to a fence rail. "How about the mules?"

"They're wagon mules, but the one on the end is saddle broke. She hasn't had a saddle on for weeks. I don't know if she will work for you or not," stated the quartermaster with reservation.

"It will do fine. Throw a blanket on her and stick a bit in her mouth," voiced Nick.

The soldier complied with Nick's request. Nick jumped across the back of the animal and landed on his stomach. The mule took several awkward steps back and to the side testing her strange load. Nick righted himself and held down his hand for Becky. She took his hand and with a little run and jump landed astride the mule with her dress atop her face in a most undignified pose. She quickly smoothed her dress down in front of her between them and looked about to see who had noticed her mishap. She put her arms around Nick's mid chest and held on. She could feel the heat of his back against her. This was also something she had not experienced before. It felt awkward. She quickly pushed back and held herself away as far as she could in an awkward posture.

"You better hold on," Nick ordered, " this could be a wild ride."

Nick guided the animal into the field and then down the road toward Gad. The mule's gait was horizontal causing the two riders to jerk to and fro. Observers stared at the odd sight.

The Gad Road was level from the Cross Lanes intersection for a short distance, and then it gently curved its way up a hill called Malcolm Heights and down a short valley toward Sparks. A small bridge passed the road over Meadow Creek just east of the

36

When Gauley Ran Blood

crossroads. As the pair started up the hill, Nick saw soldiers in gray and butternut with rifles stalking along the side of the cornfields which flanked the road on both sides. He recognized the soldiers as Confederate troops. They were headed for the Union camp just past the crossroads.

Nick knew he had to avoid the soldiers. He was afraid they might shoot at him so he turned the mule to the right into one of the cornfields. As soon as he entered the field, a cannon shell exploded behind them, scattering dirt on their backs and causing the mule to flinch and start a full gallop. A series of explosions followed and intense rifle fire commenced. A bugle could be heard in the Union camp calling the men to arms.

Becky had a bear hug around Nick to keep from falling from her mount. She was familiar with horses from her youth and comfortable with bareback riding, but this exercise was taxing her limits. The mule remained in the cornfield and started up a hillside. From that vantage point, Nick could see a continuous line of color from the road at Carnifex to the base of the hill they were climbing. It was now clear the Rebels were attempting to attack Colonel Tyler's camp on both flanks. Nick could not see any opening in the lines because of the height of the corn. He could see the corn stalks below him moving in a wave as the army advanced. Most of the firing was from the troops along the roads where their sight was not obscured by the corn. How had he gotten Becky into this? How was he to get her out?

His only escape was to go back toward the Union camp and pray they weren't shot for sesechs. In civilian clothes their chances were not good. Many of the southern troops were without uniforms. This made anybody fair game for a piece of lead. Anything was better than trying to get through the solid skirmish line formed by the advancing Confederates. Nick guided the mule in a great semi-circle back toward the crossroads. As they approached just east of the intersection he could see the soldiers in camp dropping their knives, forks, tin cups and plates and scurrying for rifles and bullet pouches. He thought to himself that they would be fighting with their knives and forks. They had been taken completely by surprise while trying to eat their breakfast. The camp was in turmoil.

37

When Gauley Ran Blood

Lines were starting to form when he and Becky started back toward the intersection in front of the advancing Confederate army. Nick knew there was Meadow Creek to cross and had an idea. Meadow Creek paralleled the Carnifex Ferry Road that intersected with the Gad Road. If they could travel below sight in the creek bed, they might have a chance of escape. The corn also provided good cover.

When they got to the creek, they found it half way up its banks from the recent rains. Nick eased the mule into the water and started upstream back toward the intersection they had left moments earlier. The mule would slow when it waded into mud and sand bars in the bottom of the stream. Nick guided the mule up the creek and behind the Campbell house. Becky glanced at the home and there was no sign of life, but an upstairs drapery was pulled to one side of the window. Just past it on the other side of the road at the Vaughn house, she saw a young Union officer leaning against a porch post with his hand to his face. As they passed he fell forward as if the wind of death had drawn the life from him.

The sounds of the battle were like nothing either of them had ever heard. There were wounded men yelling for help at the top of their lungs. Officers were trying to rally their men. The Confederate charge was now synchronized with the horrifying Rebel yell. The deadening drone of shell explosions and rifle fire filled in any lulls. Tassels fell from corn stalks as minie balls clipped the plants as they headed for their fleshy targets. Smoke rings puffed from the Confederate artillery. Clouds of smoke from the rifles and shells were joining with the smoke from the campfires, the morning fog, and the rising red sun, to create a surreal sense of hell on earth.

Could this watery route be their source of salvation from certain death? Nick feared suffocation from the grip Becky now had on him. He squirmed and managed to get her arms below his chest so that he might breathe. The mule was splashing water up in front of them and made it difficult for Nick to see. He periodically ran his hand over his face to clear the water and mud so that he could see.

When Gauley Ran Blood

They reached the bridge and it was too low to go under so they had to stop. Nick yelled at Becky to hold fast and headed their mount out of the streambed and onto the Gad Road again. If they could only get ten feet to the other side and back into Meadow Creek, they would be out of danger. He knew the Rebs were advancing toward the intersection and that they would very likely draw their fire. As they started across the road, Nick could see that a small Union skirmish line was forming. The Union soldiers were finally returning some of the fire, but the ranks were not forming as they should and there was a great deal of disorder. A nearby rifle fired and the mule jumped straight into the air leaving Nick and Becky high in the air long after it had made its descent. When they landed, Nick heeled the animal, and it stood still as if frozen. It just stood there. Nick repeatedly heeled and slapped the mule with the reins, but it just stood there.

Becky, feeling as though she was having a bad dream, looked toward the Union line and saw a familiar face. For a moment, she felt comfort in seeing someone she thought she knew and then realized it was the stocky chicken stealer from the morning. He was rodding his rifle when he looked up and saw Becky. He smiled a broad smile with one upper tooth missing and then raised his Springfield in the direction of the two stranded escapees. Becky closed her eyes and thought, "Help me Jesus! " Then there was the sound of a rifle discharging at close range. Becky felt the mule lurch forward and opened her eyes to again see the aiming soldier now with his gun on the ground tearing at his clothing in a desperate search of the source of the fiery pain that possessed him.

One of the Rebels, making his way along the edge of the road, had made good his aim. She had never seen anything like this before. The fear on the wounded soldier's face shocked her with cold shivers as he fell to the ground continuing to tear at his now blood soaked clothing. The nurturing side of Becky wanted to console and comfort this man in spite of his deeds, but Nick seized the opportunity of his again moving transport to resume their escape. He guided the mule off the edge of the road and back into the stream on the opposite side of the bridge.

When Gauley Ran Blood

They were on their way again. Becky looked back across her shoulder and saw the wounded soldier slide into the water. She saw his blood mix with the chalk colored muddy water of Meadow Creek and head downstream for the Gauley. She threw up as they made their way to safety on up the creek.

Nick exited the stream onto the road that went up Meadow Creek. As he checked the road, there was nothing between them and the Union army at the intersection, but ahead of him was a retreating Union wagon. The road forked and the teamsters took the left fork which went to Whitewater Creek and then to Peters Creek. How appropriate that a Union outfit should seek refuge along Peters Creek. The stream had been named for a slave that had been left alone at a camp on its banks by his master to survive the winter.

Nick and Becky both breathed easier the further they traveled up the road along Meadow Creek. She loosened her grip on Nick. The battle continued but the sound faded as they got further away. As they passed the Halstead farm on their way to Gad, the battle sounds ceased with only an occasional rifle discharge.

Nick stopped at the Halstead place and spoke with Becky. He told her he had to go to Amanda. She was so near the battle. Becky was safe now and only a couple of miles from home. It was time for him to protect his family. He had been gone much too long. The Halsteads were friends with the Hugheses, and they could provide shelter if Becky did not want to try and make it home. Becky agreed wholeheartedly and slid off the side of the mule. She thanked him for saving her life and told him that he was a true friend and that she would be forever grateful.

Nick continued on the short distance to Gad. He would go from there on to Sparks and then on foot back to his house and the waiting Amanda. He wanted to avoid Cross Lanes at all cost.

Becky walked to the Halstead house. They had a beautiful farm. The corn grew tall in the bottom along the meandering stream. The house and barn sat at the base of a small hillside pasture that contained two huge maple trees that shaded the cows in the summertime. The Halsteads had gone to Becky's church and she was familiar with their son John. He was so handsome and

40

intelligent. John once told her that she was exquisite. She liked the sound of foreign languages and knew it was intended as a compliment. At one time she had an eye for John, but nothing had come of it. They were friends now. She shouted from the yard to rouse someone from the house. There was no response. Perhaps they had heard the battle and fled to the woods. She tried to raise someone several times and finally gave up and started walking for home. It was only mid morning, but what a morning.

As she walked over Gad hill, she pondered the events of the last twenty-four hours. She had not had so many cataclysmic events in her entire 18 previous years of life. She wanted to be strong, but right now all she wanted to do was to go home, to be with her parents again. The battle of knives and forks had been too much. The look on the wounded soldier's face, his frantic searching for his wound, and the sight of his blood mixing in the brook haunted her. It made her sick to her stomach. What evil was this that had crept into her quaint little world?

When Gauley Ran Blood

Chapter 4
Soldier Boy

What a dream that was, the soldier thought to himself. She was a goddess. She was Venus. Had God smiled on him today? Her auburn hair and rounded features rolled over and over and over in his mind. He longed to touch her white skin. It looked like bleached cotton. He knew he had seen what he should not. It had already happened. He could not undo what had been done or could he? He wasn't to blame. He was doing his job – his duty. Would he ever see her again? Surely he had been dreaming. He was unconscious again.

Chris rolled over onto his side on a flat rock along the bank of the Gauley. He didn't feel right. He felt like his guts were on fire and assumed his previous position on his stomach. In a half daze, he could see a dark red line running from beneath him toward the river. Was he still asleep? This was no dream. He raised up a little and put his hand to his chest. He looked down at his hand and saw the same dark stain. It was then that he realized he was hurt and hurt badly. He obviously had lost a lot of blood, but he didn't remember a sniper's bullet or the cannoneer's projectile.

Several days earlier his company, the 22nd Virginia Infantry, had been making their way from White Sulphur Springs, Virginia to join Confederate Brigadier General John Floyd's army near Meadow Bluff. General Floyd, a militarily inept political appointee, was attempting to cut off Union Brigadier General Jacob Cox, who was commander of the Federal troops in the Kanawha Valley, from Brigadier General William Rosecrans, who was headed south to join him with approximately 8,000 troops.

General Rosecrans, the commander of Union Department of Ohio, which included western Virginia, had replaced General

43

When Gauley Ran Blood

George McClellan, who followed his call to serve in Washington. Following the Union embarrassment at Bull Run or Manassas, General McClellan was placed in command of the Federal Division of the Potomac by President Lincoln to replace Major General McDowell.

Cox's outpost was at Gauley Bridge and Rosecran's base of operations was at Clarksburg. If Floyd could get north of Cox with a sizeable army, he could cut him off from Rosecran's support and drive him out of the Kanawha Valley. It was important to the South because of its salt producing capabilities and the access it could provide to the Ohio Valley. Once there, he could travel up the Ohio River to Wheeling and destroy the branch of the Virginia government that was trying to organize, that was loyal to the Union. This was the gist of Floyd's battle plan.

Confederate Brigadier General Henry Wise had just withdrawn from the Kanawha Valley having won a small battle at Scary Creek. A sizeable Federal force under Cox had advanced up the Kanawha River behind Wise's retreat to their current position at Gauley Bridge. Wise, a former governor of Virginia, was offended that General Floyd had been placed in senior command and therefore provided a minimum of cooperation. Chris' regiment had recently been placed under Floyd by orders of General Robert E. Lee. General Wise rested his troops at Meadow Bluff, while General Floyd was on his way to Carnifex Ferry. Wise would soon follow in that direction.

The Confederate army was naturally concerned about Federal troop movements to the south. The routes were limited, but they still had to be patrolled and watched to prevent the enemy from attacking them in the rear. A critical route south ran directly from Summersville and across Hughes Ferry via the Wilderness Road to Meadow Bluff on the James River and Kanawha Turnpike.

Chris had been in camp the day before, and a request for volunteers was made for special picket duty. The entire Cavalry had gone off on patrols and as pickets to various destinations from Gauley Bridge to Bunger's Mill. Any man who was familiar with a horse and able to ride was summoned to help with picket duty. Chris had worked with drafthorses on his dad's farm since he was a boy. Now at twenty-five there wasn't a team that he couldn't handle. Admittedly, riding horses was not his forte, but he had been walking for days. He liked the lay of the land in this part of the world and desired to see a little more of it. He thought a little change would do him good.

With the captain's orders to report back at the first sign of significant Federal forces, or to come back in two days, Chris and another soldier were off on their horses to watch the Wilderness Road and Hughes Ferry. It was customary that an officer of the day visit the outposts at least one time per day, but Chris was told that they would be too far down the Wilderness Road and that nobody would be coming to check on them. It took them hours to cover the distance. The countryside they witnessed was mostly virgin forest with a cabin and fields here and there. Vast acreage of huge virgin hemlocks that towered over the trail dwarfed them. There was a heavy blanket of hemlock needles that covered the land. At places, it even erased any evidence of a road passing through them. There were also damnable thickets of impassable laurel and rhododendron. The mountain streams, though scarce on top of the ridge where the road was located, were cold and clear. Small trout could be seen in the big holes where they stopped to water the horses. Chris liked it.

He convinced his younger companion, a mere boy, that he should cover the ferry since he was older and more skilled in the ways of soldiering. The boy would be safer away from the ferry. He left his comrade at the Hominy Creek fork of the road and continued until he was within sight of the Gauley. He dismounted and walked his stallion about a hundred yards from the road where he tied his reins to the base of a laurel bush. The laurel bushes provided good cover and the horse could reach a small drain where it could get water. Chris stuck the Colt dragoon the captain had loaned him in his belt. He took his rifle in his hand and quietly walked downstream a short distance from the ferry site to where he had a good view.

The never ceasing roar of the Gauley enchanted him. After spending several hours on guard, with the howling stream in his ears, he lamented that it was like a lion warning an adversary of its strength. All that energy going to waste. What a huge grist mill you could build here. Time slowed for Chris.

The ferry watch that evening and night was boring. He spent much of the evening in a tree watching the ferry site. The flatboat was tied to a tree on the opposite bank. A rope was stretched from one bank to another. You could see where the road disappeared into the river at the ferry landings. It was very distinct. There was a split rail fence along both sides of the road leading to the ferry on the north shore. The fence guarded a green pasture and barnyard on the left and a garden on the right. He could see the ferryman's gray weathered house and barn above the landing on the opposite bank. With nightfall, he came near the south ramp of the ferry and got positioned in the bushes so that if he were to doze, he would be awakened if there was any activity at the ferry. The ferry was located in a long eddy, and the river was not as boisterous there. He did nap once or twice during the warm summer night but was awakened by intermittent showers.

At daybreak, Chris' eyes were heavy. He took a hoecake and a piece of cooked beef out of his haversack and ate it for breakfast. He cautiously made his way down to the river and had a drink from a pool just below the first falls downstream of the ferry. He took this opportunity to fill his canteen. As it slowly filled, he thought how pretty it was there, and his mind wondered. Probably good fishing he bet. Little pieces of driftwood danced at the water's edge along the sandy bank of the river. Large rocks bordered the pool downstream and on the opposite bank. He was exposed, yet reasonably well protected from sight at this watering spot.

This river was nothing like the streams he grew up on in southwestern Virginia. Craig Creek near his grandfather's mill was the biggest river he had spent much time on. He had seen the New River at Pearisburg several times. It was a little more like the Gauley in size but nothing to match its ruggedness. He liked to fish and there was none better than Craig Creek. He had spent hours pulling in trout, youpine suckers and chubs during lulls at his grandfather's mill where he often helped. The mill was located on a small stream that emptied into Craig a short distance away.

When Gauley Ran Blood

He was Lewis Francisco's grandson. His strong willed German lineage was of a hearty breed. Lewis's father Ludowick had been a farmer, land manager, and had served as a captain in the Virginia militia of his day. Ludowick's father was the infamous Ludwig Christophel Franciscus of Pennsylvania and Virginia.

He had purchased land from an Englishman named William Penn. He moved to one of the first settlements in Lancaster County, Pennsylvania, known as the Conestoga Settlement on Pequea Creek. A famous type of wagon had been invented at the settlement to convey goods to and from Philadelphia. The story about "Olde Chris," as he was known, had been told many times by his grandfather.

"Historians said Kentucky had a Boone and Pequea a Franciscus. It was also said the current of daring runs in the blood of the Franciscuses. His sons, after him, and his son's sons, and grandson's sons have, since the old man's day, been known as stout men. They made many a fellow cry out. "

"Of Daniel Boone, the Kentucky adventurer, it is said, he slew a bear; of Franciscus and his daughter, it is related, they eviscerated a wolf, with a similar weapon, a butcher-knife." said Daniel Rupp, an author of that day. He went on to relate a newspaper account that appeared in the *American Weekly* newspaper in 1729.

At Conestoga, near the beginning of this month, a stout action was performed by Christopher Franciscus. He had gone to bed and soon after heard a great disturbance among his sheep, which made him suddenly rise and send out his dog, and later hasten after to his sheep pen, where a large wolf was alarmed and was leaping over the fence just as the careful husbandman got there. The wolf being delayed by slipping one foot into a cranny of the fence, the man had time, and resolution to take him in a strong grasp by the neck with one hand, and by the hind leg with the other, and so pulled him down; and shifting his hand from the wolfs leg to his ear, and forcing his knee on the struggling

47

animal's body, so held him without being bitten though very hard to prevent, because the trusty dog worrying at the wolf's hinder part, the more enraged him. Meanwhile the man had not neglected to call for help. He was heard by a daughter of his who had the courage and faithfulness to bring a knife and relieve her father by letting out the entrails of the wolf.

Chris thought of how exciting it would have been to wrestle a wolf, and then he thought of the courage that it would have taken to kill the beast with a butcher knife. Did he have that kind of courage? Would he respond courageously when called to do battle, or would he falter and fail? The knowledge of his lineage built his nerve. He felt empowered by his roots. He was no coward. He was fit and could handle himself as well as any man. He was of medium build but had broad shoulders. He had brown hair that he covered with a butternut colored felt hat and a short stubby beard that allowed most of his cheeks to show through. His eyes were unusual in that they were as bright as emeralds. Enough vanity he thought, I need to be at my post.

He returned to the tree that he had spent time in the previous afternoon. He laid his rifle near the base and climbed to a height that allowed him to see both landings of the ferry. He pulled himself up past one of the tree's branches and then sat on it. His feet dangled near a lower limb. Periodically he would hold tight to the tree and put his weight on his legs and stand with his legs bent to reposition his seat on the branch. The branch was not as large as he would have liked, but it appeared green and healthy and had not given any sign of yielding under his weight.

His wait was boring. He carried with him in his haversack a handfull of small fresh cuttings from a birch tree sapling. He enjoyed chewing the birch-flavored bark from the cuttings. He ate every one that he had. He now knew how a squirrel lived since he had eaten so much bark. Finally...activity. He heard something approaching the ferry from the south road.

The driver of a wagon, pulled by a team of oxen, rang a small brass hand bell that was tied to an ironwood tree near the south ferry landing to summon the ferryman. The wagoner was a local farmer most likely. He didn't look like someone who would have anything to do with the army. The ferryman brought the flatboat to the south side of the river and briefly talked to the wagoner. The wagon was loaded onto the boat and a sack of something was unloaded from it onto the ferry. The passage was then made and the wagoner continued on up the road toward Summersville.

The ferryman was a milksop, but then he wasn't very big. He couldn't even carry a sack of grain. He fell flat on his face when he tried to lift it onto a sled. Chris had carried many sacks of grain at his grandpa's mill near New Castle. Even as a boy he could handle a man's size load. Maybe he should offer to help the ferryman. He had never been one to sit idle when there was work to be done. At second thought, he figured it best if he remained hidden.

Chris was tapping out a jig on the lower branch with his feet when he heard a splash above the drone of the river. He flinched and grabbed for his Colt. The sound came from the river behind him and not from the ferry. At first glance, he thought it was a beaver swimming, but when the head of a person appeared out of the water, he didn't know what to think. He didn't move a muscle or bat an eye. He placed his hand on the grip of the pistol and left it there. The person swam downstream toward the sandy bank where he had gotten a drink.

"Lordy, it's a woman!" he thought.

He could tell from the length of her hair and well ... he was sure it was a woman. She was naked! Without a doubt the loveliest example of womanhood he had ever seen. In fact, it was the only woman he had ever seen *ala naturale*. She was standing in the water just out of his sight behind the foliage of a bordering tree. From his vantage, he couldn't tell exactly what she was doing so he stood on the lower tree branch and leaned out holding on to upper branches. She was thrashing about so he feared she might be in trouble, so he leaned out a little more to check on her... she was a woman all right. He sensed there was something wrong, not with her but with him. He had that feeling a person gets when they're about to participate in a horrible accident. His inactivity was being inundated with arousal, and his head could only swim. It was then that he realized he had gone out on a limb for this woman and couldn't get back to the tree trunk. Was he in trouble or not?

The trigger guard on his Colt, which was tucked into his britches at the waist, was now firmly hooked on a small dead broken limb on the branch he had been sitting on. Squirm as he might, he couldn't get the Colt released from the branch. He feared if he pulled too hard, he might drop the captain's pistol to the ground and damage it, or worse yet, cause it to discharge and blow his leg off. If he let go with one of his hands, he could try to free it, but wait, there was another way. With just a faint bounce, he tried to free the weapon. Just a little more ...a little more... and the limb he was standing on snapped. With split second thinking, he released his grip from the upper branches and flung himself across the limb he had been sitting on. That branch, determined to ignore the laws of physics, resisted for several seconds, a seeming eternity to Chris, the shear forces acting upon it. Then it severed cleanly from the tree. Chris could now remember flowing like candle wax over the side of the chair-sized rock that caught him just before he became unconscious. His picket duty was over for now.

He remembered. It wasn't a dream after all. His lips were dry and cracked. The lower one enormously swollen. He managed to pull himself to the edge of the water and drank from his hand. He felt his lip, and it was the size of his thumb. He could see blood dripping from his hand into the Gauley as he scooped up another handful of water. Then he splashed water on his head and face. It was cool and refreshing. He could feel his senses returning and also the pain. His face grimaced as he unbuttoned his jacket and shirt and viewed the two rib bones penetrating the flesh of his side. The wound had stopped bleeding. He knew he had to somehow get back to camp and find the captain. He reckoned that tree must have been a Yankee tree, because it had whipped him good.

Chris stood in amazement that his legs were not broken after the fall. He breathed in short spasmodic jerks. He managed to get back to his watch tree and fetch his rifle and hat. He started for his horse and made it as far as the road near the south ferry landing. He attempted to cross a barkless tree trunk, that high water had floated to a position adjacent to the road. He straddled it like a horse and that was as far as he got. His vision blurred and he slowly rolled back into the bushes, unconscious again. His rifle remained at the side of the road.

***

Madison twisted the hemp tightly and pushed it into the crack between the two boards in the bottom of the ferry near the corner. He took a wooden wedge and tamped the hemp out of sight between the boards with a wooden mallet. The caulk always pushed out at that spot because it was where the ferry hit the landing. It constantly needed fixing. He then took a Mason jar of pine pitch and with his wooden wedge smeared a dab of tar along the seam.

"That'll fix ya." said Madison as he unhooked the ferry and started into the Gauley to check out his patching job. He gave a couple of strong tugs on the ferry rope, and the flatboat glided freely across the water without any heavy load on board. He couldn't see the crack making any water and again complemented himself on a fine repair job.

"Ma-di-son, din-ner, come and eat before it gets cold," yelled Mirriam from the front porch of the house. She took down a blouse and pair of pants that draped from the clothes line on the porch and yelled again, "Ma-di-son, din-ner."

Madison stood erect and responded curtly, "I hear ya, I'm comin' in a minute. Just hold your horses, Maw."

He saw something out of the ordinary on the opposite bank. He pulled the ferry to the south landing and tied it to an ironwood tree. He walked a short distance up the road and saw a fine Mississippi rifle laying at the edge of the road. Upon examination it looked like a new one. It must have fallen from the gentleman's wagon this morning he thought. He looked at the grip and it appeared wet. He ran his hand over the grip and the faint color of blood rubbed off on his fingers. He now knew there was foul play afoot. He looked to the side of the log and saw Chris' hat. When he looked past it, he saw Chris in his helpless state.

Madison cocked the rifle and prodded Chris in the ribs. Chris raised his head and screamed as though he would die.

51

When Gauley Ran Blood

"Now that's enough of that, fellar," replied Madison. "You better hush. What's a matter with you, anyway?"

Chris rolled over to expose his bloody jacket.

"You been shot plum through!" exclamed the ferryman. "Are you gonna die? Who shot ya?"

Chris only shook his head and passed into the darkness again. Madison could see he was still breathing and decided to take him to the house to let him die. He dragged the man to the ferry and pulled him on board. As Madison pulled the boat across the Gauley, he screamed to Mirriam, "Maw, Maw, we got a wounded soldier boy. He's shot plum through and is gonna die! Fetch the horse and sled."

Mirriam scampered toward the north landing where the horse and sled were located. She must have said "Oh, my!" no less than a dozen times. "Is it Prottman? Is it Prottman? " she asked.

She arrived about the same time as her husband, and the two pulled Chris onto the sled and then took him to the house. She could see that it wasn't her son, Prottman. She breathed a sigh of relief.

"We'll make him comfortable till he goes, Maw. It's the Christian thing to do," spoke the compassionate older man.

"He's still got good color to his face, Madison. Maybe he'll be all right. Let's clean him up and see what the matter is."

Mirriam worked hard removing his blouse and shirt. She could see the nature of his wound now.

" He's not shot. His ribs are poked through his side. I can fix this one. He's just like Edward when that tree he was cutting fell on him. You rip this sheet into strips while I cook a mess of pigeon soup."

The kind lady worked over the young man as though he were her own. She missed her boys and didn't get to see them much since the war had started. She thought he was a fine looking soldier boy and some mother's son. If her boys needed help, she hoped and prayed that someone would be there to care for them. Her baby boy, Prottman, now a soldier in the southern army, was in her thoughts constantly. She wondered if this boy knew her son, and was anxious to ask him. She cleaned his wound and wrapped his chest as best she could. He had completely stopped bleeding. Considering the nature of his wound, this was a miracle.

Chris awoke mid afternoon and drank some soup. He then slept until around 9 PM. The couple had not gone to bed at dark as was their custom, but chose to sit by him and just watch him, as if that would help.

Becky hadn't returned. That wasn't like her. She could be headstrong at times, but she never caused her mother to have to worry. Mirriam knew Becky could care for herself, but things were changing in Nicholas County. Men were becoming hateful and doing evil things. Maybe they shouldn't have let her travel so far. She had done it O.K. before. Did this soldier have anything to do with her being late? But he was on the opposite side of the river. Mirriam tried not to worry, but such is a mother's curse. Madison dozed and Mirriam prayed, on and off, through the evening hours.

"Could I have a drink, ma'am?" said Chris as he forced a swallow. Mirriam helped him with the water dipper as he drank. He then sat up in bed and drank more soup.

"Feeling better soldier boy?" asked Madison.

"I think I'll live," replied Chris.

"What is your name, son?" inquired Madison.

"Private Hughes, sir. Private Christopher Columbus Hughes."

"Would you hear that, Maw. This boy's a Hughes. Where you from?" inquired the ferryman.

The two men clicked. They talked like long lost relatives. They discussed numerous Hugheses but could not come up with a common relation. Chris' Craig County roots apparently didn't grow from the direction of western Virginia. They told hunting, fishing and horse trading stories until almost midnight. Mirriam, like a mother talking to her misbehaving sons who refused to go to sleep, forced the two men to turn out the lamp and say their good nights. She laid awake most of the night and worried about her Becky.

Chris slept well in a real bed. He hadn't been in one for weeks. He was awakened by the smell of bacon frying in the house. This was truly too good to be true. These people were the nicest folks he had ever met. There was something different about

53

When Gauley Ran Blood

them. A genuine sincerity in their deeds and a kind'a sparkle in their eyes caught his attention. He couldn't put his finger exactly on it just now. Madison reminded him some of his grandfather, Lewis Francisco. He was meek, yet you knew he held real strength. Chris knew he also had to get back to his unit.

Mirriam fed him a king's breakfast of biscuits and bacon gravy with strawberry jam. Chris ate until he could hold no more. She apologized for not having coffee, because it was all but impossible to find these days. He took her sassafras tea instead and said it was the best he had ever had.

"Do you know my boy, Prottman? Issac Prottman Hughes is his name. He'll be 18 soon. He is with the 36th Virginia Infantry, McCauseland's boys," Mirriam asked.

"Mrs. Hughes, I know the 36th very well. We have been in several scrapes together, but I can't recall that name. I will make it a point to look him up when I get back to the regiment," Chris responded.

He could walk in a very guarded posture and told his hosts that he really had to go. Madison ferried him across Gauley after Mirriam packed a half dozen bacon biscuits in his haversack. She softly and carefully hugged the soldier, as if he were her own son, and watched from the front of the house as the two new friends crossed the river on the flatboat.

The men started their conversation again, and Chris caught himself and told his senior friend that he just had to go. They shook hands and Madison told him to come back sometime. Chris, being polite, said he would like that. He knew most likely that he would never see the kind gentleman again. He moved his hand in a good-bye wave to Mirriam across the river and was off to his horse. He was in pain as he walked, but without the help of these two kind hillbillies, he dared not think what would have been his fate.

Madison returned to the north shore and was met by his daughter, who had just walked down the road to the landing.

"Becky, is that you, girl? What happened to you?"

"It's me, daddy. I'm sorry if I made you worry. Amanda had some problems I had to help her with. It was nothing much, " said Becky, smiling as she pondered what she had said. "Who was that? It wasn't Prottman, was it?"

"No, he's a soldier boy from the south. Real nice fellar. He had a little problem your mother and I had to help him with. It was nothing much. I am glad you're home. I believe your mother would like a word with you."

When Gauley Ran Blood

Chapter 5
Death in the Wilderness

Chris found his horse disagreeable, having not been fed for two days. He patted him on the flank and spoke, "Can you get me back to camp, boy? I don't blame you for being upset. I'd be mad too. I'll get you something to eat in short order if you will just get me back to the captain."

He mounted and went pell-mell back toward the Confederate camp. His ribs ached after only five minutes in the saddle. Had it not been for the scenery his trip would have been most unbearable. He marveled at the size of the gray and white sandstone cliffs along the Gauley River. At some places they looked like clouds peering through the green forest canopy. Boulders bigger than houses lined his path along the road. A forest covered a great deal of his route. Giant hemlocks and poplars that started growing centuries earlier were plentiful. Some areas had fiddler ferns three feet high. They reminded him of the green fields of tobacco he had seen in his youth in the Shenandoah Valley.

He would stop briefly to let his horse eat where there were patches of grass. This normally was where a tree had fallen and allowed the sun to reach the ground and illuminate the small tender meadow plants. The horse would have to be goaded to continue his journey. Chris hated to mistreat the animal, but such was the life of a cavalry mount. He would do what he could for him.

Chris approached the place where the road forked and went up Hominy Creek. He had left his comrade here two days earlier. He called out, "Willie. Willie, are you out there? Hey Willie."

He called and searched for thirty minutes and decided that the soldier had most likely started back to the unit. He found where grass had been grazed short. Willie had allowed his horse to eat. He also found tracks in the sand that headed back toward camp, but they were old and partially washed away by one of the showers that morning or the night before. Chris couldn't tell. He determined he needed to head back to camp. He might run into Willie on the way back. He broke off a sprig from a young birch tree and commenced to chew the bark from it as he steered his horse down the pike.

Chris had ridden several miles down the Wilderness Road when he spied several sets of fresh tracks. He had passed half a dozen small farms that looked like the men folk had left. The fields had been taken over by weeds and even the house gardens looked overrun with weeds. There had not been any tracks from those places. These horses were traveling cross-country. Chris followed the tracks for about a quarter of a mile and then they left the road and went along a split rail fence near another small farm. He could hear a bird whistling. It was like no other he had ever heard. He turned and started back toward camp and a small lad of seven or eight appeared beneath a huge oak tree. The shoeless boy was dressed in brown linen trousers and a dirty white shirt. His blonde hair grew long and straight out of his head, and he looked like a dandelion flower that had gone to seed.

"Howdy mister," spoke the youngster. "You're a Johnny Reb, ain't ya?"

Chris responded in a kind, but authoritative voice, "That's right, son." He thought he might as well fish for any information the youth might have. "Have you seen any other Johnny Rebs around here?"

"Sure did, mister. Last evening afore dark. They came through here."

"What do you mean they?" Chris queried. Had the captain sent men for them and somehow he had missed them? His curiosity was pricked.

"One fella dressed like you and four others dressed in coats. They all had guns, but the one dressed like you. They rode out toward the Benford place," spoke the lad.

"You mean rifles?"

"Yea, they were rifles," stated the youngster.

"What is your name, boy?" asked Chris.

When Gauley Ran Blood

"Odie Nutter. Odie Ray Nutter," replied the boy. "I'm Dane and Opal Nutter's boy. We live down yonder." The lad pointed to a gray weather beaten house at the foot of a hill in a clearing carved out of the hemlock and laurel.

"Is your dad at home?" inquired the soldier.

"Pends," said the boy.

"I don't understand. Explain yourself, boy." Chris said in a scolding voice. He was gravely concerned about Willie. He didn't even know Willie's last name. He thought it was McGraw. He had to find out what was going on.

"Pends upon whether he wants to see ya or not," responded the kid.

Irritated he asked, "Well do you think he wants to see me?"

"You a Reb, ain't ya? He's a sesech. He'll see ya. Come on." The boy climbed over the fence and opened the gate for Chris' horse. They made their way down to the cabin. A light skinned woman was working in the well-manicured garden. She wiped the sweat from her face with her soiled apron and placed her hands on her lower back as she stood erect. Chris saw that the woman was exhausted. Her face was emaciated, and her eyes were receded into her skull. She was walking dead. Chris was speechless.

"What can I do for you mister? You might as well not ask for food cause we ain't got none. Bunch of bushwhackers wiped us out Monday two weeks ago. We're making it on blackberries and huckleberries now. A little squirrel and groundhog when we can find em. We'll be having beans in a couple more weeks once my garden comes in," said the woman.

"No ma'am, I don't want your food. Your garden looks fine. I'm looking for one of my fellow soldiers. Man named Willie McGraw. Your boy here says he went through here yesterday evening," inquired Chris.

"I can't tell. You best talk to my husband, Dane. Dane, can you talk to this fellar?" asked the woman. She looked toward the woods as if to be addressing one of the trees.

Chris saw the shoes and then the legs and body of a man extend down from one of the branches of a tree near the cabin. The man slowly lowered himself to the ground from the tree at the edge of the woods. He straightened his gray kepi hat and tucked his shirt into his trousers as he walked to the house.

"You with Floyd's bunch?" asked the man.

"Yep," replied Chris.

"My name is Dane Nutter. I wanted to join up with them boys, but a while back a gang of bushwhackers come through here and took most every thing we had. They took our cow, two hogs, every chicken on the place, and even the meat out of the smokehouse. Left us nothing. People are desperate these days. We have about starved the last two weeks. There is no way I can leave until the garden comes in here for Opal and Odie Ray. Odie Ray is my scout. He watches the road and whistles when anybody comes around while I'm trying to work. If anybody shows up, I make it for the woods until they pass on. You're a Reb in that uniform. Me too. I would have voted to pull out of the Union. I don't want Mr. Lincoln telling me what to do," stated the man.

"This boy tells me a soldier and some other men were through here last evening. Did you see them? Do you know where they went? I need to find my friend," spoke Chris as he dismounted from his horse.

"I wasn't here. I was over near the Benford place picking berries. I did see a Reb with four men. I was off the side of the road in the blackberries when they came through. If that was your buddy, I got some bad news for ya. They kilt him. Shot him right in the back of the head. They were the same ones that took our stuff. Rough bunch they are. They killed him like he was a bug. He thought all they wanted was his horse and gun. He thought he was free. After they left I covered him with a pile of rocks to keep the varmits from pickin' at him," explained the man.

The man instructed the boy to stay at the house. As he walked with Chris to the grave, he told him how he was picking berries along side the road to the Benford place before dark the previous evening. He explained how they stopped a short distance from him so that he could hear every word. He heard one of the men say that they had gone far enough and that it was time. One of them told the boy that they were going to let him go now, but that they would need his horse. He dismounted and started to walk down the road. They had taken everything he had including his shoes. All he had left was his uniform and hat. He hadn't taken ten steps when two of them put up their rifles and shot him in the back. One of them on a big gray horse shot him right in the back of the head. The soldier boy sure was a mess. The man showed Chris an enormous dried bloodstain on the wagon road and then a large pile of rocks along side the road.

"I put him in here," said the man as he pointed to the pile of rocks. "I didn't know what else to do with him. He ain't stinking yet, but he will be. I'd a put more on him, but it was getting dark. I took his hat. I didn't think he would need it. I'll give it back. "

The man helped Chris uncover the body. With Chris's ribs in the shape they were, he relied heavily on the man to lift the big ones. He didn't appear to mind.

Willie had been only a boy of eighteen. His stiff corpse could have been anyone. The size was right. One side of his face was missing and the other side was disfigured beyond recognition. He looked at his trousers and found the little half-square hole at his thigh he had noticed two days earlier when the couple had ridden out on picket duty. It was Willie. Chris grimaced and rolled his lips between his teeth to keep back the tears. He was just a boy.

Mr. Nutter helped Chris secure the body onto the back of the horse. As they lifted the body across the horse, a piece of paper fell from the boy's shirt. Chris picked it up and saw that it was a letter. He stuck it in his watch pocket and got on his horse. He told Dane to keep the hat and passed him a piece of cloth that contained the biscuits Mrs. Hughes had given him. He needed them, but these people needed them more. The soldier thanked Mr. Nutter for his help and was off again for camp.

Chris pulled the letter from his pocket and read it as he rode along.

Picket Duty Near Gaulee River
August the 25th 1861

Dear sister
I was pleased to receive yours of the 12th of June. Does old Brandy still have the colic. He has been a good horse and if he were to go I wod shure miss him. Your letters help take my mind

off being away and this frightful war. I rite from my post. This duty is most boring. My love I sent to mother and father. The package with the socks and dried fruit arrived. The fruit didn't last long. Sis, tell Amie Souders I should like to call on her when I return. (if she is amind.) She is in my thouts dailey. I wood answer her letters quick if she would kindly rite.

Here it is pretty and screne. I magine heven will be like this. Very quiet beneath the trees. I am looking for Yankees. Came here with a new friend. His name is Christopher Columbus Hughes. I had a good laugh over his name. He is a good man. He will be a good friend I no.

If God wills that I return ...

The letter obviously unfinished pulled at Chris's heartstrings. Now his chest ached inside and out. He hardly knew the boy, and yet he said he was his best friend. He knew he was homesick. All soldiers get homesick. What if the boy had gone to the ferry, and he had stayed at Hominy? Would he be the one draped across the back of the horse? And what of his sister's letter? Chris paused to let his horse graze. He sat down upon a fallen chestnut tree. He removed a pen and ink from his haversack and finished the letter for the boy. It was the least he could do for the young soldier.

If God wills that I return ... or not I shall always be your most loving brother.

Willie McGraw

Miss McGraw,

Willie asked me if I would be kind enough to finish his letter for him. I regret that your beloved brother is no longer with us. He is now with other heroes of faith with the Lord almighty. He gave his life for mine in an engagement near Gauley River in Virginia. He was a brave soldier and a friend that put the life of his friend before his own. May the grace of God be with you and your family.

When Gauley Ran Blood

I will always be indebted to your loving brother and will remain your humble servant.

Pvt. C. C. Hughes

Chris knew that could just as easily have been him on the back of the horse instead of young Willie. In a real sense he owed him his life. He blew on the ink to dry it and then folded it as Willie had. He would see that he posted it as soon as he arrived at camp. Someone had to know where he was from. He could find an address. He was back on his way in minutes, and his mind pondered the waste of human life the war was causing. The broken dreams and the ruined lives caused by this beast were too costly for any country to pay. He rode on.

Not long after he came to the intersection of the James River and Kanawha Turnpike near Meadow Bluff, Chris came within sight of where their camp had been. There was no one in sight. It had become a ghost camp. He was exhausted from his long ride. He left the road and went down over the hill to a rhododendron thicket. He wrestled Willie's body from the horse and placed him on the ground. He took his blanket from the horse and wrapped it around the body. He then quickly pulled the blanket from Willie and wrapped himself up in it. He didn't think Willie would need it. He laid down with his rifle on one side of him and felt the grip of his Colt in the front of his trousers. He'd be fine. He closed his eyes and he was asleep. He didn't move until morning when the snorting of his horse awakened him. He loaded up and was off again.

All he could do was follow the path made by the wagons to the west and hope to find his unit. This was an easy task because the road was rutted from the heavy wagons traveling on the rain soaked surface of the pike. At places the road was a sea of mud from earlier showers.

Chris's stomach growled and he had nothing to eat, but a half dozen green apples he had gathered along the road. He rode by a birch tree and broke off a small limb. He gnawed at the branch like it was a piece of fried chicken. It wasn't much and only marginally better than nothing at all. He graciously stopped and allowed his horse to chew a few morsels of grass when he would pass a green area along the pike.

Chris knew it was well into the afternoon and that it was going to get dark before long. He started looking for a place to stay or camp for the night. He saw a church up ahead and decided it might be good for a night's rest. As he got closer, he saw a wagon and team tied in the yard. The teamster sat on the steps of the church and spit tobacco as Chris approached.

"Lookin' for the 22nd Virginia. Have you seen them?" asked Chris.

The man returned dialog with a high squeaky voice. "Their wagons were travelling in our caravan. We were with the 36th. We were headed for the Sunday Road not up yonder too far. Hear tell they were goin' to Carnifex, ...Carnifex Ferry. We hit a rock back in one of them mudholes and broke a wheel. Fixed it well enough to get out, but it's in poor shape to travel," he paused and spit a brown stream with a small slobber refusing to leave his chin, "We're waiting for a replacement from the quartermaster. He was ahead with General Floyd's army. We been waiting about all day."

"You mind if I wait with you a while? That saddle is growing into me. I'm in the infantry, but had special picket duty. I'm not accustomed to sitting a saddle. I got a couple of bad ribs, " said Chris.

"I'd enjoy the company. What happened to your man there?" replied the teamster as he spit again.

Chris told him the story about Willie's death as he slid him from the horse and placed him beside the wagon.

The soldier said, "Well I declare! I never hear such. Just shot him in cold blood, did they? You want something to eat?" He spit again emptying the tobacco from his mouth. He hawked and spit several times before he was comfortable that he had cleared his mouth. He wiped his mouth with the back of his hand.

Chris found it difficult to discuss the boy and eating in the same breath, while the man practically puked in front of him, but he had not eaten for nearly two days. The man offered him boiled beef and potatoes and, although cold, they tasted good to an empty stomach. The soldier was afraid to build a fire because of it drawing the attention of federal scouts or worse yet, bushwhackers.

When Gauley Ran Blood

They talked into the darkness. Chris took his blanket from the horse and wrapped up in it in the cool damp air. It was after nine when they heard a horse neigh down the way. Chris walked to the edge of the church building and cocked his Colt. The teamster did the same with his Enfield rifle. They could hear the squeak of a wagon wheel and knew no one would try to sneak upon them with a team of horses and a squeaky wheel.

"Howdy gents," yelled the teamster, "I have a wheel for your wagon, soldier. Colonel McCausland sends it with his complements. Fresh from the victory over the Lincolnites at Cross Lanes."

"They have a battle?" asked the soldier.

"Battle, it weren't no battle. It was a massacre. Them Yankees didn't know what hit 'em. That's what the captain told me. He was in the middle of it. He otta know," stated the driver. "Looks like I'll be spending the night with you gents. I can't go on in the dark. I'll end up like you."

"Whatcha hauling?"

"I got sick and wounded boys from Cross Lanes. I'm headed for Lewisburg. That is, me and my partner here," stated the driver as he stepped from the wagon. "I got twelve boys in there. Two of them are hurt real bad. We gotta build these boys a fire for tonight."

"What about bushwhackers?" asked the soldier.

"You talking to the army that just whipped up on the Yanks. Do you think they are going to come back for more of the same? Half that army has done run to Charleston by now. No need to worry now. Help us get these boys out and we'll start a fire. Lord won't mind if these men sleep in His house tonight," replied the teamster.

Chris and the teamster helped the sick and wounded out of the wagon. Two had measles and the rest had bullet wounds. The two sickest men did not need help. They were already dead. A fire was built out of split rails from the field behind the church, and all the men gathered about it from the cool damp August night. It was an interesting menagerie of mankind with no one in charge.

When Gauley Ran Blood

The men talked about the battle. It was the first major battle many of them had been in. It was quite a tale. Chris listened intently.

The men knew that ever since the Confederate victory at Mannasas or Bull Run when Union General McClellan took over the Army of the Potomac from General McDowell he and his subordinate General Rosecrans were eager to control western Virginia. Confederate General Lee and two of his generals were contrary to those actions. General John Floyd and General Henry Wise were both former governors of Virginia. Both were Brigadier Generals and pains in the side of General Lee because of their constant bickering. Their meetings were very loud and often turned into shouting matches. The men sensed the friction between these two long time political rivals. Floyd was none the less the senior officer and therefore in charge. There was some question whether he was in actual control because of their feud.

Floyd was determined to cut off Union Brigadier General Jacob Cox from General Rosecrans' support from the north. He and Wise devised a plan to put Cox in a pincer position between their forces. Cox would have to vacate his position at Gauley Bridge and withdraw from the Kanawha Valley. Floyd knew that the upcoming vote in this part of Virginia for the formation of a new state could well depend upon the success or failure of this mission.

General Floyd had moved his troops across Gauley River at Carnifex Ferry. This was a most difficult task. The Federals had sunk the flatboats at Carnifex. Floyd had them raised along with some smaller bateaus to cross the raging river. The first casualties occurred when one of the boats carrying the cavalry broke free from the towline and crashed into boulders and rapids below killing six men and two horses.

Floyd's counterpart, Wise, and his troops did not cross. Instead they traveled on down the James River and Kanawha Turnpike toward Gauley Bridge to occupy Cox and prevent him from attacking Floyd's rear.

General Cox had scouting reports of the Confederate's activities. He skillfully deployed the 7th Ohio Infantry under Colonel Erastus Tyler on the north side of the Gauley between Gauley Bridge and Summersville. Cox used Tyler's scouting and defensive measures to confuse Floyd while he awaited the reinforcement of his army by that of General Rosecrans'. With all the jockeying for position going on, it was only a matter of time until one of the armies ran into another. This happened at Cross Lanes.

The soldiers said Floyd called his new position above the cliffs at Carnifex, Camp Gauley. Wise had cautioned him about crossing the river. He said that if Floyd got into trouble that he couldn't withdraw his army fast enough across the bottleneck at the ferry. He would be better off on the south side of the river. Floyd ignored Wise's suggestion.

The men explained how they arose at 3:00 am and were told to cook and prepare meat for two days rations. The Rebs were off at dawn. Shortly after sunup they received orders to form ranks across a cornfield that was located near the intersection of the two roads at a community called Keslers Cross Lanes or just Cross Lanes. They soon found out that Tyler's camp lay just beyond the intersection. The Rebs attacked the left and right sides of the Federals. The Lincolnites were eating breakfast and appeared unconcerned about defending their position because they were taken totally by surprise. The Confederate soldiers laughed at the magnitude of the Rebel yell that echoed across the valley amid the cannoning and gunfire. People could have heard it in Summersville eight miles away.

Tyler had no choice, but to withdraw his men to avoid a disaster. All of the Rebs agreed that the soldiers they fought that day were brave men and that they fought with daring. They never had a chance. They were outnumbered two to one and they never really got organized from the first. When the battle ended after about an hour, there lay dead or wounded nearly 150 men. The North had five times as many casualties as the South. Floyd's forces also had taken about 150 prisoners.

Colonel Tompkins of the 22nd attacked on the left and caught many of the Federals trying to withdraw through a mountain pass. The Union death count would have been much higher, but he ordered his men not to fire and yelled out for the Federals to throw down their guns, and they would not be touched.

When Gauley Ran Blood

The Union forces had been routed. General Lee sang Floyd's victory song a few days later.

From: HEADQUARTERS,
Valley Mountain, August 31, 1861.

To: General JOHN B. FLOYD,
Comdg. Army of Kanawha, Camp Gauley, near Summersville, Va.:

> *GENERAL: I take great pleasure in congratulating you on the dispersion of the forces of General Tyler and the handsome victory gained by a portion of your command. If it will result in cutting the communication between Generals Cox and Rosecrans, it will be of effectual service in future operations. To do this it will be necessary to call to you all of your force that can be spared from your center and such aid as can be obtained from the loyal militia. A movement of the troops south of New River to a favorable point of the Kanawha will cause the retirement of General Cox from Gauley Bridge and enable you to unite your troops for an effective blow. I understand that the North Carolina and Georgia regiments that have been ordered to join you are on their march. I have the honor to be, your obedient servant,*

R. E. LEE, *General, Commanding.*

The significance of this battle echoed all the way to Washington. General McClellan, as the new Commander of the Army of the Potomac, was outraged. This battle, although small, would reflect negatively on his new rank. General Rosecrans received a telegram that expressed McClellan's response to the Rebel victory and summarized his course of action.

When Gauley Ran Blood

AUGUST 29, 1861.
Brig. Gen. W. S. ROSECRANS,

Clarksburg, Va.:

> *There is no excuse for Tyler being surprised.*
> *Concentrate everything possible against Floyd. Let*
> *Cox leave the minimum force required to hold the*
> *Gauley, and with the remainder of his troops attack*
> *Floyd from the south at the same time you attack*
> *from the north. Your continued presence at*
> *Clarksburg excites comment.*

G. B. McCLELLAN.
Major-General, Commanding

The wheels of the great Union Army had been set in motion. The small Confederate force was about to experience the wrath of the Federal invaders from the north.

A story circulated in camp about a sight that was seen on the field that day. Early in the attack, men reported seeing a man and woman on a mule racing back and forth through the cornfield. Many thought they were trying to warn Tyler's troops. Others thought they were owners of the cornfield and were trying to protect their property. Still others said they were lovers that had been caught in the cornfield.

Chris commented that if that were the case she was certainly his kind of woman and laughed heartily. Little did he know the veracity of his comment. The men told other tales until late in the evening.

Chris slept by the fire with many of the men. Others took comfort inside of the church. Chris did not sleep well due to the sick men milling about all night. His ribs didn't hurt so much after seeing some of the wounded in the wagon. He was glad to see the morning. He ascertained that the 22nd was at Camp Gauley and that they had been involved in the battle at Cross Lanes. He was anxious to see his old crew and left early after securing passage of Willie's body to Lewisburg with the teamster. He followed the

69

directions the teamster gave him for finding Carnifex Ferry. In his conversation with the driver, he realized that he had ridden many miles out of his way to return to his unit. If he had only known they were at Carnifex, he could have been there in two hours from Hughes Ferry instead of the two days it was taking him to travel the long route of some 50 miles.

He rode down the Sunday Road to Carnifex Ferry arriving just before noon. Meadow River emptied into the Gauley at this place. The ferry site was a hub of activity. The flatboat was similar to the one at Hughes Ferry. Two towropes were used at the site. One stretched from the north side of the river to the south below the confluence of Meadow River. This route connected Summersville with Dogwood Gap. The other line started at the same location on the north shore, but angled up stream to the opposite shore of Meadow River. This road led to Mt. Lookout.

Soldiers were busy building a footbridge downstream of the ferry. It was a hodge podge of posts set into rocks across the river. They were connected with rough cut boards and split timbers with cross braces sporadically placed. No railings were present to prevent a man from falling into the rapid current below the ferry. Chris remembered the story told by one of the soldiers the night before about the flatboat breaking up and the men and horses drowning. He now more that ever realized that it was no tall tale. Again he was awestruck by the Gauley.

The entire affair looked like plastering scaffolding stretched between beanpoles. He was glad he was on a horse, although probably not for long. He soon would be back in the ranks and on his feet. Two soldiers directed him onto the ferry, and they pulled him across. There were several cavalry soldiers waiting on the other side for a return trip. He exited the ferry and climbed a steep poorly cut wagon road that took him past astonishing views of the river gorge. The hillsides were steep and carelessness on horseback or on foot could be deadly.

When he reached the top of the hill, he could see a labyrinth of tents, campfires and soldiers on foot and horseback going to and fro among them. He asked for directions to the 22nd, and the private responded that they were an infantry group not a cavalry regiment. He indicated he knew that, but he wanted to know where they were. The private directed him into the woods toward the west end of the camp. He spotted his Uncle John and felt a certain relief that he was back with people he knew.

"Where you been C.C.? Thought you'd taken a minie ball and I'd lost my tent companion," asked Uncle John Hughes as his nephew dismounted. He often called Chris the pet name of C.C. in spite of his age. He didn't do it to agitate, but to poke fun at his brother's son. "It's good to see you, boy. Where did you get the horse? Did you go and join the cavalry?"

"You're full of questions today, Unk. Aren't you?" replied Chris as he walked in a bow legged fashion holding his ribs. "Hear you fellars had some action while I was gone."

"Yes sir, we did. We had us one fine time scaring the dickens out of them boys in 7th over at Cross Lanes. They'll not be back for a while. How did your patrol go?" inquired John.

Chris started to speak, but Captain John Halstead interrupted him.

"Where did you come from Chris? I thought you had gotten lost. We missed you at the battle day before yesterday. How did your picket duty go? You need to talk to Colonel Tompkins as soon as you can."

"I was about to tell Unk here that Willie got bushwhacked," said Chris.

"Bushwhacked! Did he get hurt?" inquired the captain.

"Cap, Willie's dead. They shot him up something awful. I sent his body on the quartermaster's train with some of the other dead to Lewisburg," responded Chris.

Captain Halstead stated, "I encouraged him to go. He was just a kid. I thought it would be safe duty for him. Darn it anyway! He was always talking about horses. I don't know why he didn't join the cavalry to begin with. I'll have to write his maw."

"I have a letter for his sister I had to finish. Can you post it with yours?" said Chris.

"Sure thing. You need to see the colonel. We'll talk at supper," replied Captain Halstead.

Chris returned the horse to the quartermaster and went directly to Colonel Christopher Tompkins's tent. He had been in charge since Colonel George Patton had been seriously wounded at

When Gauley Ran Blood

Scary Creek and forced to convalesce while he awaited a prisoner exchange that would allow him to return to action. The men loved him and Colonel Tompkins. Great leaders seemed to run in Patton's family.

The colonel sat on a stool at the front of his tent writing on a crate that was turned upon its side. Chris simplified his report to the extreme. He had not seen any Federals at Hughes Ferry, and he was injured by a fall. Bushwhackers had killed Willie.

The colonel expressed his dismay with the senseless murder of the boy. Chris gave considerable more detail to the circumstances surrounding young Willie's death. He elaborated on the story Mr. Nutter had related to him. The colonel asked if appropriate arrangements had been made for the body and if the family had been notified. Chris indicated that all was in progress.

It was assumed by the colonel and others who had gathered that an unskilled infantryman acting as a horseman could most likely have an unfortunate fall. The colonel did, however, remember that when Chris volunteered he had stated that he was "good with horses." He said nothing to embarrass Chris since he had in fact volunteered for the duty. The colonel expressed his concerns and told Chris that he should consider a visit at the surgeon's tent. Chris had heard the cries from that place before and had no desire to seek their source. The colonel thanked Private Hughes and told him he had done a good job.

Chris could not help but feel guilty about the events of the past few days. He had done nothing wrong, but he also had done nothing to contribute to Willie's defense or the battle he had missed at Cross Lanes. He returned to his tent and slept until Unk awakened him for the evening meal.

Chris ate as if there was a hole in his stomach. Boiled beef, potatoes, beans and cornbread disappeared as fast as they were placed on his tin plate. He ate with a spoon that folded out from his pocketknife. He drank coffee from a tin cup. First coffee he had had in a while. He wished he could get a cup to Mrs. Hughes at the ferry to repay some of her hospitality. The coffee was part of the plunder the soldiers had reaped from the previous breakfast raid at Cross Lanes.

When Gauley Ran Blood

Captain Halstead pulled up an empty cartridge box near the fire where Chris sat Indian fashion. He asked, "How did it go at the ferry? Did you see the Hughes? They are friends of mine."

"Yes, I saw them. How did you come to know them?" responded Chris.

"My home place is just over the mountain on the other side of Cross Lanes. We went to the same church for years. Madison and my dad are very close. I've hunted with him and his boys many times. We used to mill cane sugar most every summer. I've eaten at their house with the boys many times," stated the captain. "I just saw their son, Prottman, when we came across the Gauley at Carnifex Ferry. Colonel McCausland had him running the flatboat. Lord knows the boy grew up on his dad's ferry. They went on to Summersville after the battle. He's probably eatin' home cookin' by now."

"Yep, that Mirriam can really cook," blurted Chris. He spoke the words without thinking and hoped he hadn't been heard.

"You met Mrs. Hughes did you?" replied John.

Chris knew he had already stepped on the dog's tail and would have to feed it more to keep it from barking. He and John Halstead had become close during their brief stay in the 22nd, and he felt he could safely confide his story to him. Reluctantly, he told him about the woman he had seen and about his fall. He told him about how they had taken him in and provided care. Madison and Mirriam were, in fact, people you had no choice, but to like.

"What did you think of Becky?" asked John.

"Becky, Becky who?" queried Chris.

"Their daughter. She's probably the one you saw in the river. She's a pretty little thing with reddish brown hair. I had an eye for her one time, but I spent so much time with her brothers she was like a little sister. You know? She was always around like one of the boys. So, she broke your ribs. Can you imagine that?" chuckled John as he stood and started for his tent. "Good night, I'm going to bed. I have 2:00 AM watch."

Chris's stomach now floated, and he thought he might up chuck. He wasn't hungry anymore. It sounded like the same woman. So, Becky is her name. Probably Rebecca he thought. Why wasn't she at the house? Maybe he was too sick to remember.

No, he would have remembered her. Would he get to see her again? Rebecca Hughes, humf!

Chris had no idea of the ordeal that awaited him in the days to come. The conflict he was involved with would take his mind far from the young mountain girl he had made the object of so many thoughts. His battles had not yet begun.

Chapter 6
The Meeting at Camp Gauley

Becky had settled into her work again at home and at the ferry, and things were somewhat normal. Her mom and dad could not stop talking about the young soldier that had visited with them during her absence. To hear them talk of the gentleman, you would think he was a cross between General Thomas Jackson, whom they were now calling "Stonewall" because of his stand at Manassas or Bull Run, and grandpa Jeremiah O'dell, Mirriam's father, of Revolutionary War fame. She regretted not getting to meet him. She had inquired what battles he had fought in and neither could answer. They didn't even know how he had been wounded. All they knew was that he had been on a special mission. He didn't say what it was.

Mirriam found a hole in Becky's scarf large enough that she could stick her finger through it. She inquired how she had so damaged it and Becky could only truthfully answer that it must have happened on the way back from Amanda's. She did not elaborate on the details of the dilemma Nick and she had found themselves. She said they had witnessed part of the battle, but had run to keep out of the middle of things. She laughed to herself when she realized what she had said.

She tried to change the subject and started discussing Amanda. The new baby was doing well and looked like his daddy. She said that Nick had been away and that Amanda had been worried. Becky told them that a soldier had tried to steal a chicken, but had been unsuccessful. She failed to mention her arrest or how she had gotten up with Nick. She said she had gardening to do and hurried out of the house toward the barn. She closed the door with a sigh and her conscience knotted in her stomach. She did not want to mislead the people she loved, but neither did she want to worry them. She was all right and nothing had happened to her. She wondered if a Yankee bullet or a Rebel minie ball had made the hole in her scarf. She felt her head as if to be searching for a missing hole in her skull. Admittedly the experience was exciting, but it was not something she would want to go through again. She could still see images of the dying soldier tearing at his clothing trying to find the source of his internal fire. It actually made her look forward to a quiet morning's work in the family vegetable garden.

She had a plan for the afternoon. Her taste of fresh coffee at the Union camp after a long hiatus reminded her of other things she had not been able to get since the war had begun. Summersville, the closest community to the ferry that came close to resembling a town, had no stores. It did, however, have a Union occupational garrison with supplies. She had now been in one of their camps and felt she could get by, being somewhat familiar with their ways. It was obvious that diplomacy carried great weight in the military. She had spent most of her young life arbitrating between and among her five brothers during their sibling disputes. She had become a master.

Becky knew they most likely also had coffee and her plan was to trade food or garden vegetables for coffee and maybe even sugar if they had any. Her mother loved coffee but, not having any, had been instead serving sassafras tea. She had been doing this for months. Mirriam was not one to complain. She, like many mountain women, was content to have a healthy family and food on the table for them. Becky's desire was to please her mother in this small way. When her vegetables were ready she would barter them for goods, but for now she was going to try baked goods. She had placed her order for three pones with her mother that morning. Becky supplied the kindling for the fire before she left for her work. She knew she could tempt the angels from heaven with corn pone, fresh butter and honey. Would the Union soldiers go for it? Time would tell.

Her garden was growing well, and the side dressing of aged manure she used for the plants would put them in great form for bearing their fruit. She enjoyed the hard work and the joy of seeing the seeds become plants and the plants bear fruit. A process that could only have been created by God she thought. She hurried through her work anxious for her visit to town. She hurriedly lifted the latch to the granary door and swung it open. She placed her hoe beside the others in the corner and started for the barn. She wanted to harness Maude, their horse, to the wagon before she put on her good clothing for fear of soiling them. Having completed this task she went to the house and bathed.

Mirriam asked, "Rebecca Jane, your appetite has most certainly grown these last days. Are you well? You'll have me wear out my Dutch ovens."

"I am fine, but for the blister I picked up on my pen hand this morning from my hoe. Daddy's gloves are much too big for me, and I don't want the bulk of them in my way. Someday someone will make gloves for women. We all can't stir pots all day. With all the men gone, someone has to do the outside work," replied Becky.

"Momma, those pones are not for me. I am going to sell them for things we need. I think they will fetch a smart price with the soldiers in Summersville," she added.

Becky washed with a cloth and water from a porcelain basin. Her skin was smooth and soft. When she wrung out the cloth, her newly acquired blister burnt inside her fist. She opened her hand and looked at her palm. Her hands were callused from tugging on the ferry towline, but the hoe had worn the skin loose near the thumb. She started to pull the little flap of skin from the sore spot, but hesitated and thought to herself, that she needed to be on her way.

She finished her bath. Then she slipped into a nightshirt and took the basin out to the front porch of the house. With a mighty upward motion of her arms, Becky threw the washwater to ground alongside of the house. There was a bare spot at that place. Becky always figured it was from the lye in the soap they used for bathing. She wondered if she would put the water around her plants in the garden if it would kill the weeds. Oh, but it would kill the plants too! Her mind never stopped its quest for exploring new arenas of endeavor.

Becky dressed in a simple, but attractive olive colored dress with matching bonnet. It made her hazel eyes shine like halos. She peered in the small looking glass that was the pride of her mother. Mirriam had received the plate sized mirrored glass as a wedding gift from Madison. Becky tucked the edges of her temple hair beneath the bonnet. She gathered her baked goods and amenities into a hand basket and started for the wagon. The chickens in the barnyard scattered as Becky passed through as if to announce that there was a new woman today out to seek her place in the world. With her basket safely stored in the bed of the wagon, she was soon mounting the wagon she had tied to the hitching post outside of the barn.

She took the lines and with an up and down motion of her arms whipped them against the tail end of the horse.

"Ha-yi. Ha-yi," she cried.

The horse jerked awkwardly and then stepped toward the worn wheel path that led to the ferry road. She was on her way.

She enjoyed the ride up the picturesque Salmons Creek Valley. The road wormed its way up the green tree clad valley. The road was rough and giant mudholes plagued the way. Becky was tossed up and down in the wagon by the bumpy road. The road passed through the stream no less than six times between the ferry and the foot of Grose Hill. This was a formidable hill that was actually part of the great mountainous plateau on which Summersville sat. She had considered going via Irish Corner Road, but that route was longer and the first leg of it was the road up the Joe Branch that was always wet and muddy. She liked the scenery, but didn't want to risk getting stuck in the mud.

Becky topped the brow of the hill and heard similar words she had heard before.

"Halt! Give the sign."

This startled her, but she immediately stopped the horse.

"What is your business, ma'am?" asked a soldier dressed in a gray uniform with a butternut colored slouch hat. He stepped out from behind a clump of bushes by a tree and pointed his gun in her general direction.

Becky pulled back on the lines to stop Maude and said, "Whoa, whoa Maude." She used her hand to push an unruly lock of hair beneath her bonnet.

When Gauley Ran Blood

"Sir, I have business in Summersville today," she responded tersely. She was shocked that a Confederate soldier would be this near the Union garrison.

"Just what exactly is your business?" inquired the soldier. "You looking for them boys from Ohio? Last heard they were plum down Charleston way and not looking back. We licked them good at Cross Lanes. Put 'em to flight."

"I certainly am not looking for any Yankees. Who would be in charge of this operation, soldier?" asked Becky in her most mature and authoritative voice.

"That would be Colonel McCauseland with the 36th Virginia Infantry in Summersville, ma'am. Floyd is at Camp Gauley."

"Then that is who I will speak with," responded Becky. "Did you say the 36th? My brother is in the 36th."

"Yes, the 36th. I can't promise the colonel will see you. His headquarters is just past the crossroads," said the soldier. He backed away and allowed the attractive young woman to pass, but not without an appropriate viewing.

Becky whipped the lines against the horse and again started toward town. She smiled a sheepish grin at having passed the sentry. Where to now? Would she get to see her baby brother, the little Rebel?

She guided Maude and wagon on down the road toward the crossroads at Summersville. The road in town was a muddy mess. Bottomless ruts criss-crossed enormous mudholes. As she approached the intersection of Peters Creek Road, she could see more than two dozen houses and buildings dispersed along the roads and hillsides. Above the intersection on a small hill which overlooked the main road of the town was situated a multitude of tents of different shapes and sizes. Crowning the hill was a church with a steeple. The tents spilled over into the adjacent fields and along the roads. Soldiers were innumerable looking like ants on an anthill scurrying about their activities. The main road was busy with horsemen going in all directions at once. Teamsters were busy unloading their haul among the tents. A Confederate flag hung limply from a tall slender poplar wood flagpole.

She could only make out two or three figures that were not in uniforms. One of them was approaching the wagon through the oozing earthy goo. She recognized the man's face. It was Mordecai Halstead, her friend John Halstead's father.

"Rebecca Hughes, what on earth are you doing here? You going to join the army?" asked Mordecai.

"Hello Mr. Halstead. Oh, no I wouldn't do that. I am going to sell or trade some baked goods," she replied. "How is John? I was by your place the other day and no one was at home."

"John came to see us just the other day. He has made captain. He said he has met a soldier who knows your parents. He told us General Floyd's Corp will have a dress parade tomorrow and that we must visit him. Reverend William Downtain will deliver the message at 11:00 AM. Would you and your parents like to join Margaret and me? We will be leaving at nine if you wish to ride in the big carriage with us. Margaret will pack a lunch for all of us. Tell Madison I said hello. You be careful out like this. There are ruthless vagabonds on the prowl these days."

"Thank you Mr. Halstead. I will give your message to dad. He and mother really need to get away more often. Traffic at the ferry has slowed, and daddy hates to miss any fare that he can get. Please give my regards to Mrs. Halstead and the boys," said Becky.

"Mr. Halstead, do you know where Colonel McCauseland's headquarters might be? I must check with him about doing my trading," continued Becky.

"Would you like me to introduce you to the colonel?" inquired Mordecai.

"That would be nice," responded Becky.

Mordecai helped her from her wagon and tied her horse to a fence post along the road. At her request, he fetched a small basket covered by a bright red cloth from the back of the wagon. They walked a short distance to a large tent with a table at the front of it. A tall dark haired man with a long mustache in a Confederate uniform and hat sat at the table.

"John, excuse me," interrupted Mordecai. "I have someone I would like for you to meet."

When Gauley Ran Blood

"Yes, Mr. Halstead, back so soon? Did you not get enough for your cattle?" asked Colonel McCauseland.

"You were most fair, sir. This is Rebecca Hughes, Colonel. Her father operates the Hughes Ferry south of town. She wanted to meet you," stated Mordecai. " I must be on my way. I trust you will see to her needs. Becky, perhaps I will see you tomorrow? Good day, colonel."

"Call me Becky, please, Colonel McCauseland," said Becky.

"Most pleased to meet you, Becky. What can I do for you?" replied the colonel.

"With the war and all, my family has a difficult time of getting staple items such as coffee, sugar, and spices. I have prepared two corn pones I would like to trade to someone in your regiment that might have a surplus of these items for trade," stated Becky.

"Miss Hughes, excuse me, Becky, the Confederate States of America does not normally do business at this level of commerce. We naturally prefer to purchase large lots of goods so that we get them at the very lowest price. Much like the cattle we have just purchased from Mr. Halstead. But, it has been months since I have tasted the fairer side of a dinner menu, and I might like to sample your products. What do you have to offer?" asked the colonel.

Becky lifted a cloth from her basket and revealed her prize of round golden yellow pones wrapped in a tablecloth and two small blue glass jars. One contained butter and the other poplar bloom honey. The colonel swallowed and unconsciously licked his lips. He was reminded of his mother's corn pones on baking day and how she always allowed him a fresh warm piece from her oven. Becky was right. The angels would have to get in line behind the colonel if they wanted a piece of her pone bread.

"What would you have for this delicacy?" inquired the colonel.

Becky quickly responded, "I would like coffee, sugar, peppercorns and cinnamon bark." She felt brazen in asking for so much, but as always she started bargaining at the high end.

81

When Gauley Ran Blood

"I might find five pounds of coffee beans we relieved from the Lincolnites a few days ago. Such other indulgences in the spice line I cannot help you with," said the colonel.

"That will be fine," spouted Becky. She wanted to jump for joy, but restrained herself in proper female fashion.

"Would you care to join me for dinner, ma'am?" asked the colonel surprisingly. His only intent was to be polite.

"Ah, sir, thank you so much for the invitation, but I really must return to my parents. They are older and I don't like to leave them alone for long periods. It is so kind of you to ask." Becky innocently crossed her fingers and realized she had stretched the truth to its very limit and maybe beyond. Both of her parents were quite capable of caring for themselves, but they were in fact "older."

"Another time perhaps?" inquired the colonel.

"We will see, sir," played Becky, completely missing his intent.

"Captain, would you see that Miss Hughes is accommodated with a few rations of coffee beans for her baked goods. Ah, and prepare her a pass for the sentry. Good day, Becky," said Colonel McCauseland.

"Thank you so much. Oh, Colonel, I believe my brother Prottman is in your service. Do you think I might be able to visit him?" Becky asked at departing.

"If he is not on duty, I am certain he would love to see his sister," replied the colonel. "What company is he in?"

"I believe he is in Company F. They call themselves the Mountain Riflemen," she added.

"You will find them directly below the church in the area of the flagpole." replied the colonel.

She was led to a wagon containing part of the army's provisions and the deal consummated. She held back one of the pones hoping to have a prize for Prottman. A soldier guessed at five pounds of coffee beans he removed from a large burlap sack and placed them in a cloth in Becky's basket. She removed the final pone and wrapped it with a scarf. She then placed the basket in the wagon and was off with the cornbread to find her brother. The soldiers were aware that there was a young woman in camp, and many volunteered to help her in her task. She inquired about his whereabouts and was told he was on patrol near Powell's Mountain north of Summersville. She asked if she might leave a package for him and was directed toward his tent. An obliging private promptly answered her request for pen and paper. She bent near an ammunition crate and wrote:

Dearest brother,

I had occasion to visit town on business today and was raptured to find that your company was here. It has been so long since you were home. We have received not one letter. Have you received any? I regret that you are on a mission, I hope this note will let you know the place you have in my heart. I miss you dear brother.

I believe that Colonel McCauseland is quite a gentleman and that you should be proud to serve under him. The treatment he offered your sister was kind and generous. I rejoice that I have secured coffee for mother. She suffers so with her boys all gone from home. To provide this small pleasure to her will indeed be a joy. It could only be topped if her youngest were there to sip it with her. If she were here, I know her tears would warm your heart and encourage you in your endeavors. Being so close, please try to visit if you can. May God watch over you, and I pray that He spare you from harm. Until we meet again, I shall always remain your loving sister.

Rebecca

She folded the note and wrote *Prottman Hughes* on the outside. She entered his tent and placed the note and scarf containing the pone on his straw bed pallet in such a fashion that he could not miss them on entering. In short order, she and her arabica prize were back on her wagon and headed home. Her gain as valuable as gold. She sang as the wagon bounced down the pike. She felt great.

When Gauley Ran Blood

Amazing grace, how sweet the sound.
That saved a wretch like me.
I once was lost, but now am found.
Was blind, but now I see.

She truly was light of heart. She regretted not getting to see Prottman, but she didn't know he was even in the area. When she sang praises to God, she would often be overcome with joy. In spite of the state of the country and her local community, she could still praise her Creator. She knew because of her faith that everything would work out for the best. She could not see the big picture as He could. He was in control. She was elated over the prize she had obtained for her mother.

When the sentry stopped her, she showed him her pass and he allowed her through. She felt a sense of importance having been shown such respect.

Becky arrived at home in the early afternoon. Mr. Halstead had made her job much easier and faster with the introduction to Colonel McCauseland. She tied the horse to the hitching post outside of the barn and went into the house to change clothes before putting the horse and wagon away. She carried her coffee beans with her.

"Prottman's regiment is in Summersville," she excitedly told her mother. "But he was on duty, and I didn't get to see him. I did leave him a note and one of your pones."

She showed her coffee beans to her mother and told her about their invitation to join the Halstead's for the picnic and visit to Camp Gauley. She quickly lost interest in her arabica beans and moved on to the exciting happenings at Camp Gauley and in Summersville.

"Do you think dad will go?" asked Becky.

"Madison will not hear of it. He won't leave the ferry, even if it is only for a short time. Since your brothers have left he has hardly been off the property. Did you hear any word from your brother?" Mirriam asked.

"The soldiers only showed me his tent. They didn't have any news on him, but they said there was quite a battle at Cross Lanes," answered Becky. " I guess I knew daddy wouldn't go, but I

84

can watch the ferry. You haven't seen Margaret in such a long time. You and daddy go and have a good time."

"We'll see. It would be nice to see Margaret and Mordecai again. They must be excited about seeing John in his uniform. Wouldn't you like to see him? " replied Mirriam.

"Mother, John and I are friends and nothing more. I would like to see how he is," stated Becky.

"Is that why you put charcoal on your eyebrows and strawberry stain on your cheeks that last Sunday we went to church. I could have sworn I saw you and John holding hands after church," Mirriam said as she walked from the house to take down laundry. It hung on a line that extended from the porch post to a maple tree in the side yard.

Becky changed into a blouse and her brother's trousers and hat. She went directly to the barn and took the bridle loose from the horse. The girth strap was loosened and the harness pulled from the animal with the collar, wooden hames and traces. The harness was hung on pegs placed in the stalls in the barn. She walked the horse to the barn field, opened the gate and turned it loose in the pasture to graze.

Becky walked to the ferry to see her father, who was just arriving at the north landing with a rider on a horse. She pulled the railing from the front of the ferry and placed it on the storage posts by the road. Her dad tied the ferry to the ring in the sycamore tree. The passenger mounted his horse and rode up the road toward Summersville.

"Becky, that fellow said the Confederates is thick over on the pike about Dogwood Gap. He said he heard they have built a camp at Carnifex. They had a battle with the Yankees at Cross Lanes and run them off. Maybe this war will be over soon? How did your business go?" Madison asked.

"Prottman's unit is in town. I didn't get to see him though. I got five pounds of arabica from the Confederates," replied Becky.

"Confederates? In Summersville? Praise the Lord they're already moving north," Madison exclaimed with jubilation. His enthusiasm for a southern victory was sincere, but premature.

Becky told her father about her trip and about the invitation to go to Camp Gauley with the Halstead's. He spoke earnestly.

"You and your mother go on. Now, you know I have to tend the ferry. Your mother hasn't been out for ages. She needs a visit. A talking spell with Margaret will do her good."

"Please, Daddy, you take her and I will tend Gauley," pleaded Becky.

"I'll hear no more about it. That is it," concluded the ferryman as he shoveled horse manure left by his previous fare from the ferry.

This was not what Becky wanted, but she knew her father. He was a Hughes, and there was not a more stubborn creature alive than a Hughes once they had made up their mind about something. She knew any further persuasion would only lead to frustration by both of them. She was going to Camp Gauley!

She didn't sleep well thinking about all the soldiers and events that were to take place the next day. Who would she see that she knew? Who might see her? Would one of the soldiers recognize her as the damsel trailing the mule-riding scout a few days earlier?

She had heard that the Bailes boys had joined the men in gray. Several of the Dotson men had also joined the Rebel forces though some had gone west to Ohio country and joined with the Federals. Summersville had contributed an entire company of men called the Nicholas Blues. Then there was Prott's bunch called the Mountain Riflemen. She wasn't sure of all the men that had joined with them. Of course she would see John Halstead. He was a little older at 24, but still handsome. He was a talented leader and a good man and Becky thought fondly of him. She wondered if he would notice her.

It wasn't first light when Mirriam touched Becky's arm and said, "Becky, it is time for you to get up. We need to be on our way."

It was clear that Mirriam was also anxious for the day. It wouldn't take an hour to get to the Halstead's. Mordecai had said to be there at 9:00. It wasn't 6:00.

Mirriam had prepared Becky's breakfast with her dad's. She sat in her chair by a coal oil lamp reading her Bible while waiting on Becky. Madison had gone to the barn to prepare the horse and wagon. He returned to the house and entered saying, "Alright, ladies, your carriage is ready. I want you to take my rifle and hide it under a quilt in the wagon. You may find it a comfort. I hope you see Prottman. Give Mordecai and Margaret my regards and tell Johnny boy I ask about him. Don't be out late. The roads are becoming really dangerous these days. Don't dally on your way! "

Becky put on the same olive green dress from the day before. She added her best two petticoats to fill out the dress. Her father positively forbid the wearing of hoop dresses. He thought they were decadent. She, however, spiced up her wardrobe with a knitted white collar and matching green bonnet. Mirriam had knitted a border of white along the edge of the bonnet, and the contrasting colors along with Becky's auburn hair and green eyes made her hard *not* to notice. She shawled her shoulders with a piece of black lace. She had traded for it early in the summer and had never worn it before. It made her feel elegant and was quite a contrast from her dirty worn wool trousers. She knew it was going to be warm, but the light fabric would be just right for a wrap on such a day. She hoped John would notice her.

Becky could only convince her mother to wait thirty additional minutes before leaving. It was the best she could do. They were going to be at the Halstead's before they were out of bed at this rate.

Madison took the squirrel rifle from its pegs atop the entrance to the house and placed it inside a fold of the quilt Mirriam had placed in the wagon. He kissed Becky and helped her onto the wagon. He repeated the process for his wife.

"Careful girls. Stay away from them soldier boys," he said with a grin as the girls rode off up Salmons Creek on their way over Gad Hill.

Becky allowed the horse to poke along. Her intent was to use as much time as possible. She feared they would arrive unfashionably early at their hosts. As she crossed the creek, she allowed the horse to water, and her mother scolded her for taking so long. They crawled over Gad Hill and down the McKees Creek side. Sooner than she would like they crossed McKees Creek at the ford and were heading up Halstead Hollow. She guessed that it was almost 8:00 when she turned off the main road and rounded the corner past the Halstead's barn. There sat Mordecai and Margaret in their two seated carriage wearing very sober faces.

"Decide to sleep in, did you?" barked Mordecai. "We've been waiting nearly an hour." He was intent on not missing a moment of the activities of the day.

"Now Mort," soothed Margaret. "We have plenty of time to get to our Johnny's parade. Mirriam, tie your horse to the post and let's go. Now!"

Her impatience also was beginning to show. Her fried chicken was also getting cold in spite of her attempt to keep it warm in a Dutch oven wrapped in linen sheets. Mordecai helped the two ladies into the rear seat of the carriage and they were on their way to Camp Gauley. He expressed his regret that Madison was unable to join them.

They retraced the road Becky and Nick had taken during their escape from the Cross Lanes battle a few days earlier. Mr. Halstead drove the horse at a soft trot, and the holes in the road bounced the passengers up and down and back and forth. The bouncing caused Mirriam to give an uncharacteristic breakfast belch that could be heard above the carriage noise.

She placed her gloved hand over her top lip and said. "Oh! Excuse me."

Becky girlishly grinned and chuckled. Mrs. Halstead curled her nose indignantly. It appeared that all parties were guilty of putting on airs this day. It was a special day for them. Little did they realize the impact this day would have on the rest of their lives.

A guard at Cross Lanes challenged them and Mordecai displayed a note from Colonel McCauseland. The guard rested his rifle and allowed them to pass. Mordecai sat high in his seat as they passed the guard. His display went unnoticed by a community that appeared as a ghost town. The few scattered homes revealed no inhabitants. They were gone or hiding. This often happened in a war zone. The Vaughn house was alive with soldiers. It had been turned into a hospital since the Cross Lanes battle. Margaret mentioned that a Union officer had actually died on the back porch of the house.

"Bled to death, he did," she stated unequivocally.

When Gauley Ran Blood

Becky relived her ride through the cornfield with Nick and the horrors of the day. The cornfield now looked worse than a mangy dog. Only sporadic corn stocks grew in the field. No ears were noticeable. The armies had stripped every last ear for personal consumption or to feed their stock. There were large areas in the field that were completely devoid of plants, most likely the source of a quartermaster's cattle fodder. There stood Zoar Church, a survivor. God's lighthouse she thought. A testament to His sustaining grace.

They rode on toward Camp Gauley down the Ferry Road. The road in places was a sea of mud. It was well worn from the traffic of General Floyd's Confederate army. A hot sun was helping to dry the ruts.

They passed the Patterson farm and a soldier leaning against a porch column in the front of the house greeted them with a raised hand. Mordecai tipped his hat with a bowed head and drove on by. They could see more activity ahead as they neared the camp. Again the road became a long ribbon of mud from the traffic of nearly 2,000 men with wagons, horses and other accoutrements. Soldiers were going in all directions among the city of tents that was erected in the woods and in clearings along the road to Carnifex Ferry. Many were well dressed with navy blue trousers and gray jackets. They wore gray or butternut hats or kepis. Some wore soft slouch hats, better to keep the rain and sun from your eyes. Others were dressed in civilian clothing, some barefooted. They were right off the farm or from the streets. They were soldiers none the less. Smoke rose from innumerable campfires. Flags of the various units hung limply from their poles, the pride of each corps. Some troops were drilling in the open field just past the Patterson house. A number of cannons could be seen at the brow of the hill where the Ferry Road topped the height of the ridge. The road leveled off for a quarter mile at this point before it started its treacherous course down the mountainside to the ferry site at the mouth of Meadow River. Some two dozen wagons and carriages were parked at the edge of the woods near the cannons. He pulled his carriage into an open spot and stopped.

Mordecai asked one of the soldiers where the 22nd Virginia Infantry was camping. He was directed into the woods along a spur from the main ridge. He told the ladies to wait on him, and he would find where the activities of the day were to occur. Several other ladies were seated on their wagons or in their carriages. The men were standing in groups talking. Mirriam saw an old friend, Eleanor Dotson, and waved. Eleanor saw her and waved back. Eleanor sat with a young woman about Becky's age. They appeared to be in a heated discussion judging by their countenances. The woman got down from the carriage and followed the muddy path Mordecai had taken into the woods.

Mr. Halstead walked for five minutes down a trail cloaked with tents on both sides. Then he saw a flag with the 22nd Virginia Infantry emblem on it. He stopped and looked around, but no one was in camp. He started back to the carriage when he met a young woman holding up the edges of her light blue dress to prevent it from getting muddy. Some of the black trim along the bottom was already covered with the bright yellow mire.

"Excuse me, sir. Could you tell me where I might find the 22nd Group?" asked the young woman. "Mr. Halstead, is that you?"

"My name is Halstead," replied Mordecai.

"My name is Ginny Dotson. Jacob Dotson is my father, Mr. Halstead. I'm looking for my brothers. I was told that some of the men who joined the army in Summersville were assigned to this unit. I was hoping to find them here," stated Ginny.

"I can't tell you about that, and there is no one here to help us. Let us walk back to the field and see what news we can gather," answered Mordecai.

They walked together back through the tent village. When they reached the carriages, they each went their own way. Mordecai asked one of the men standing at the carriages what time the parade was to begin. He replied that the parade was at 10:30, and that Reverend Downtain was to speak at 11:00. Mordecai looked at his watch and it was not 10:00 yet. He went back to the carriage and waited with the women.

The marching drill and parade began exactly on time. The Halsteads and their guests walked a short distance to a drill field on the east side of the Ferry Road. They joined a group of two score that had already assembled. Across the field was a group of military officers on horseback. Becky supposed one of the men was General Floyd. A dozen officers assisted him. Floyd raised his sword and the drum cadence began. Troops marched from the south to the north. Each man had a rifle resting on his shoulder. Some of the front ranks were perfectly in step and marching to the cadence of the drums. Others in the lessor ranks tried to keep up, but their jerky attempts to keep in step resulted in them looking palsied. The cavalry was in the rear of the procession. It was truly an impressive sight. Becky had never seen such an exciting display of military arts. The troops would swing to the right and then to the left. Some would kneel and aim their weapons, and others would stand and aim. The horses would race up and down the sides throwing large pieces of sod into the air above their heads. Becky was awe struck.

Colonel Tompkins rode in front of the 22nd Virginia Infantry. He sat on his horse gallantly and with pride. Margaret Halstead was elated when she saw her Johnny with the stripes on his sleeves marching near the head of a column of men. She jumped up and down by flexing her toes and yelled, "Johnny, Johnny, meet us at the carriages."

Mordecai quieted her with a hard look and said, "Leave the boy alone. It is his day, today."

Then he added, "That a boy, John."

He was a very proud man at that moment. The thread of patriotism that ran through his veins for his beloved state of Virginia brought a tear to his eye. He quickly wiped it away with his thumb so that no one would see him. He had felt the urge to join the war effort before. Today it was overpowering. He could help to end this war.

Becky and Mirriam both waved at John when he passed. There was no acknowledgement. Becky curled her lip. He tipped his hat to someone several steps down the line. Becky saw that his mother preceded her in the line and knew it wasn't to her he was paying his respects. She stretched her neck to see.

Mirriam looked down the line of soldiers and saw a familiar face. Who was that she thought? Then it came to her, the soldier boy. What was his name? Chris, that was it.

She quickly yelled, "Hurray for Christopher!"

When Gauley Ran Blood

She began waving. Chris heard his name and glanced over his shoulder to see Mrs. Hughes. Then beside her he saw Rebecca. He swallowed, stood as tall as he could, which was about 5 feet 6 inches, and squared his chin. His heart raced in his chest.

With Mirriam's enthusiastic yell, Becky took a long look at her mother and said, "Christopher who?"

The response of Margaret and Mordecai was equally puzzling.

"Remember the soldier boy I told you about Beck. That's him, Christopher Columbus Hughes in the flesh. Imagine that, I figured I'd never see him again. He sure was bunged up, "Mirriam uttered.

Becky and her mother made their way back to the carriage where they met their hosts. Reverend Downtain was walking toward one of the cannons, which was set on a high mound at the break of the hill. The people and soldiers followed. The scene resembled a Bible picture of Christ's Sermon on the Mount of Olives with the throngs of followers scattered around him. The preacher's message however came from the upper room discourse.

Bill Downtain did not pussyfoot around. His scripture reading included the Gospel of John, chapter 15, verse 13; *Greater love hath no man than this, that a man lay down his life for his friends.* He explained over the next sixty minutes how Jesus had been sacrificed for the sins of mankind, and by believing in Him, you could spend eternity with God in Heaven. He also pointed out how many of the men there that day would have to lay down their lives in battle so that others might live. It was a very emotional and soul stirring address. At the end, an invitation was made and hundreds of soldiers with tear filled eyes knelt to receive Jesus. Many were joyfully on their knees in the mud.

Chris listened intently, but seeing Rebecca earlier had distracted him. During Downtain's message, he thought of Willie and how by providence his own life had been spared. A simple task such as selecting a guard post could determine who lived and who died. Had Willie died by mistake? Should that have been my post? Was there something to this Jesus stuff? Many men he highly respected believed this Jesus was God. It seemed too simple to Chris. Admittedly, he was confused.

His confusion was shared by many. How could God be part of such a monster as this war? If He was in it, each side wanted Him to take their part. The commanders of both armies earnestly pleaded with God to side with their cause. Lee and Jackson of the Confederacy were devoutly religious men. There were also those from the North. An order from the commanding Union General McClellan may have expressed many of the military leaders' views of this "holy cause".

GENERAL ORDERS No. 7.

HDQRS. ARMY OF THE POTOMAC,
Washington, September 6, 1861.

The major-general commanding desires and requests that in future there may be a more perfect respect for the Sabbath on the part of his command. We are fighting in a holy cause, and should endeavor to deserve the benign favor of the Creator. Unless in the case of an attack by the enemy, or some other extreme military necessity, it is commended to commanding officers that all work shall be suspended on the Sabbath; that no unnecessary movements shall be made on that day; that the men shall, as far as possible, be permitted to rest from their labors; that they shall attend divine service after the customary Sunday morning inspection, and that officers and men shall alike use their influence to insure the utmost decorum and quiet on that day. The general commanding regards this as no idle form; one day's rest in seven is necessary to men and animals. More than this, the observance of the holy day of the God of Mercy and of Battles is our sacred duty.

GEO. B. McCLELLAN,
Major-General, Commanding.

Whether they believed in God or not, they would accept any edge they could muster. For the men who fought the war, God became real much sooner than He did for the commanding generals who sent their forces into battle. Bullets were persuasive evangelists. This day was not the Sabbath, but Chris pondered Downtain's words none the less. He allowed his mind to wander back to Rebecca. He spent much of his time looking for her in the crowd. Midway through the service he spotted her standing beside Mirriam and another couple. At the end of the service he made his way toward them.

The Halsteads and company made their way back to the carriage in the crowd. Mordecai then disappeared into the crowd.

Margaret stated, "We must find Johnny so that we can begin our picnic."

Becky responded, "I'll fetch him." She too was off through the crowd.

Chris plowed through the web of soldiers and civilians to the carriages. He spotted Mirriam and made his way to her. Suprisingly, Mirriam immediately hugged him as if he were her own son.

She kissed his cheek and said, "Chris, it is so good to see you again. How are those ribs? "

"They are healing up quite nicely, thanks to you," he responded. "How is Mr. Hughes?"

"He is busy at the ferry. He just won't leave it," replied Mirriam. "Let me introduce you to my friend, Margaret Halstead."

Chris extended his hand and asked, "You're not related to Captain John Halstead by any chance? He is the captain of my company."

"Johnny is my son," replied Margaret.

"I want you to meet my daughter, Rebecca. Oh, Rebecca. Where are you?" inquired Mirriam.

Chris's mind went into overload. Could this be happening? He asked himself. He was finally going to meet this woman. Admittedly, his first impulses may not have been totally pure, but getting to know her family and the love that her family displayed helped put his thoughts into line. If she were a young version of her mother, what a genuine treasure she would be. He was thankful he had gone to the river that very morning and bathed. He had even changed his inner undershirt to his outer undershirt beneath his

94

jacket and his inner socks to his outer. His beard had not been trimmed, but he had cut his hair just two days previous. His expectations skyrocketed. He was as ready as he would ever be to meet her. He hoped he would say the right words. His thoughts were interrupted.

Margaret Halstead spoke, "Mirriam, Becky has gone to get Johnny. She is a helpful girl. You know, I think they make such a fine couple. When I ask Johnny about them, he always denies his feelings. I know he is sweet on someone. I can just tell. I know he is writing to someone because the last time he was home he took all of my stationary and a bottle of ink. Who knows, Mirriam, someday we may become mother-in-laws of our kids."

The last bullet Margaret fired caught Chris in the throat, just above the heart. He remembered John had said they were friends. Why would he lie about his relationship with Rebecca? Maybe for the same reason Chris had not wanted anyone to know about his voyeurism. People do strange things. He had become John's friend, and he would not do anything to jeopardize that. They had to depend on each other. He couldn't let a woman come between them. His heart was beginning to run out his eyes, and he knew he had to get away.

He spoke hastily, "I must get back to my company. It was nice meeting you Mrs. Halstead. Mrs. Hughes, give your husband my regards. I really have to go."

He was off with his hand crossing his face as if to be wiping the sweat from it. Chris feared they might see the disappointment on his face. Sure, he was disappointed, but he was going to be a man about it. He could pout later.

Meanwhile, Becky searched feverishly in the hot sun for John. All the soldiers in their uniforms looked so much alike. She stared into each face atop the uniforms seeking John Halstead. She paced the edge of the drill field without success. She felt something wet surround her foot when she started to cross the road. She had stepped in a caramel colored mud puddle. She could feel the water squish between her toes as she continued to walk. She saw that Columbus guy mother knew. He was handsome she thought, but he looked ill. His face was so red around his beard. He must be sun burnt. "I wonder what he looks like without the beard?" she asked herself.

Then she saw John. He had his back to her and was talking to someone. She started toward him and had only taken two or three steps when she saw him pick up a girl in a blue dress and carry her across the muddy road and set her down. The girl giggled as he carried her. Becky knew her. It was Virginia Dotson. Ginny, they called her. She was just a child. Couldn't be more than 14 or 15. What could John possibly see in her? Becky did an about-face and started back to the carriage. Her appetite was lost for food and men. Unfortunately, she had to endure both during the Halstead's picnic.

Margaret Halstead had prepared two large baskets of food. The main course was fried chicken and fresh baked bread. John's favorite of course. He sat with Ginny on a small log and ate, and she giggled. Becky sat with her mother and the Halsteads on a blanket on the ground. How "romantic" she thought sarcastically. Margaret had also brought out fresh green beans and corn on the cob from the garden, pickled beets and boiled potatoes. They drank from a crock of sassafras tea. She crowned the affair with fresh apple dumplings.

Becky noticed that John ate voraciously. She only stirred her plate to make it appear as if she had eaten. She would not dare hurt Margaret's feelings since she had gone to such trouble. The little "priss" ate from John's hand like a trained canary. Becky thought she would not last long. Sure, she was petite and pretty, but men like strong women. This girl child is too soft and delicate. She is not John's type.

At the conclusion of the feast, John stood to his feet, removed his hat, and said, "Ladies and gentlemen I would like to announce my engagement to Miss Virginia. We plan to be wed at the end of this conflict, God willing."

Becky choked on a pickled beet and blew a scarlet spray across the blanket.

Mordecai stood to his feet as if he had been challenged and proposed a toast to the newly betrothed couple. "May God richly bless you two. I also have an announcement of my own to make.

As of today, I have enlisted in the Army of the Confederacy. I report for duty tomorrow."

Having heard Mordecai's announcement, Margaret got to her feet in a daze and promptly fainted back onto the blanket. Losing two men in one day was too much for her.

It was a long ride back to the Halstead's that afternoon. No one spoke a word.

Later that evening, Chris sat at the fire with John and several other soldiers. He was uncomfortable, but knew that if he didn't tough it out, he could never live with them for the ribbing if they suspected he was upset, especially over a woman. As the fire died down and the soldiers one by one went to bed, only Chris and John were left.

John looked at Chris and asked, "Did you hear that I'm getting married?"

He responded, "No, but I can't say I'm surprised." He bit into his lip as he continued, "I hope that the two of you are happy together. She is one elegant lady, a fine catch."

"Well, thanks, Chris. I agree. I hold her in the highest esteem. I only hope I make it through this war to make a life with her," commented John.

Chris raised his eyebrows and shook his head in the affirmative. He thought to himself. Yes, I wish you and Becky the very best, the very best.

When Gauley Ran Blood

Chapter 7
Skirmish at Hughes Ferry

The party arrived back at the Halstead's. Becky and Mirriam said good day and quickly climbed aboard their wagon and were on their way home. Mordecai and Margaret were participating in an old married couple's game, seeing who could yell the loudest. They hadn't time to say good-byes. Margaret was dumbfounded that Mordecai would join the army without consulting with her. He was over 50 and often beset with severe arthritis. She wondered which one of the other soldiers would rub horse liniment on his shoulders when it acted up and he was unable to sleep? He was her big baby. She liked it that way and thought he did too. She walked swiftly to the house and the door closed sharply as she entered. Mordecai was having second thoughts, but he was committed now. He had to go. That's all there was to it. Virginia needed every good fighting man she could get. With the anticipated size of the Union army being several times that of the Confederacy, all the southern commanders were urged to enlist every able bodied volunteer they could get. The atmosphere at the Halstead house remained unsettled.

Becky, for a change, was in no mood to talk. She said little as they crossed McKees Creek and rode over Gad Mountain. Light rain fell on the women as they crossed over the top. As Becky started the horse and wagon on the final leg of the trip down the grade between the break in the cliffs that led to the ferry, she knew immediately that there was a problem. She could look down on the ferryboat and see that it was partially submerged about a quarter of the distance across the Gauley. She whipped the lines against the horse and it jumped forward down the gradual winding way. Mirriam held to her seat and sensed the urgency in Becky's actions.

99

When Gauley Ran Blood

"Oh my! What has happened, Becky?" asked Mirriam as she held to her seat with one hand and her bonnet with the other.

"I don't know, Mother. We'll have to find out. See if you can get the rifle from under the blanket," responded Becky as she guided the horse toward the rocky dock, fostering her mother along the way.

"It will be alright, Mom. Don't worry."

She could now see the ferry was floating awkwardly in about four feet of water. Load barrels were attached, three to a side, and they were partially submerged with the boat. The barrels were normally only used when there was a fear of a heavy load causing the ferry to swamp. They were attached low to the sides to add buoyancy. This was an old ferryman's trick to stabilize his craft.

Her dad was wading to shore in the direction of the remaining stored barrels. His face was white except for a plum colored bruise above his eye. A red gash was centered on the swelling wound. A line of blood ran from it down Madison's face to the corner of his eye and then down his cheek to his chin where it dripped into the Gauley. He looked up the hill, saw them, and started toward the landing.

Becky pulled up on the lines of the horse to stop it as she set the brake at the landing. Meanwhile, Mirriam had found the rifle and was holding it with both hands by its long barrel. At that point, she saw her husband and exclaimed.

"Dear God, Madison, what has happened to you?"

Becky took the weapon as her mother dismounted from the wagon. Becky followed her to the water's edge where Madison stood dripping in his pants and shirt.

"Madison, you are bleeding!" Mirriam said as she began to weep.

"Now, honey, I'm alright. It's not as bad as it looks," retorted Madison as his wife embraced him in spite of his soaked condition.

She kissed his cheek and took up her dress and began to wipe the blood from his face. As she touched the wound the bleeding immediately stopped.

When Gauley Ran Blood

"Daddy, what happened to you? What happened to the flatboat?" asked Becky as she too hugged her exhausted father.

The three stood at the edge of the water embracing one another. There was a moment in time that no words were spoken, but an unmistakable message was conveyed among them. They now felt the weight of the evil that was upon them. The war had reached the ferry. Madison broke the silence.

"It was bushwhackers or scouts. I'm not sure. It was a couple of riders. We don't have time to discuss it right now. We have to try and save the ferry before it sinks. I have been trying to attach the barrels to her before she goes down, but there are so many holes in her she may not make it. I only have two barrels left and one of them is a leaker. Doesn't it beat all? It looks like rain to the west. All I need is a storm," exclaimed Madison, as he started toward the two remaining barrels.

Becky, realizing that she could not work, nor swim, in her dress, quickly loosed it and removed it along with her petticoats. She barked at her mother to fetch her work clothes from the house while she aided her father. He rolled one of the barrels into the water, and she followed with the second. They each waded to the boat with their barrel and tied them to one side and then the other of the ferryboat. The south end of the boat was high in the water, and the north end was under water. She could see brightly colored spots along the bottom of the boat. She knew they were bullet holes. Laced among them were fist size holes that looked as if the boat had exploded from within. These holes puzzled her.

"The boat was at the dock and I got it to these waters so that I could work on both sides to try to repair it. I can only work on one side if she's at the dock. I don't know if I can fix her or not," Madison stated earnestly.

The couple made their way back to the dock and Mirriam was waiting with Becky's clothes and dressings for Madison's injury. While the two ladies worked on his head, he explained what had happened.

"I had just finished eating when I heard the bell across the Gauley. I saw two men on horses across the river. They summoned me to carry them. As I towed the ferry across, I could see neither of them had on a uniform, but that they were heavily armed. I

When Gauley Ran Blood

guessed them to be scouts. One of them gave me two bits and we started back across the river. Neither of them said much 'til we got across. The one on a big gray horse asked if I was a sesech. I told him I wasn't taking sides, but that I didn't think it was right for Mr. Lincoln's government to be getting involved with everybody's business. It ain't the part of government to do that, I told him. He asked if I was going to vote for the new state of Kanawha, and I told him Virginia was plenty good for me. He said that made me a sesech and that there was no good coming to me. He said he didn't want to do business with no sesech and asked for his two bits back. I wouldn't give it back, so he took out his pistol and started shooting the boat. He said he would take his two bits out in wood. I tried to stop him, and his companion whipped me with his rifle when I started at him. It pulled the rug out from under me. I woke up over there by the gate, and they were gone. They cleaned my pockets before they left. By the looks of the boat, they must have shot holes in the bottom of it before they left. It was going down fast when I woke up and that's when I started tying barrels to her and getting her away from shore. People these days got no scruples at all. I think them fellows was Union Scouts."

"Well, thank God you're alright. You're lucky they didn't shoot you through. Let's get you to the house and get you doctored up. I'm going to open a hospital here. First that soldier boy, and now you. I should have been a doctor. Hep me, Becky. Let's get your father to the house and get him something to eat. Margaret Halstead sent you some of her fried chicken. You always make over it so at the church picnics. It will fill your belly up and make your head stop hurtin', " said Mirriam trying to hide her anxiety.

A few droplets of rain peppered them, as they made their way to the house. Becky looked at the river and could see the color changes from the impact of the raindrops on the water surface, thousands of little concentric circles. A storm was coming. It was coming fast.

"Becky, can you pull it out? We'll lose everything if we don't get her out of the water. If this storm is a 'Gauley washer', it will take that boat plum to Carnifex," stated Madison.

He didn't have to say anymore. She knew what she had to do. She had watched her dad and two of her brothers, Mathew and

102

Virgil, hook to the boat and pull it ashore before. She could do that. They pulled it just up river a little bit so that it would clear the dock.

She stopped at the log barn to get the rope stored there and couldn't find any. The rain fell harder. The tree limbs swayed in the strong wind. Leaves blown by the wind danced at her ankles. She ran to her brother Mathew's blacksmith shed to continue her search. She found a large coil of hemp just inside the door. She quickly unhooked Maude from the wagon and hooked the harness to a singletree so that she could pull more efficiently. Maude was not the prettiest horse with her swayed back, but she could hunker down and pull with the best of them.

Becky waded with one end of the rope to the boat and secured it to the tow rope guide. The boat was almost cleanly underwater by now with just one end sticking no more that a foot out of the water and into the air. She part swam and part waded back to the horse and tied the rope securely to the singletree ring. She loosed the ferry towline so as to give out all the slack she could and then fastened it back to its ring that was set in a rock on the river bank. The rain by this time was coming down in buckets.

She guided Maude to the upriver side of the dock and yelled. "Get up, Maude, get up! Come on girl!" as she danced the lines against the back of the horse.

Runoff from the horse's back splashed as the lines contacted her saturated coat. Maude gave two quick jerks forward, and then the weight of the water filling boat stopped her in her tracks.

Becky yelled again, "Ha-yi! Ha-yi! Get up, Maude, get up."

The horse shifted her weight sideways on her hind legs and then sprang forward by stretching them. The muscles in her great legs swelled and the strain was evident. By taking up the small amount of slack in the harness, she had sufficient inertia to start the boat moving. With Becky's coaxing, the horse drew the flatboat toward the bank in the downpour.

With the rain in her eyes it was hard for Becky to see, but she continued her charge with the lines. She glanced at the boat and saw it was going to hit the landing, but knew that if she stopped the horse for new direction, she may never get the ferry started again off the bottom mud. The ferry rammed into the corner of the dock and halted Maude momentarily. She pulled again and the boat edged forward taking three of the ramp boards with it. The barrels that had been placed along that side of the boat were scraped to the back of the boat while their rings pulled free from the ropes that had bound them to the ferry. The barrels slowly floated out into the current and were swept away down the Gauley. Finally Maude stopped and could pull no more. Becky examined the boat and saw that almost a quarter of it was out of the river and on the shore. She took her towrope and double tied the flatboat to a sycamore tree a short distance from the bank. She believed it would hold. She took up the slack in the ferry towline and tied it tightly to its mooring ring. There was absolutely no way that boat could escape now.

"Let it rain," she said to herself.

Becky took Maude to the barn, removed her harness, and gave her a large full measure pitchfork of hay to eat. Maude had saved the day and deserved a reward for her efforts. Becky saw her own part as a task that had to be done. She expected no reward, other than accomplishing her goal, and most likely would receive none. After all, she was a woman.

As Becky made her way to the house the rain was subsiding, but the skies were still dark. She could see light flickering from the window coming from the coal oil lamp. She looked at the Gauley. Muddy water from Salmons Creek had already made its way to the center of the river, and the tide was rising. She didn't think it had rained so much. She entered the warm and dry house to the questioning of her parents.

"Did you get it, Beck?" queried Madison who was now wearing a swath of white cloth around the crown of his head.

"I think so, daddy. Maude pulled her heart out for me. I'm afraid I hit the dock," responded Becky.

"Never mind that. That boat has got a fine frame to it, and even if I have to replace every board on her, the salvage of that frame saves me many days of hard work. I wish the boys were here to help me get it back together," stated Madison

His daughter had just given her all to save that boat and now felt a little shorted on the gratitude list. She fought off a tear that was gathering in her eye and pursed her lips. She had had a long disappointing day. She knew her dad loved his boys and that they in turn loved him, but this awful war had separated them. She did her best, but they were a hard act to follow. They always seemed to garner his praise. She was just a woman. No better than a slave she thought. What was Mr. Lincoln going to do for her?

Mirriam called them to supper. As Madison got out of his chair and started for the table, he walked to where Becky was sitting and took his daughter's face in his coarse callused hands and said, "Becky girl, you saved my boat. You are a fine daughter. You serve well and make me proud to call you my girl."

Simple words spoken from the heart. Becky's spirit rebounded from the depths and she stood and put a bear hug on her father and said.

"I love you, daddy."

She could now no longer hold back her tears which had changed from self-pity to completely overwhelming joy of love for her father. The tears rolled from her cheeks and Madison just chuckled.

Her mother who had been looking on said, " You all quit making such a fuss and come on and eat. The food will be getting cold soon."

She turned quickly toward the kitchen so that they would not see a tearful display of love swelling up from within her. The family did not have much, but what they had money could not buy, and death could not steal. Their power was not of man.

Due to her fatigue Becky slept soundly. She awoke to the sounds of her father pounding on the boards that comprised the flatboat. He was up early and anxious to get a start on building a new boat, or at least putting new planking on the old frame. His head remained wrapped, but it was mending and the pain had subsided for now. He feared the pounding would cause it to return, but such was not the case.

The rain had fallen short of his feared expectations and he was thankful. The river was muddy, but it had only raised about a foot and a half. Many of the bottom boards were older and worn, and he had pushed hemp into the cracks until some were more plant than wood. These needed replacing, and now with the bullet and buckshot holes, they were unsalvageable and useless. He would have to pay Mr. Chapman a visit at his mill and procure the necessary boards to complete his task. He was out of business until he could get the ferry repaired. He could run the dugout canoe, but you couldn't get a wagon on a dugout, only foot traffic and riders. The horses had to swim.

Madison had sufficient old lumber to construct a dry dock for the boat. Becky assisted in all aspects of the construction. She particularly enjoyed utilizing Maude with a block and tackle to completely remove the boat from the water. Madison removed the necessary boards to allow the water to flow out of the boat as Maude inched it out of the Gauley. Several hard days of work lay ahead for the ferryman and his daughter as they stripped the old hull and placed new boards on her keel and sides. The bow and stern boards were in good condition having been replaced in the past year. A difficult task lay ahead of them, but their livelihood depended upon that ferryboat. If it didn't float, they didn't eat. For now, this ferry was closed.

This could not be said for the flatboat at Carnifex Ferry. It was in perpetual motion, back and forth between the banks, carrying soldiers and supplies to Camp Gauley. Many families were seen crossing to the south shore on the ferry in fear of pending retaliation from the Federals for the attack by Floyd at Cross Lanes. The refugees were making their way south to family or friends. Some stayed to endure the coming clash of armies.

Several days had passed since the battle. The dress parade at Camp Gauley had stirred patriotism for the great state of Virginia. The men were anxious for another battle. The officers had their hands full keeping the men from fighting with one another. They kept the men occupied by drilling.

Chris' unit drilled each day. Rain fell and made for a miserable camp. Mud was everywhere. The tents leaked and the blankets were wet. Sleeping was difficult at best. Rumors circulated through camp that Rosecrans' Federals were nearing the camp with 10,000 troops. The Confederate forces were hardly 1,800 men and the odds were frightening. The men were getting jumpy. Some of the Confederate soldiers stationed there had yet to receive weapons that had been promised by General Floyd. They were especially uneasy, but the officers assured them that when they needed them, they would have weapons.

They were not the only ones having grave military problems. Following the defeat of Colonel Tyler's forces at Cross Lanes, it became imperative that the Commander of the Army of the Potomac, General McClellan, seek a retaliatory blow to the south in western Virginia. President Lincoln was pressuring him to get his army moving. The President wanted action. McClellan had ordered General Rosecrans from Clarksburg to Summersville to crush General Floyd's army.

From atop the cliffs overlooking Carnifex Ferry, Floyd had stated that he could resist, " The world, the flesh, and the devil, " from his position.

General Wise was camped near Hawks Nest, about 15 miles away, holding General Cox at bay at Gauley Bridge. He had counseled Floyd to defend his position from the south side of the river. They were aware that Union forces many times their strength were on their way to confront them just miles from Summersville. The problems Floyd had encountered crossing on his advance to Camp Gauley could be potentially devastating if his troops were forced to retreat in haste. The high water in the river made it impossible to cross without a boat or bridge. Floyd had two small ferryboats and a makeshift footbridge that would take hours for his army to cross if he had to retreat. Floyd would soon find out that his greatest enemy at Camp Gauley was not the Union Army but topography. His lesson was about to be taught.

This period of the war was a time of learning for both armies. Many of the officers from the opposing sides had been classmates at West Point. Ironically, some of the officers from both sides had served together in the War with Mexico. Now they were fighting one another. Most of the others had not tasted war. The battles at Scary Creek near Charleston, Rich Mountain near Beverly, and Cross Lanes were the largest battles many of the men had fought. Their techniques of killing one another were still in the refining processes. As the war progressed, so did the tactics of warfare and methodologies of inflicting death. To this stage of the war, Napoleonic methods were quite common. This stand and fight method was rapidly being replaced by providing cover whenever possible for ones' troops.

Camp Gauley had been prepared for the northern attack. Serpentine trenches were constructed at the brow of the hill perpendicular to the road that led from the Patterson house to the ferry. Log and split rail fortifications were also used in conjunction with the earthworks. The trenches extended from the cliffs on the east side of the point for nearly a mile to the cliffs on the other side of the point. The trenches were hidden from view by dense forest undergrowth. Abatis with needle sharp points had been fashioned from felled trees and waited to spear any unaware over zealous advancing enemy. Colonel Guy's artillery had several cannons placed at the top of the hill behind the fortifications. They were dug in and ready for a fight.

Colonel Tompkins, the commander of the 22nd Virginia Infantry, was disgusted when he received his orders to report to General Wise at Hawks Nest. Wise feared an attack by Cox from Gauley Bridge and wanted the extra hands. Tompkins sensed the real battle was about to begin at Camp Gauley and was growing tired of being played as a pawn between the competing generals, Floyd and Wise. His regiment was continuously put in the lead when attacking and at the rear when retreating. He was a good soldier, however, and obeyed his orders and reported to General Wise.

Private Christopher Hughes found himself on the march again. He knew after the first few miles of walking that riding was his preferred method of travel. The steep grade up Sunday Road after crossing Carnifex Ferry was an exhausting climb on foot. They continued on this road until they joined the Kanawha and James River Turnpike near Dogwood Gap. They marched another ten miles until they came to the Wise camp near Hawks Nest.

Chris marveled at the view of the great bend in New River from his lofty perch atop the cliffs. He knew that up that river some distance was the mouth of Sinking Creek. If he traveled up Sinking Creek and then through Rocky Gap he would be at his home on Johns Creek. He missed his mother and family. He wondered if he would ever see them again. His father had died years earlier and only his younger brother and two sisters were at home to help his mother. His had two brothers who were also in the Confederate Army, and an older married sister. When he saw middle aged women anywhere, he thought of his mom. He loved his mother. Now he had a bad case of homesickness, but he was so tired all he wanted to do was find a place to sleep. He was given a piece of bread dough that he baked by 'snaking' it around a sapling and holding it over a fire. He ate it with a piece of beef left over from the day before and went to sleep in his blanket. He dreamed of home, Becky, and flying like a bird off the high rock pinnacle at Hawks Nest.

The 22nd Virginia Infantry's stay with General Wise was a brief one. The threat of attack from General Cox proved to be false, and they were ordered back to Camp Gauley. They no more than spent the night, and they were off again retracing their march of the previous day. Marching in those mountains was no easy task. The rains made the roads wet and muddy. Their feet were always wet. After a few steps the mud on a man's boots made him feel like he was dragging anvils. Add in the stress from the fear of an ambush at any time, and the exhaustion multiplied, but they marched on. They had been marching all day and were headed back down the Sunday Road toward Carnifex Ferry when the colonel ordered a halt and for the men to set camp. They were going to spend the night in a small field at the Reynolds family's farm.

Chris and the other men were preparing their tents and gathering wood for fires when Captain Shelton of Company D, - called the Nicholas Blues, and Captain Halstead of Company C, Chris' group, - called the Mountain Cove Guards, came back from a meeting with Colonel Tompkins.

Captain Shelton addressed Captain Halstead, "We need men familiar with the area. Colonel Tompkins doesn't want a greenhorn out on picket duty. If Rosecrans is a coming south and tries to cross at Hughes', we need somebody who can give him torment. I can only spare two men. We'll need every man at Camp Gauley if that's where we're to have it out."

"I better go myself. It's easy to get lost going through the Mt. Lookout route. I have one man who has been to Hughes Ferry and I'll probably take him. Have your men meet me here in ten minutes with the horses," responded Captain Halstead as he left his colleague and searched for his unit.

"Private Hughes, Chris, ready for a ride?"

Chris was sitting on a log cleaning his rifle when he looked up from his work with bewilderment and said, "We have been marching all day and now you want to ride? You are kidding aren't you, John?"

"No, Private, I am not kidding. I need you to volunteer to go to Hughes Ferry and keep watch for Rosecrans' bunch. If they try to cross and come in from behind, General Floyd wants to know. Just today he gave orders for us to return to Camp Gauley and to post pickets at Hughes Ferry. He wants Colonel McCauseland's men outa' there and back to Camp Gauley. He doesn't have a man to spare," replied the captain.

"It's forty miles to the ferry by the Wilderness Road. It will take me better than a day to get there," Chris said with reserve.

He remembered his last visit at the ferry, and his ribs were still sore from his fall and sleeping on the hard ground.

"I'll get you there by another route, but I'll have to go on to Camp Gauley. If we cross Meadow River at Carnifex and go by way of the McClung Settlement at Mt. Lookout and on to Collison Creek, it's not more than fifteen miles. It's rough, but the horses can make it. It's better than walking. I thought you were just griping about the march," stated John. "Get your stuff ready. I'd take two days rations if you can get it."

Chris thought he knew why John wanted this duty, but he wasn't sure he wanted to go back there. There was no woman waiting for him. He did think it would be nice if he could see the Hugheses again. He might get the chance.

It wasn't long before the men from Company D arrived with horses for their journey.

"Privates Dotson and Baker reporting for service, sir," said one of the young men from his horse.

Chris was given a brown and white mare that looked more dead than alive. The filly had oozing sores on her back beneath the saddle. He hated to do it, but he mounted and waited for John. Soon they were off and within an hour they were at the Carnifex Ferry. On their way down to the ferry, they had met a few civilians and some sick men who were headed for Lewisburg. No one had any news on the advance of the Federals. Two privates pulled the towline to get the four men and their horses across Meadow River. The same ferry could also be used to cross Gauley River to get to Camp Gauley. The camp lay about a half-mile north and about 400 feet above the ferry.

The pickets climbed a winding grade to the top of Mt. Lookout and rode a short distance. They stopped at the McClungs and Captain Halstead made arrangements for them to feed and rest the horses in the barn for a few hours. Chris slept. The Union Army 20 miles north also slept that night, but briefly.

General Rosecrans and his 8,000 troops spent the night north of Summersville near Mumblethepeg Creek. Before 4 AM, they were aroused for another long march. The dew was heavy as was the low-lying fog. Rain could not have produced the dampness that permeated the small wedge tents of the soldiers. They ate hardtack and beef with their coffee. The hardtack was a three-inch square soda cracker. Some of the men ground up their hardtack and made gravy with beef suet and water. They would use it as sop for their crackers. Some claimed they ignored and ate the ever present weevils, but others carefully picked them out of the sauce claiming they were too bitter. The breakfast was shortened by the bugle calling the men to march and the officers shouting, "Come alive!"

The entourage made its way toward Summersville, at times reaching more than five miles in length. There was, of course, the infantry. The cavalry riders and a long train of supply wagons appeared endless. There was even a company of artillery, know as the 'Jackass Battery,' because mules rather than horses drew them.

The road was more like a trail, and mud was an ever present enemy. The Rebel cavalry made the going that much harder, always staying one jump ahead of the superior forces sent by Rosecrans to clear the way.

As the Rebel cavalry withdrew through the small community of Nicholas Court House, which some called Summersville, word spread that ten brigades of Lincolnites would soon over-run the hamlet. Many of the inhabitants were Secessionists and had left their homes and taken to the woods and countryside to hide. Others had left the day before and gone with

111

When Gauley Ran Blood

Colonel McCauseland when he pulled his troops back to Camp Gauley. All that were left were advance pickets to warn of the advancing Federal Army. These were positioned at Summersville and at the Hughes Ferry south of town.

The people of the small town had pride and had watched their community grow. Now they were in fear of destruction. For the many years that court had been held in Nicholas County, Virginia, the records had continued to grow. The county clerk, determined not to leave his post, was gravely concerned about his records. He had heard rumors of entire towns being burned by the advancing armies from the north. Robert Hamilton was determined not to see his work and the records of nearly forty years go to ruin. He helped his son, Alex, load the records into a wagon and started him in the direction of Greenbrier County and safety via the Wilderness Road. As Alex crossed the final hill of his beloved town he could see the Union Army Cavalry entering from the north. He guided the team of horses with haste, and the books and papers bounced beneath the canvas covering in the back of the wagon. In his scrambled exit, twice he had to stop and gather the archives into a heap. Finally, with the aid of a large rock strategically placed atop the canvas covering, he managed to keep the records from escaping. He made his way down the Salmons Creek Valley, through its many fords, and arrived at Hughes Ferry hoping to quickly cross the Gauley River.

He was stopped by Rebel pickets at the top of the hill and explained his dilemma. Being part of Colonel McCauseland's 36th Virginia Regiment, they were keenly aware of the advancing army. They wished him well and sent him on his way.

Madison and Becky had just gotten the flatboat back into the water after nearly a week's work, replacing the sides and bottom. They were pounding tarred hemp into any seams that showed signs of leakage. At one point, they had to pull the boat back out of the water when they launched it due to the number of watery cracks displaying small fountains. With time, hemp, and coal tar they managed to repair most of the percolating leaks. They were now working on getting the smaller seeps under control. In time, this also would be cured. They halted their work to see Alex approaching hastily in his father's wagon.

Becky looked up and said, "What bug's under his harness? He sure is in a hurry."

Alex yelled, "I have to cross the river. I have the court records here, and the Federals are entering Summersville. Can you ferry me?"

"I spect. If you can give us a minute to put back these towline ramp boards. Cost you 25 cents for the team and wagon," responded Madison.

"You don't understand. There is an army on its way here. They may kill us all! Especially if they think you're a sesech."

"I'm not takin' sides. I'm not a soldier and I'm not fighting any war. I'm running a ferry. You want to cross, it will cost you 25 cents. I just had to rebuild this flatboat and that wasn't for free. I'll help you any way I can, but I gotta make a living," stated Madison.

"Tell that to those Rebs that stopped me up there on the hill. They know Rosecrans is coming with enough men to stretch from here to Summersville."

"Help him, Daddy. We have to do our part. He can help us test the ferry," Becky gingerly requested, so as not to make her father think she was trying to tell him what to do.

Both she and her father were unaware that eyes had been watching their activities. There was nothing they could do about it now. A pulse of fear seared through Becky as she wondered if another Cross Lanes was about to happen at her own home with a clash of armies anxious for battle.

Just then the sound of the summoning bell was heard across the river. The bell startled Becky.

"Help us with these boards. We'll get you across," replied Madison ignoring the bell.

Soon the walkway was in place and the towrope was placed in its guides. Alex guided his team onto the flatboat, and he and Madison were on their way across the river.

"Becky, you and your mother get a few things together. I want you to go to the sanctuary as soon as possible and stay there until I come for you. Do it quickly," shouted Madison.

Becky knew the sanctuary. Becky and her brothers sometimes played there in the winter. She had been there many times in her youth. Up river of the ferry, past the Joe Branch, and near the falls of Campbells Branch, a massive chunk of solid sandstone from the cliffs had dislocated and shifted toward the river creating a large unroofed room the size of two houses. The smooth straight walls of the room reached a height of eighty feet and more. One side of the block sloped outward into the room and provided cover during harsh weather. Interior of the sanctuary were two hemlock trees. The one with a five-foot diameter dwarfed the smaller tree reaching a height of well over 150 feet. Its boughs spread to provide shade to the entire room. Pine needles shed by the giant tree had accumulated in the chamber for hundreds of years and softened the harshest sound to only a whisper. Thus, the place was dubbed the sanctuary. It was easily accessible to those who knew its secrets. One entrance was through a rock-fall cave that wasn't used in warmer months because of the fear of snakes. The other entrance was through a tall narrow passageway where the large block joined the cliffs. This entrance provided easy access; however, smaller rocks and laurel thickets camouflaged the actual opening, and you could easily travel along the base of the cliffs and pass by it without ever knowing it was there.

She hurried to the house and coaxed her mother to gather blankets and a few morsels of food. Becky led Maude for fear of the soldiers killing or taking her. Many of the farm creatures were liberated. She opened the chicken coop and beat on its roof with a stick. The chickens scattered in all directions cackling as though they had met their death. On her way, she left the pasture gate open and the cows and sheep began to scatter along the fields by the river. The pigs and guineas were no where to be found.

Becky and Mirriam were off in short order, and within thirty minutes arrived at the sanctuary. They no sooner had arrived and Mirriam asked Becky. "Beck, go get your father. That stubborn Hughes will get himself killed. You have a way with him. If he complains about you coming back, tell him I sent you after my Bible."

She had left Maude in a laurel thicket near the base of the cliffs at Campbells Branch. She walked the horse along the pathway until she got to the trail at the Joe Branch, and then she mounted and heeled the horse to a full gallop in the open lane.

When Gauley Ran Blood

As Madison offloaded Mr. Hamilton and wished him Godspeed on his mission, a boy carrying a small gunnysack approached the ferry. Obviously the one who had been impatiently ringing earlier. Alex flipped the lines against the backs of the horses and they bolted off the flatboat and down the Wilderness Road toward Meadow Bluff. Madison asked the boy his business.

"My mother has sent me with food stuff for my father. He's in McCauseland's band in Summersville. Are you the ferryman? My mother said to give this nickel to you," stated the lad.

"Keep your nickel and come on, Son," replied Madison, seeing no reason to stop his philanthropic giving at this point. This ferry will be the death of me, he thought.

The boy said his name was Johnny Blizzard and that he was from Mt. Nebo. He told Madison that he wanted to kill Yankees like his father, but his mother wouldn't let him sign on. Madison told him he would have to hurry to catch McCauseland. He figured they would be leaving Summersville soon if Rosecrans' army was coming. Madison did not know they had left the day before.

Not five minutes after Madison had delivered the boy, he looked up to see his passenger walking back down the road toward the ferry with a Rebel soldier. At this same time, the bell across the river began to ring. He looked across to see three horsemen waiting at the dock. It was Chris and his companions coming from the McClung Settlement. He pushed off the dock for the south abutment.

There were actually four soldiers waiting. Chris had checked his horse's saddle and blanket and found them infested with maggots. They had been feeding off of the raw back of the poor filly. She may well have worn the saddle for days without having it removed. He had not noticed it the night before when he pulled off the saddle. He refused to ride the animal in that condition and John agreed to double with him.

Captain John Halstead yelled, "Madison, Madison Hughes. It's John Halstead. How about a ride? Can you help us across?"

After recognizing John, Madison pulled hard on the towrope. A small wake pushed in front of the flatboat.

When Gauley Ran Blood

"Where you headed John? I haven't seen you for a coon's age," spouted Madison. "Christopher Columbus! Is that you? Why boy, I thought I'd never see you again. How are those ribs doing?"

"Good, Mister Hughes. Thanks to you," replied Chris, feeling somewhat embarrassed with the flippant use of his name. He was defensive about his name sometimes.

He rolled off the back of John's horse and caught the boat with his foot as it contacted the shore. The other riders also dismounted and started to walk their horses onto the ferry.

"Wait a minute men. You two find cover on this side of the river and set up watch. Chris is going with me to see what orders that soldier has. He'll join you in a few minutes.

"That is a Reb coming down the road?" asked John. "What's he got? A prisoner?"

Madison returned, "Yea, I just rode the boy across. Feller just passed through said there were Reb soldiers watching the ferry. It must be one of them."

Chris helped Madison tug on the towline as they made their way to the north side of the Gauley.

"I hate to say this Madison, but you need to get your family out of here for a while. Reliable reports have it that a General Rosecrans is coming south and that there is going to be a showdown with General Floyd. Floyd's got a camp at Carnifex Ferry, and he's itching for a fight. I am on my way there now. I had to drop off these boys here to keep an eye on your ferry. They have to make sure them Yankees don't go this way, and get behind Floyd, " said John as he remounted his horse just before the boat contacted the north landing.

Chris was dumbstruck that he hadn't asked about Becky. Wasn't she the girl he was going to marry?

"I've sent Mirriam and Becky up Campbells Branch. They'll be safe there," said Madison.

John rode ahead to meet the soldier and the boy, and words were exchanged. The boy got on the back of John's horse, and the soldier turned and started back up the road to his post. John spoke as he returned to the ferry.

"The boy's going to Camp Gauley with me. His dad is there. I can't turn him loose with them Yankees all over the place.

Those boys are from McCauseland's unit. I told them they were relieved of their post and they're starting to Camp Gauley. Do I hear a rider coming in?" asked John.

At that moment Becky came riding in on Maude from up the river.

"Dad, Mother wants you to come to her," huffed Becky who was out of breath from clinging to the horse at a gallop. A saddle would have helped her ride.

"Hi, John. How's soldiering?"

"It's not much fun at present. I'm trying to convince your dad that he needs to take you and your mother and go to the woods," replied John.

When Chris saw Becky his spirit lifted. She was something. He had never seen a woman wear pants before. She had them on all right and a felt hat like a man. Admittedly, she wasn't too appealing in her get up, but still she wasn't hard on the eyes. John certainly did not make much over his betrothed girlfriend. He had not finished his thought when the sounds of "bam" - "bam" echoed back and forth among the cliffs. The direction of the shots was hard to judge with the echoing effect.

Everyone at the ferry looked up and saw the two soldiers running down from the top of the hill shouting, "They're coming! They're coming! Yanks are coming. Cavalry is coming. Hundreds of 'em."

The boy holding onto John became excited and dug his fingernails into John's side causing him to flinch by arching his back. John started to issue a command, but instead grabbed at the boy's hand and asked him to let up. The air was thick with excitement.

Without hesitation Madison yelled to Becky, "Come on, girl. We got to go to your mother! Let me get my gun."

Madison ran to the barn where he had started leaning his musket in one corner after his attack at the ferry. Becky followed him on the horse. The two soldiers ran to John. Their faces were white, as though they had seen a ghost, and their eyes were the size of white saucers. Chris could feel his heart bouncing against his still tender ribs.

117

When Gauley Ran Blood

"We gonna fight 'em here, sir?" asked one of the out of breath soldiers.

"No. Take the ferry across the river and defend it from that position. I have two men there now. Fight until it gets too hot and then get outa there," exclaimed John.

He was perplexed about what to do with the boy and how he could get to Camp Gauley. He didn't feel right about leaving his men in a pickle. He had to think fast. He could hear riders at the top of the hill who were most likely Yankee cavalry. Madison and Becky were both on Maude, and returning from getting his weapon. As they passed John in the road, they wished him good luck, and he yelled to Chris.

"Hughes, take my horse and the boy and race to Camp Gauley. You can take the shortcut through the Slippy Gap, then out through the Bend and down by the Long Point. You can follow the river from there to Carnifex if you must."

"Yes, sir, but how far is it to the Slippy Gap?" Chris responded in earnest.

"Bam - pop, bam - pop," could now be heard as the soldiers across the river were taking shots at the advancing Federal Cavalry. The sounds of their rifles could be heard along with the pop of the sycamore leaves as the bullets pierced the tops of the trees, " Bam - pop, bam - pop."

"John, I know how to get there. Let me help. Daddy, stop!" exclaimed Becky as her dad paused and she slid off the rear of the horse like a cowboy in a Wild West show.

"Becky, take my horse and the boy. Wait for us at the Point. Chris, come with me. We'll get on top of the cliffs on this side of the river and get these Yanks in a crossfire. You boys, get that ferry outa here," barked John, who only had seconds to make his decisions.

The two men worked the ferry towline feverishly. The front of the boat lunged out of the water when they pulled in tandem, with no load aboard. In seconds, they had made their way across the river and were scurrying up the road to join their comrades who were encouraging them to hurry.

Becky and the boy were off along with Madison, but in different directions. Madison went up the river to the sanctuary and

Becky went downstream to the first low gap in the ridge known as the Bend. She wasn't much bigger than the boy who held to her sides. Madison thought of helping in the fight. He had heard the stories of his Uncle Jesse Hughes, the famous Indian fighter. His family had been massacred and he had sworn an oath to bring justice to the guilty. In his zeal for justice, he was known to pass over the line into vengeance; and mete out punishment, even to the innocent, based solely on the red color of their skin.

Madison's pistol whipping was fresh in his mind. Could he just kill one to restore his pride? No. These men had not harmed him. In fact, he didn't know that the men who had taken arms to him were Lincolnites. How ironic, he desired to kill, like his ancestor, based not on the color of their skin, but that of a mere uniform. No. He would not kill this day; unless it was to protect his wife or daughter.

John and Chris ran with their rifles by the barn and house, over the bank and through Salmons Creek. They made their way up the hillside and positioned themselves on the top of the cliffs overlooking the house and ferry landing at a distance of 150 yards. They were not in position a full minute when riders stopped at the ferry, but they weren't in uniforms. Had the soldiers on watch been mistaken?

Soon men joined them in blue uniforms. They had hats with one side turned up with feather plumes attached. They had swords flashing at their sides. The firing continued from the Confederates on the south side of the river. The dragoons returned fire but appeared to have primarily small arms, as was the custom of the cavalry, and only a few rifles. Their return fire was very ineffective from the small weapons. It appeared that the leader of the group realized his need for bigger arms to reach across the river, and he returned to his regiment to seek assistance.

As one of the men who remained at the ferry site made his way from the split rail fence that lined the road to the landing, a "pow" was heard on the opposite side of the river. A "thoop" sound was heard and the man collapsed at one side of the dock. He attempted to steady himself at the side of the landing but fell into the Gauley grasping his leg. The Confederates on the south bank let out a yell when they saw the man fall. Soon a crimson vortex

119

was seen swirling by the landing. The man lay silent, but in great pain in the mud at the side of the landing.

A series of cheers was heard up the Salmons Creek Road as the officer was returning with additional men, "Hurrah for the mighty 10th! Hurrah! Hurrah!"

The officer had summoned 10 men, but his order was misunderstood, and the bulk of the 10th Ohio Volunteer Infantry Regiment responded. Each man was anxious for his moment of glory. Hundreds of men from the 10th made their way at double-quick pace to reinforce their brothers under fire. There were no braver men to be found anywhere as they charged down that road to the ferry.

The Confederates continued to fire, but the smoke from their rifles gave their positions away. The Ohio men poured the lead to them. A deafening thunder and pounding of the air resulted when hundreds of blue clad soldiers fired their weapons across the river at the Rebs. During the volleys, the leaves on the opposite side waved as if in a strong wind. However, the air was still as witnessed by a fine line of smoke, rising straight into the sky from the chimney of Mirriam's kitchen. The smell of gunpowder mixed with the aroma of the fried chicken Mirriam had left in a skillet on the fire. Combined smells one would expect at a 4th of July celebration, not a battlefield.

The infantry held back nothing. Under this cover of shots, two of the scouts slipped out of their clothes and swam across the river to where the ferry had been left by the last two Southerners to cross. With the ferry as a shield, they swam and pulled the flatboat along toward the north shore.

The Confederates across the river began to withdraw under the heavy fire, but stopped when they realized they possessed adequate cover to return fire. Captain John and Chris had held their fire to avoid drawing attention to themselves and the fleeing couple. They had to act now for the sake of their comrades across the river, and began firing upon the boys in blue. By now there was a sea of blue at the ferry site. As they sensed being caught in a crossfire, many of the soldiers took cover behind the rail fence that lined the road. Some entered or stood behind the barn and blacksmith shop, and yet others bravely stood in the open firing their weapons time and time again. Now and then you would see a man spin violently and drop to the ground as his body was pierced by a piece of Southern metal. Immediately, he would be helped to cover by his companions.

John was not sure of the motives of the northern force. They appeared to be more interested in destroying the ferry than crossing the river. That being the case, he felt he and Chris should make it for Camp Gauley, and the main body of the Confederate force. They could gather Becky and the boy from the Point and then go on to Carnifex. Going via the Long Point was not the easiest route, but he suspicioned the roads would be thick with Yankees. He had hunted much of the area for most of his life and knew where most of the gaps were in the mountains and the breaks in the cliffs they would have to pass through. As with the boys on the far side of the river, the smoke from their weapons was their traitor. They had been spotted, and the fury of a regiment stung by bushwhackers was unleashed against them. The popping of leaves being pierced by bullets caused them to simultaneously look at each other and commence running in unison without a word being said. A half dozen mounted men in blue left the group to attempt to flank the fire that had come from the two that were in flight. Their unfamiliarity with the topography of the area and cliffs frustrated their pursuit. Chris was struck in his leather cap pouch at his waist, which held his rifle percussion caps. The round had ricocheted from one of the rocks along the cliffs and had lost its sting. It didn't even knock him from his feet. It did motivate him for a brisk retreat.

With the lull in the firing, the men from the army attacked the ferryboat with fervor. They used Madison's own saw to bisect the work of his hands. Chris' last glance, through the trees in the direction of the ferry, was of the two sections of the boat approaching the rapids below. The towline tethered from the south bank like a great fishing line. The ferry had been destroyed!

Some minutes later, the Union riders had found a break in the cliffs and were cautiously hunting their attackers. John and Chris ran along the crest of the ridge called the Bend that led to the Long Point. At the snort of a horse, both of the men made their way into a thick growth of rhododendron and hid as best they could. Chris had a clear shot at the rider but did not take it for fear of drawing the whole of the Yankee forces upon them. They watched as the rider rode out the ridge, turned, and rode back past them. After his passing, the two were again on their journey to the Point and in a short time, heard Becky calling from behind a downed rotting log.

"John, is that you?"

"We're here, Becky, where's the boy and the horse?" asked John.

"He is here, with me, and the horse is over the hill tied in a laurel thicket," she responded.

John was again faced with making a decision about what directives to give. He knew he needed to warn Floyd of the advancing Union troops. This had to be his priority. He had no other choice. He had to get the others to the Confederate lines someway. He could not send the civilians back to the ferry. The feelings would be running high among the Union soldiers at the wounding and possible death of their fellow campaigners, and they might take their frustrations out on them. The safest place for them would be behind the Confederate forces that were well dug in place at Camp Gauley.

"Becky, can you show Chris and the lad how to get to Carnifex? I've got to take the horse and warn Floyd as soon as I can that Rosecrans is coming. You and the boy will be safe there. Chris, you can watch over them until they're in the clear and then find the 22nd." With those comments, he was off to find his horse, and Chris and company were on their way to the Point.

It was a short walk to the laurel thicket that hid the opening of the passageway through the cliffs. As they approached the Point, Chris saw through the leaves the profile of a Union Cavalryman positioned near the abyss, observing the countryside below with a pistol in his hand. He grabbed the boy and Becky and shoved them into a heavy stand of laurel. He then dove into the thicket landing astride both Becky and the boy.

They could hear the clickety-click of the horse's shoes against the exposed rock atop the cliffs at the Long Point as they lay there motionless and in total silence. This was not the time for fantasy, but as they lay there, Chris was aware of Becky's sweet breath against the side of his face and the expansion and contraction of her chest as she attempted to catch her breath. A strange thought entered his mind as he listened and gazed for the mounted Yankee. His thoughts were not of desire, but of a deeper, more meaningful nature. He thought of what the preacher had said some days before at the camp about how God had sacrificed his Son because he loved the world. He died for people who didn't deserve it. Here he was now, in the midst of a conflict, and he knew in his heart he could die without reservation for the woman at his side. It seemed so simple. Was this that kind of God love? Maybe at another time they could have gotten acquainted and been friends. Maybe in other circumstances he would be telling Captain John about his bride to be. For now, he knew he had to protect his friend's fiancée even at the cost of his life.

He quietly asked, "How far to the passageway?"

"It's just there in the next thicket. If we could only get there, I can guide us through," she whispered as she pointed as if to touch the passageway hidden in the next thicket only a few feet away.

Chris raised from the leaf-covered ground and picked up a dead branch. He threw it as hard as he could in the direction opposite where Becky had indicated hoping to attract the soldiers attention away long enough for them to make good their escape. The broken limb made a thrashing sound as it slapped the leaves on trees as it flew, end over end, down the hillside. It struck a tree much closer than Chris would have liked, but he purposed to make the most of his ruse. The soldier heard the noise and quickly turned to the sound. As predicted, he left the edge of the cliff and rode a short distance over the hill, and out of sight to investigate the disturbance.

Chris was quick to start the group in the direction Becky had indicated. They were running as they cleared their blind. A bullet from the gun of an another unseen cavalryman shattered a sapling at Becky's right.

Chris yelled, "Go on. Don't stop!" as he turned and fired at the Yankee who was positioned some distance away high on the ridge above the Long Point.

He began reloading, instinctively, determined to confront the soldiers to allow Becky and the boy to escape. He bit the paper end from a cartridge and poured the powder into the barrel of the gun. Then he dropped the bullet into the barrel of the rifle and rodded it home. He fired again and again. The Union cavalryman withdrew for cover from Chris' persistent fire but returned to view in seconds with the other mounted soldier at his side. The two fired their pistols repeatedly as they charged his position. The pistols cracked with their exploding rounds, and the foliage surrounding Chris was buzzing with lead.

Becky reappeared and said, "Chris, come on! Please, you're gonna get killed!"

He fired one last time in the direction of the oncoming soldiers and ran toward Becky and safety. Becky sensed that he was going to sacrifice himself, for the benefit of her and the boy. She was touched by his gallant gesture, but also knew they had an excellent chance of escape if they all could get to the passage.

They entered the thicket and slid down the leafy ramp into the maze of passageways. They could hear the Yankee soldiers running through the brush above and plotting aloud their strategy for killing the bushwhackers. Becky led the way, followed by the boy, then Chris. Unlike her last visit there, the cooler weather apparently had kept the rattlers in their dens. Not one was seen or heard until the pursuing soldiers turned into a corridor that led to an outside opening high on the cliffs. The intermittent sun had lured one rattler into its rays to warm. The rabid soldiers charged into its midst and met with its wrath for being disturbed. Chris heard cursing and then a shot that reverberated back and forth through the rocky labyrinth.

Becky bravely continued along the ledges and through the corridors. When she reached the ramp that led to the exit where she had gotten into a nest of vipers some days earlier, she spoke.

"Watch yourself through here. We could have additional crawling Rebels we don't need."

Chris could not help but smile at her display of cautious humor at such a time as this. He liked it.

They were clear of the cliffs, and as Chris had suspected, they drew fire from the soldiers who had withdrawn back to safety at the top of the Long Point. He glanced back and saw one of the soldiers firing his pistol at them. The other was rolling on his back with his shoe off, and his pants leg pulled up grasping his leg. One of the crawling Rebels had apparently struck him just above the top of his boot. In seconds, they were out of sight and range of the cursing soldiers.

They ran and walked at an aggressive pace. They did not pause as they made their way down the Gauley. Becky led them surely along the path she knew so well. Chris was taken by her courage, intelligence, and beauty even in her unladylike garb. In her defense, he wondered why women had not worn pants earlier in doing garden work or even when riding horseback. They seemed much more practical than bulky dresses and hooped petticoats. He admired his friend John who was very fortunate to have such a prize fiancée.

They stopped and allowed the boy a drink at the mouth of McKees Creek. Chris took the opportunity to acquaint himself with his friend's betrothed.

"Are you and John going to live at the ferry, or on McKees Creek?" asked Chris in a loud voice to be heard over the roar of the Gauley.

Becky responded with a puzzled look and a strained voice so she too could be heard, "He'll live at McKees Creek, and I'll live at the ferry."

Chris was shocked at this arrangement. He had never heard of anything quite like it.

"Will you not share the same house?" he asked with inflection on each word.

"What for? He practically lived at the ferry when he was a boy. Played and hunted with my brothers all the time," she responded irritably.

Chris was growing more confused by the second. He knew the people in the mountains of western Virginia were a different breed, but this culture she outlined, he never dreamed existed. In desperation for understanding, he asked again with great inflection.

"Will you have children?"

125

"I hope to when I am married, but I don't really think that is any of your business," she responded. "Mr. Hughes, is there something you want to ask me? I get the impression that you don't believe what I say. Do you want something?"

Chris hesitated but stated, "I think the place for a wife is with her husband."

"Me too," she said.

"I think a husband and wife ought to live together."

"Me too."

"Then why would you live at the ferry and have John live at Gad?" Chris finally said, "I just can't figure that."

"You talk like he and I are getting married. Mercy, who knows what will happen in our lives by the end of the day, let alone the end of this war. People's feelings change. Marriage is a commitment, but he could change his mind by the time the war's over. Who knows who will end up with who?" Becky replied as Johnny joined them, and she turned toward him and away from Chris, so that he could not hear her over the roar of the Gauley.

"Besides, Ginny and John make an attractive couple. She's not so bad and John is a great fellow. I wish them well."

"What? I didn't hear..."

His sentence was interrupted by the sound of rifle fire somewhere to the west of them. They all paused and listened intently.

"We better go," he said.

He thought Becky was certainly displaying an offhanded attitude about her relationship with John. He agreed that John is a great fellow. Where was she coming from? She sounded distant from John. He knew she would never wish any harm come to him. Hillbillies are a strange breed he thought. Who can understand them? He remained intrigued by this woman with whom he was so smitten.

Chapter 8
Engagement at Carnifex Ferry

John soon found his horse and backtracked to a low gap in the Bend. He turned the horse to the west and headed for Camp Gauley. His route was difficult but shorter than the one taken by Rosecrans' troops. His horse was near death when, after much hard riding, he reached the first Rebel pickets outside of Camp Gauley just before mid afternoon. With little fanfare, they waived him through and he reported to Colonel Tompkins who, with the 22nd, had just arrived. They had crossed Carnifex Ferry only minutes earlier.

After a briefing with General Floyd, Colonel Tompkins spoke to the leaders of his regiment.

"Men, our job is to defend the far-left flank of this position. On our right will be Colonel McCauseland's 36th, and then Colonel Reynold's 50th Virginia Infantry. The front left flank will be Colonel Wharton's 51st Virginia Infantry, and part of the 36th. They will branch to the left of the 50th and be in front of us, so take careful aim that you don't shoot our own men. On the right of the 50th will be four of Captain Guy's cannons at the high point of the fortification. Heth's 45th Virginia Infantry will hold the right flank. It is about 400 feet down to the river at that point. If the Yankees want to come in that way let them. They will be so tired from climbing the mountain, we can whip them with a club."

A hearty, but nervous laugh went up from his men.

He continued, "Reynolds has recently withdrawn from his camp at Cross Lanes and McCauseland from Summersville. Everyone, but us, is dug-in and ready for a fight. Have your men clear as much brush as possible and build whatever protection you can. Keep them low. Make certain each man has forty rounds of ammunition. The supply wagon has not arrived yet, but we expect it any minute. Major Smith, you will please mount-up and check on the disposition of the supply train. Hurry them up a bit."

John told the Colonel of the skirmish at Hughes Ferry and about the massive troop movements that had been reported. Tompkins acknowledged that he had heard similar reports given by Colonel McCauseland's forces. Tompkins knew that Floyd had not more than 1,800 men but that he had requested more from Wise and Lee. It would take no less than a miracle to defeat Rosecrans' force of 8,000. Colonel Tompkins had a great deal of respect for his fellow West Point alumnus, General Rosecrans. They had also had business dealings prior to the war. It was unfortunate that the war should cause them to take arms against one another.

John told Colonel Tompkins of the plight of Private Hughes, Becky, and the boy. The colonel told him he could look for them for thirty minutes, but he was very short on men, and his company needed him. He would have to return as quickly as possible. Captain Shelton of Company D assured him that he would take care of his company until he returned. John was off to find the party that was traveling on foot. He knew Becky would lead them down Gauley, past the mouth of McKees Creek, and then through a low gap in the mountains toward Camp Gauley. She would guide them through the gap and down the valley of a small stream that emptied into the Gauley a half-mile upstream of the northern most trenches of the Confederates' right flank. The fortifications, however, lay some 400 feet above the river at a bend where the Pierson Hollow converged with the river.

He had taken a route north of the one Becky and company were on which was more accommodating for the horse. He was familiar with her most likely route but knew his chances of finding them were slight because of the vast area each had to travel. There was a narrow corridor between the cliffs and Gauley they would have to pass through. He chose this as his interception point. He had confidence in Becky's guiding abilities and knew he could depend on Chris in a fight. But, he didn't know if he could find them.

When Gauley Ran Blood

John rode past the cannons and down the road toward Cross Lanes. After he passed the Patterson farm, he guided his mount to the right and down the Pierson Hollow toward the Gauley. He knew this would be his quickest and best chance of helping his friends get to safety behind the Confederate lines. He paused just before he started down the long steep slope that led to the river and heard gunfire in the distance. It came from the direction of Cross Lanes. Were Rosecrans' forces arriving already and driving in the Rebel pickets? He didn't know if the advancing Union army would allow him time to find his friends, but he had to try. He felt badly about leaving them behind.

He had to dismount to navigate his horse down the steep slope to the river. He couldn't have ridden anyway because of the low branches hanging from the trees. Not half way down, he gave up on the horse and tied it to a pine brow. He finally reached the bank of the river and took a brief drink from a pool with his cupped hand. He could no longer hear the distant gunfire over the roar of the river. He started upstream over large boulders and driftwood logs in search of his band. In places the river met the bank at large rocks too high to get over or massive laurel thickets too dense to penetrate, and John was forced to travel around them. In desperation, at times, he would crawl on his hands and knees beneath the laurel to make his way through often ending up on his stomach to clear the impenetrable mass. He had never been at this particular area on the Gauley before and now knew why. Lizards and snakes were the only creatures built low enough to the ground to allow convenient passage through this jungle of green.

As John had speculated, Becky, in fact, had brought her party through the low gap and had made her way down the Gauley to a point a short distance above the Pierson Hollow. It had taken her much longer than she had expected, but they were experiencing the same problems John had encountered. They had been walking for four hours. His thirty-minute jaunt was beginning its second hour. During one of his crawls, he looked up at a distance and saw movement. He brought his rifle around and aimed at the movement. He then observed Becky, crawling as he was, with her hat in her hand. The boy and then Chris followed her.

129

"Don't you have anything better to do?" John asked jokingly.

Becky was startled and jerked her head up against a branch when she looked up. They stood between laurel thickets with Becky rubbing her head. The boy brought up the rear but looked in better form than the others.

"Am I ever glad to see you all. I was just about to turn back," said John.

Chris spoke in a musing tone while he picked laurel leaves and cobwebs from his beard.

"I think I'd rather take my chances with the Yankees than with this laurel mess. I have been scraped, scratched, poked, flipped and gouged. All them Yankees are gonna do is shoot me! Where do they want me to stand? I'll turn my weapon over to Mr. Lincoln."

"They'll have their chance, mister. You can't hear it, but I think things are heating up at Camp Gauley as we speak. I could hear shooting before. You can't hear it now for the river. We have got to hurry and get to the camp," said John.

The four stood in a small clearing devoid of laurel. That was an anomaly for that section of the river. Dispersed among the expanses of laurel was an occasional giant hemlock or poplar tree. Gray and white cliffs were sporadically visible on both sides of the Gauley. The constant roar of the river seemed almost unnatural in the serene setting as the sun was setting out of site behind the high point of the mountain that was called Camp Gauley.

"What are we going to do with Miss Hughes and the boy?" asked Chris.

"They should be alright when they get to Carnifex. It's not more than a couple more miles down the river. We'll go back up the way I came down and cross behind our lines until we get to where the 22nd is positioned. We may have to kill a few Blue Boys to get there but we'll be in good shape then," replied John.

"We need to make tracks. Becky, can you manage with...," he hesitated not knowing the boy's name.

"His name is Johnny Blizzard," voiced Becky. "His dad is with the 36th."

When Gauley Ran Blood

"I'll speak for myself, thank you," said the boy. "If it is all the same to you, Captain John, I'll fight with you. I have always taken my own part in things, and this here war ain't no different. I can shoot, but I need a gun. I would be obliged if you could get me one."

The trio of adults was shocked, not only could this boy handle himself on the go, but he was also very articulate for his age. A reasonable sign of maturity, John thought.

"I can take care of that when we get to camp, Johnny. I just hope we can get there without getting shot. We'll all travel together. Follow me," commanded John.

The four walked, crawled, and climbed until they made it to the mouth of the Pierson Hollow. Then they started the exhausting climb out of the river basin toward the Cross Lanes road, to the Rebel right flank trenches, and reasonable safety. There was no trail so travel could only be made between rock outcrops and boulders as they climbed the mountain. The laurel was a constant menace. They would make an occasional swing to the left or right of the hollow's center to avoid having to climb large moss covered boulders or rock outcrops.

As the drone of the river faded and they made their way up the mountain, the sound of cannon fire could be heard. It was unmistakably coming from Camp Gauley. There would be an initial boom and then an echoing effect from numerous cliffs that sounded like distant thunder. As they rose higher up the mountain, the sounds of firearms could be heard. At times the sound was a splattering of gunfire, and individual rounds could not be distinguished. Cannon and rifle fire had replaced the drone of the river. Becky had heard these sounds before, and she was anything but anxious to experience them again. Her good intentions had gotten her into this, and it appeared the good Lord would have to get her out.

John and Becky had made their way to the right center of the hollow some distance ahead of the others. The boy was growing anxious, and he and Chris had paused behind a boulder below a rock ledge on the left side of the hollow while he relieved himself. Johnny buttoned his pants and started around the boulder and was met with the barrel of Chris's gun against his chest. Chris

131

motioned with his index finger to his lips for him to be quiet. He then nodded with his head for the boy to look up the hollow. Blue uniforms covered the cove. John and Becky were rounding a ledge higher on the hillside than Chris and could not see the enemy approaching directly above them. He put up his rifle and took a bead on the first Blueboy determined to shoot him through. He paused and thought, after he saw dozens of uniformed Lincolnites behind the first, his zeal to draw first blood might put John and Becky in a hornet's nest of blue. He felt helpless but could only look on down the sights of his gun.

The soldiers he saw were part of the 23rd Ohio Volunteer Infantry. They were part of Rosecrans' forces. All the Union forces had reunited after the ferry skirmish and made their way toward the abandoned camp of Colonel Reynolds of the 50th Virginia Infantry at Cross Lanes.

General Rosecrans and Brigadier General Benham of the 1st Brigade rode ahead of the troops advancing on Camp Gauley to the break of a hill to assess the Confederate position. Benham was ordered to reconnoiter the area with the 10th Ohio Volunteer Infantry. At mid afternoon as they made their way to Camp Gauley near the head of a fork of the Pierson Hollow, they traveled down a gentle wooded hillside to the edge of what had been a cornfield. The nearby Southerners had stripped it of all its bounty and fed the fodder to their horses. Only a small patch of deep green remained near the Henry Patterson home on the opposite side of the field. The gray weathered two-story structure, with a large front porch and kitchen to the rear, was near the center of what would become the battleground that day. A pavilion stood guard over the dug well in the front yard of the house. No one stirred in the yard, but activity could be seen through a window of the house. A barrage of musket fire broke the calm stillness from the hidden Rebel fortifications on the opposite side of the house about a 100 yards from it. Brave soldiers twisted in their shoes as the Rebel bullets ripped their flesh. Others gnashed their teeth and gripped their weapons as they watched the bright red blood flow from their comrades' blue uniforms that day. They aimed their rifles at an invisible enemy. Where were those cowardly Gray Jackets? They were hidden like bushwhackers.

When Gauley Ran Blood

From his horse, Union General Benham extended his telescope in the direction of the house and put it to his eye. He saw nothing, but just as he was about to take down the glass, he saw a woman with a small child in her arms run for her life from behind the house toward the woods to the west. He repositioned his telescope and ran it past the house and along a road to the brow of the hill. The Rebels began a horrendous barrage of cannon fire from their position on the opposite knoll. The ground exploded in front of his horse. He calmed his mount and again repositioned his glass. The trees above the Union men came alive with shot from the Rebel guns. The Confederates threw a great deal of grapeshot, so named for its appearance as large round grapes, from their cannons at the Union forces that day. Its impact was deadly and its affect demoralizing.

"There, there they are!" exclaimed Benham.

He had caught sight of the fiery blast from the end of one of the four cannons in Captain Guy's battery located behind the breastworks.

"They're dug in like moles. There's that scoundrel Floyd. He's standing on a chestnut stump looking like Napoleon. Bring up the 10th, 12th, and 13th. Have McMullin's mountain howitzers placed here on this knoll. I'll give them some of their own medicine. We'll see how them cotton pickers like that," snarled Benham.

After nearly a twenty-mile march that had begun 12 hours earlier, the Union forces were now engaged at Camp Gauley. After little or no rest, Benham's 12th and 13th regiments were sent against Floyd's right just above the southwestern lip of the Pierson Hollow. They attacked ferociously, with a constant firing of their weapons from the east, and drove Heth's 45th away from the flank toward the center near the artillery. They were aided by the bombardment of the Confederate ranks by Benham's artillery. Colonel William Smith, leader of the 13th, reported back to General Rosecrans and General Benham that with additional support he felt he could take the Southern right flank. His support would come from the 12th and 23rd.

Colonel John Lowe navigated the 12th across the open cornfield toward the Patterson house where they could shelter from the torrent of Confederate bullets. As he led his troops to challenge the Rebel works, he heeled his horse and with the reins in his left hand and his sword swirling above his head in his right he cried, "Follow me, my men, charge!"

A Rebel bullet in his forehead halted his heroism. His men looked on as he fell from his horse and made a feeble attempt to land himself on the ground. He briefly held himself up from the ground and said in a daze, "Oh, my dear!"

Seconds later canister fire from one of the Rebel guns exploded atop his legs and shredded them. The brave mutilated leader lay dead in a bloody shell hole. His troops and others cried out for revenge of his gruesome death when word reached them.

Moments earlier, Colonel Lytle and part of the 10th Ohio Voluntary Infantry had started the battle by making a valiant charge against the Rebel artillery. They sustained heavy casualties in nearly the same area as Lowe's troops - near the Patterson house. Lytle was hit in the leg and knocked from his horse. The horse was mortally wounded and ran riderless toward the Rebel abratis that protected the artillery. The soldiers looked on expecting to see the horse impale itself in the sharpened spears of the protective lattice. Its mane danced to and fro as it jumped over the abratis and into the Southern works. With great lunges, it made its way down the line continuing to toss its mane until it fell. The beautiful creature lay dying; spasmodically flinching for several seconds until it took its last breath.

Colonel Lowe had made the 1st Brigade proud. The loss of his horse was trivial compared to the deaths of 10 men and 50 wounded by the enemy fire. Brave and fearless men shed their blood on the field that day.

A non-lethal Yankee bullet had also struck the Confederate General Floyd in the forearm during one of the bullet exchanges. He would survive, as would most of his dug in troops. The 22nd had not had time to prepare their defenses properly, but they too suffered minor casualties.

They were positioned on the Confederate left flank and were hit with cannon fire and shot from the Northern troops. They were positioned in such a fashion that the cannon fire from the Union troops was parallel to their lines, not perpendicular to them.

When Gauley Ran Blood

The Union Army had positioned their guns so that the projectiles launched at the Confederate artillery traveled directly at the 22nd position. They were pelted with canister, solid shot, and shrapnel from exploding shells. They were fortunate that only a few men were stung with Yankee steel.

Rosecrans launched a two-fold plan against the Confederates late in the day. Colonel Smith of the 13th would be joined by the 12th and 23rd and again hit the Rebels' right flank. The 2nd Brigade including the 9th, 28th, and 47th Ohio Volunteer Infantry under Colonel Robert McCook was to strike the center of the Floyd line concurrently. As they awaited the attack by Smith to the Rebels' right, the 28th was called to join and support him, the 12th, and the 23rd in the Pierson Hollow.

A company of the 23rd led by Major Rutherford Hayes cautiously made its way down the Pierson Hollow toward the travelling quartet. Chris and Johnny could only watch as John and Becky made their way up the hollow toward the enemy. As they were crossing beneath the brow of a cliff, Hayes' men surprised them. They were told to halt by a young soldier standing atop the cliff.

John started to put up his gun when he saw numerous dark colored figures outlining the horizon. He lowered the rifle as he whispered, "Becky, follow my lead. Please, just follow my lead."

John yelled as he dropped his rifle and threw his pistol on the ground, " I surrender! Don't shoot! I surrender!"

He looked up at the cliff and a young soldier was staring down his sight at him and Becky.

Again he spoke softly to Becky, "Lose the hat and let your hair down. Pull out your blouse and act like a lady. I'll try to get you out of this. "

A dozen others now joined the single soldier. Each had their gun aimed at the couple.

" Let's kill-em!" yelled one of the privates.

John wondered now if he had made a mistake in not trying to fight his way out. He wanted to try and save Becky any way that he could.

"No! They're my prisoners. Let them be," scolded the first soldier. "You, down there, put your arms above your head and don't move a muscle. Somebody get the Major. He'll know what to do with them."

"Shoot their brains out. Like they did to Colonel Lowe. They're Rebel scum. Shoot them through," repeated another of the soldiers.

They had heard of the valiant death of Colonel Lowe by the Rebel bullet and the near obliteration of his corpse by the cannon shell, and they were anxious for revenge.

"I said no!" the initial soldier repeated loudly. "They've surrendered and we're not going to murder them. You, Johnny Rebs, come on around the rocks and come up here. Keep your hands in the air where I can see them."

"Hey, Bill, that's a woman. Well, I never, she has pants on," jeered one of Union soldiers.

John and Becky walked up along the side of the rock cliff to the top with their hands above their heads. Becky tilted her head and her hat fell off. Then she shook her head to help her hair fall from the tight bun it had been in atop her head. Chris looked on from a distance, but he and the boy remained still and took no action for fear of placing the couple in jeopardy.

"What's your regiment soldier?" the soldier asked John.

"22nd Virginia," he replied.

"Are you a soldier?" he asked as he stared at Becky.

John interrupted, "She is my wife, sir. She's no soldier."

John knew there was a slim chance of her being set free, but he figured he had nothing to lose since they had not been shot already. He only hoped Becky could play along.

"I was taking her home to safety from the camp and thought we were clear of the fighting. She's got nothing in this. Please let her go. Let her go home."

"What do you have there, Private McKinley?" asked Major Hayes as he arrived on the scene. "Men, keep spread out and your eyes open. There may be others about."

McKinley replied, "A Reb and his wife. He says he was taking her home from the camp. She had no weapon, sir, when we come upon them." His compassion, for the pathetically dressed but attractive woman, was obvious. He appeared relieved that he had not had to kill them.

When Gauley Ran Blood

Becky placed her forehead into her hand and pretended to sob as she shook her head.

" I just...I just wanted him to know about the baby. "

"What is it, ma'am?" asked the Major.

"We're going to have a baby. I just wanted him to know before he went off to war," stated Becky as she pretended to sob.

Becky lied, trying to appear innocent. Her spoof was as good as if she were acting in a New York City theater. John was surprised at her boldness and silently prayed that she wouldn't over act or take things too far.

"Very well. Let's get them to the rear for now. We've more important business at hand. Escort them to General Rosecrans' staff. They may have information of value," said Major Hayes as he led his men on down the ravine that Chris and Johnny had just left.

Chris observed that John and Becky had been taken prisoner and not shot, as he feared. With at least the comfort that they were alive, he and the boy made their way around the steep cliffs on the Rebel right flank and into the rear of Heth's troops. The boy was quite adept at scaling the rocks and cliffs late that day. Chris had to tell him to wait up on more than one occasion to keep from losing site of him. Johnny said he played on rocks a lot when he was growing up.

Only occasional firing was heard as they entered camp. Chris was directed west along the trenches to the location of McCauseland's 36th where Johnny was relieved to find his father. Chris then made his way to the 22nd and was reunited with his company. He had arrived in time to miss the peak of the action, but Chris' day was only just beginning.

As Chris and the boy escaped, John and Becky led Private McKinley back up Pierson Hollow at the point of his rifle. A soldier of the 13th challenged them.

McKinley spoke, "I am under orders from Major Rutherford Hayes to deliver these prisoners to General Rosecrans. You need to let us pass."

His request was granted and they continued their trek.

When Gauley Ran Blood

McKinley asked the private who had challenged him, "What's your unit? You're marching to the rear. The battle is in the other direction. What's going on?"

The private quickly responded, "They called off the assault. Something about it was too late or dark or something. I'm with the 13th. The 28th is back there somewhere pulling up the rear. I just want to go to sleep. I haven't gotten to sit down one time today. I haven't had a drink since noon. We have been on the go for 16 hours today. Tell you the truth, I could sleep right here."

They continued on their march and John brazenly asked, "Why don't you let her go? She doesn't have any part in this battle. Please, let her go home."

The expression on the private's face was awkward. John could tell he was uneasy pointing a gun at a civilian - especially a supposedly pregnant female civilian.

"I've got orders. I regret your circumstances, but I can't do that. I'm confident that the general will deal with her fairly," replied McKinley.

He could see up ahead that there was a column of soldiers on the march toward the road that led to Cross Lanes. It was nearly dark when he saw the distinct fire from a rifle on his left, then another, and another. They had obviously gotten too close to the Rebel lines and were now being fired upon. The company ahead returned fire in a deafening barrage of fiery shot and blinding smoke. The still cool air of the September evening held the smoke in its place. They could not see the enemy for the smoke and fading light, but the gunfight continued. Both sides delivered horrendous volleys at the other. McKinley had John and Becky sit at the base of a large poplar tree away from the firing, and he, likewise, stood on the side opposite the action for protection with his rifle now pointed toward the opposing Southerners.

John tried one final time, "You're going to get her killed, you Yankee devil. Let her go. She can save herself if only you'll let her. Please, let her go!"

This was no ruse. John was scared. He was scared for his life and for Becky's. Becky sensed his fear and her mouth dried and her heart raced. She could feel the blood surging through her temples. It is bad enough to take aim and to kill in the light of day, but night fighting is extremely dangerous and only for the insane. He and Becky stood as the smoke from the intense fighting surrounded them.

"Go! Run if you can! " barked the private at Becky in the privacy of their smoke cloud, "Just get out of here, now! Hurry, run."

"Oh, thank you, thank you," she said, "Good luck, John."

Becky was off in the direction opposite the gunfire, and towards Cross Lanes. It was late in the evening and getting very difficult to see. Becky knew she could travel east a mile or so and intercept the trail that ran through the low gap they had come through earlier in the day, but not at night. There were too many boulders and rock cliffs to fall from. She would put distance between her and the battle, then find a place to rest for the night, and retrace her path back home to the ferry at first light. She thought of going to Amanda Ramsey's house but figured the Yankees would be thick in and about Cross Lanes. She would be better off just laying low for the night and starting fresh in the morning. She was concerned for her parents and prayed that no harm had come to them.

As Becky made her escape, John thanked the private and told him how much he appreciated what he had done for them.

The private responded by saying, "This never happened. Do you understand? This did not happen."

John acknowledged and told him he understood. The shooting had stopped and the smoke cleared. They continued their walk and came upon a company of Union soldiers who had been shot up badly. Other soldiers were attending to them.

A passing officer was heard saying, "Calm down men. Hold your fire till further ordered. Hold your fire."

It appeared that the fight was over for the day. It was now time to withdraw the rest of the troops and avoid a counteroffensive by the Southerners. Rosecrans would prepare for an all out assault at the break of day. He knew the soft underbelly of the Rebels lay at their right flank. His forces would attack that spot with vigor, but for the remainder of the night, they would sleep on their weapons.

When Gauley Ran Blood

Word passed through the corps that in the confusion of withdrawing from the battlefield in the darkness the 13th and 23rd, which had been at the front on advance, upon withdrawal, had doubled back on the trailing 28th Regiment. For an unknown reason, someone had opened fire not knowing in the darkness and dense underbrush that they were firing into their own troops. Between the two groups, 30 casualties were recorded, some to never rise again. Becky's good fortune of being released during the conflict had unfortunately been a disastrous time for some of the combatants, and Captain John Halstead remained a prisoner of Federals.

As the Northern Army marched to the ferry road, the Union batteries gave a great volley of cover fire to aid the withdrawing Federals. Ambulances and litters were seen carrying the dead and wounded away from the battlefield. The cries of the wounded pierced the night air. The knives and bone saws of the field surgeons were kept busy until the early morning hours. When the final tally was taken, there would be nearly 140 Union casualties including 30 deaths. The soldiers had had a long exhausting day. Most had not taken food or water since early in the day. Many, on command, had dropped their bedrolls and knapsacks going into battle and would now have to go without their essential provisions. They would spend the night with their rifles in their hands.

General Floyd cared for his wound and pondered his fate. He sensed that, being out manned 4 to 1 with no reinforcements on the way, his tenure as King of Camp Gauley was drawing to a close. Rosecrans had ample time to study his fortifications and armaments and would charge his weaknesses in the morning light. The southern general held a confab with his officers in the evening, and it was decided to retreat across the Gauley under the cover of darkness and join General Wise at his camp at Dogwood Gap.

The plan sounded simple enough but it had its faults. How could you mobilize an entire army without your enemies, who were only a few hundred yards away, hearing the commotion? What would happen if the Federals learned of their withdrawal and attacked from the cliffs overlooking the ferry? Critics of the plan said the Confederate soldiers would be sitting ducks. The Yankees would have a carnival shoot until every last trooper was floating face down in the Gauley. How could you negotiate the narrow mountain trail with men, teams, and wagons in the darkness without enormous loss of life? How could they do it? It would take a miracle for Floyd to move 2000 men across the Gauley with only two small flatboats and a footbridge by first light.

Floyd was about to try for his miracle. Around 10:00 PM, in anything but a gallant gesture, Floyd alone crossed the river to the south side. He was followed by the troops in order of their position along the lines from the east to the west. The order of his pet regiments being first in line was questioned by some of the 22nd. The 45th, 50th, and 51st Regiments were allowed to go first. The 36th and finally the 22nd followed them. Again the 22nd found itself in the rear during a retreat. This one having particularly dangerous consequences for failure.

Chris' unit began its retreat about 12:30 AM. Their wait had been long and agonizing. The troops were leaving in ranks and the process was unbelievably slow. They had been on the go for several days without rest, and Chris' day had been long and hard. On the positive side, he had gotten to see Becky again and that was a pleasant affair. He was heartsick about her and John's capture, but there was little he could do to prevent it.

The 22nd would march no more than 5 minutes and they would be halted for 45. They were told they were waiting for the supply train of the 36th. While they waited, they heard noises from the area of Captain Guy's artillery. Everyone froze in place and not a sound was made. Major Smith rode toward the source to investigate. The wagons of the 36th were nowhere to be seen, but to his dismay, the Confederate artillery was still in place. Not a team had been harnessed to the limbers. The cannons were not ready to be moved. How had word not reached them to prepare to move out? This delay could cost the 22nd their lives.

Major Smith barked, " Prepare the cannons for withdrawal immediately. We're retreating across the river. Make haste, Gentlemen."

"But, Sir, we have no orders," replied a lieutenant.

"You do now, lieutenant. You either harness up those teams and get them limbered to the cannons and make tracks, or you will be left here to fight the Union Army by yourself," added the major as he wheeled his horse around and made his way back to the regiment.

Tompkins concurred that there was a fly in the ointment. Every moment brought them closer to dawn and the scores of Union infantry who would besiege them, hungry for vengeance of their comrades' blood from the previous day. He had Smith return and repeat the order in his name. Smith did not return to his regiment until the cannons were on the move. His astuteness could well have saved the entire regiment from capture or death. They were finally moving again. The 22nd was the last unit out of camp. Such was their lot. It was part of their duty as rear guard. Some thought Floyd had a bad habit of placing the 22nd in that circumstance too frequently.

The road to the ferry was more like a trail. It was narrow and steep and crept down among the boulders and cliffs like a great snake. It was difficult to cover in daylight, but in the middle of the night in total darkness it was nearly impossible. There was a pause after each step they took. The cannons were creating an even greater bottleneck. At places, the trail edged along the tops of high cliffs hardly wide enough for a horse. Navigating a limbered cannon along these ledges was extremely dangerous. The limber itself was not the problem. It was the combined length of the two teams, limber, and gun carriage on the narrow trail that caused the dilemma. The limber was nothing more that a set of two wagon wheels with a frame to hold storage boxes for the cannon's supplies and a tongue to attach to a team of two to six horses. The field gun carriage, consisting primarily of two wagon wheels on a small frame that held the cannon, would attach directly to the limber with the muzzle of the gun pointing behind. Sometimes, an additional larger storage chest, called a caisson, would trail the limber.

Major Smith again rode ahead to assess what was holding up the column. Time was growing short to when the great Union Army would strike. After passing three cannons he came upon the lead weapon. The horses were balking at one of the precipices. At this place the trail made an abrupt right turn. In order to clear a rock outcrop on the right side of the path with the limber, the horses had to be taken to the very edge of the cliffs. Even in the darkness, the animals sensed the risk in their path. Their managers were helpless to get them moving. Smith reported back to Tompkins of the plight of Captain Guy's batteries.

"Shall I ask him to run them off the cliffs, sir," asked Smith, who more than anyone else realized the potential for disaster if their progress was not renewed. As rear guard they could not pass the batteries with their corps.

"No, Major," replied the Colonel, "have we no one who could aid these gentlemen?"

"Hughes, sir, Private Hughes claims to be a horseman," he answered.

"Take him forward and see what he can do, Major," commanded Tompkins.

Major Smith was off in seconds to Company C to summon Chris' assistance.

"Can you help us Private Hughes? We seem to be having trouble with the battery teams. I am told that you have a way with horses. Would you have a look with me?" asked Smith.

The major offered his hand and Chris jumped behind him on his horse. Shortly, they were down the trail to the bottleneck. The column along the way was tormented. Men had squatted on the ground, some were leaning against trees, and others were sprawling in the leaves beside the trail. They had a very long day and most were totally exhausted. The waiting was unbearable. Many of the men knew they were the last regiment to leave, and with the coming of the sun, most likely, their lives would end if they didn't get started soon.

They arrived to find the drivers of the first cannon, with the aid of others in the battery, manually passing the limber and carriage through the tight spot. They had unhooked the horses, backed them up and then walked them between the precipice and rock outcrop. This had greatly shortened the turning radius required by the horses and limber. The troops of the battery were in the process of manually moving the limber and gun carriage around the obstacle. They would then reform their train and continue down the mountainside. As Major Smith and Chris looked on, they agreed that the procedures employed by the drivers were proper and effective for safe passage. The serious drawback was the amount of time involved in passing each cannon. With

143

three cannons to go they could consume an additional hour and a half. This was precious time that could cost the 22nd their lives.

In the corner of his mouth, Chris chewed on a piece of birch branch as he talked, "Major, I think I can pass those teams directly through that spot without unhooking, if they would let me try. We had a treacherous curve like this back home on Huckleberry Ridge. We used to have to take loaded grain wagons around it. It wasn't this high, but the curve and grade were about the same. You see, Major, the horses see better than we do. They have night vision. They are holding back the load and feel the pressure against them and when they get near the edge they naturally balk. They're far from stupid creatures. They sense they are being pushed toward the cliff. I can't guarantee my method, but I think she'll work."

The captain of the battery, who had been listening, was skeptical but understood the plight of the 22nd. It was his neck in the noose if he lost his battery. With a little coaxing, he conceded to allow Chris to try with one cannon.

"Wrap that rope twice around that tree and tie it to the cannon carriage. We'll use it like a hawser to hold back on the load and take some of the pressure from the teams. Let's blindfold the horses so that they cannot see at all. Your artillery horses are accustomed to that. That will help remove the fear. Swing wide to the left on your approach. Attach a lead rope to the left horse, and when they get to the edge, pull for all your worth," instructed Chris to the drivers, "Major, I've always had a habit of finding better ways to do things. Sometimes things improve and well sometimes... they don't. I feel good about this one. I think I can make this one work."

Each cannon had two teams of two horses each. The limber and the cannon carriage followed the teams. The drivers, who normally rode atop the left horse of their two-horse team, were forced to use the right non-leading horse to steer as they walked alongside. They voiced their opposition. The captain asked if they would prefer to ride and risk a long trip off the side of the cliff. They submitted by their silence. It was time for the train to move. Chris chewed hard on his birch twig and held tension on the rope that was attached to the axle beneath the cannon.

When Gauley Ran Blood

"Get up, get up," barked the drivers as they walked beside their teams straight toward the cliff in the pitch darkness.

The night air was cool but the drivers were sweating profusely. One of the lead horses flinched and snorted as its driver unknowingly steered it into a holly bush with its sharp spines. The other horses jerked as it pulled them in their harnesses.

"Easy boy. Easy," calmed the driver.

Chris held tension on the rope so that the horses had to actually pull the load down hill, which would be a more natural sensation for them. The air was thick with anxiety and excitement. Chris wiped the sweat from his brow with his sleeve.

As the teams approached the escarpment, a brave lieutenant, who had ingeniously lit a greasy ram from the cannon as a torch, watched and was to give a sign when the drivers were to turn their teams. The blinded horses crept closer to the edge. From his vantage on the edge of the cliff, the lieutenant could see the dim torch lights on the ferryboats and on the footbridge downstream. Though faint, he could make out a steady procession of the withdrawing Confederate troops which appeared as a parade of ants leading from the anthill.

Everyone held his breath as the front team approached the edge. With one more step, the horse would become airborne. The lieutenant called out softly but firmly so as to not spook the horses.

"Now."

The drivers tugged on the lead ropes and yelled, "Gee! Gee!" guiding them to the right.

The horses, nearly standing on their hind legs, abruptly turned to the right and continued their pull down the hillside. The inside wheel of the limber caught an edge of the rock outcrop and rode up it a short distance, and then fell back to the trail with a rumble and rattle from the ammunition and supplies within. The cannon carriage repeated the climb and fall. Chris released the rope and the horses were clear to travel on down the mountainside. He breathed again. His approach had worked in less than ten minutes. With little fanfare, the remaining two cannons were passed in the same process.

Chris paused and searched his mouth for his comforter, the small birch branch he had been chewing on. His tongue went from side to side in his mouth, but it was not to be found. In the heat of things he had ground it to sawdust and swallowed it. Fortunate for him, it wasn't a gold toothpick.

The column was on the move again and many of the men breathed easier, but the retreat was not complete. They had a river to cross and little time to do it. The 22nd crossed the footbridge by torchlight after waiting on the 36th. Chris watched a short silhouette cross in the darkness and wondered if it was Johnny Blizzard. The major started his men across the footbridge at about five foot intervals. The water was swift beneath the shabbily constructed footbridge that had no handrail. Less than 50 feet downstream a series of rapids churned and tossed the water so that a white cloud could be seen in the black of night. A misplaced step and you could easily be swept away to eternity. Torches were placed about every 50 feet along the bridge but were burnt to mere stubs and put out little light. Darkness was rapidly being remedied by the dawning of Wednesday morning.

Finally, the men had all safely crossed the Gauley. Several had congregated on the south side along the river to drink or wash their wounds. The current, that had just threatened them with capture or death, now carried life giving waters to them and cleansed their battle scars. As artillery fire was heard from the direction of Camp Gauley, Colonel Tompkins hastened the men up the Sunday Road but left one company to destroy the bridge and ferries.

General Floyd had received his miracle. He had fought without losing a man. He had withdrawn his entire force without incident but only with the aid of competent subordinate officers. He had left behind some of the sick and wounded and many of the Union soldiers captured at Cross Lanes, but his army would live to fight another day. General Rosecrans had missed an excellent opportunity to crush his foe. Now he would have to play a game of hide and seek with his adversary. General Floyd withdrew his troops to Dogwood Gap and then to Meadow Bluff near Lewisburg. In time, his foe would follow.

A runaway slave, who had been with his master at the camp, escaped during the night's activities. He was captured by Union pickets the next morning and reported to them that the

Rebel Army had escaped in the night. The 30th Ohio Volunteer Infantry overran the camp and secured it for the Federals.

They captured Floyd's flag that was inscribed with gold lettering that read, "Floyd's Brigade -The Price of Liberty is the Blood of the Brave."

The Confederates had left behind great stores of stock, ammunition, and other supplies. The cannons that had been firing on the camp were moved to the cliffs overlooking the ferry site. There they could see the company that had destroyed the ferry and footbridge. Though nearing the outside edge of their range, the cannons fired at the fleeing army. Their damage was slight, but the sound echoing in the ears of the retreating Southerners was mentally disheartening. They had not lost a man, yet their army was withdrawing. Rosecrans quickly occupied Camp Gauley and renamed it Camp Scott after General Winfield Scott. Later, the camp was moved to Cross Lanes.

The battleground was left to the memories of the men who had fought and died there. The fields were plowed with furrows created by cannon balls. The seed that was sown was the dry crusted blood of brave soldiers both North and South. It would take four more long years before the harvest of peace would come to the nation. A new state would be born, but the price of bearing this offspring of the war would be the tears of those mourning their lost.

When Gauley Ran Blood

Chapter 9
Privates, Pickets and Potatoes

She slowly opened her eyes and in the distance she could hear the resonating boom-boom-boom sound of cannon fire echoing back and forth across the rocky canyon walls of the Gauley. Becky had made her way in the darkness as far as she dared for fear of falling from one of the many cliffs or ledges. She had entered a large thicket of rhododendron and covered herself with a blanket of leaves from the previous autumn. Much to her surprise, she had slept soundly, in part due to the fatigue of the previous day. The leaves had insulated her from the cool September night as she slept in the comfort of her nest in the wild. Her immediate need was water. The climb up the Pierson Hollow the evening before had consumed her body's supply and her mouth was dry as dust. She knew that when she reached the river again she would care for that need. Her mind moved from thoughts of her capture to the future in store for Captain John Halstead and to the fate of her parents she had left behind. Had Chris and Johnny been taken prisoner too?

She crawled from her bed looking like a refugee from an insane asylum. Her trousers and blouse were disheveled and she had leaves by the dozen clinging to her now stringy hair that rested in all directions atop her shoulders. She attempted to part her hair with her hands and to remove the leaves using her fingers as combs. Realizing the futility of her labor, being without brush or comb, she flipped the ends of her hair by flexing her fingers into the air with an upward motion of her arms and hands. She then departed her foliage covered bedroom. She had to get back to the ferry. She crept briskly out the ridge keeping an eye out for soldiers of either army. Then she traveled down the mountain trail

149

in the direction of the mouth of McKees Creek. She planned to retrace the path she had made the previous day. From McKees Creek she would go up river to the Long Point and back out the Bend ridge. Then she would go down the Slippy Gap to the river again and then up river to the ferry. It was longer but safer. When she reached McKees Creek she cupped her hand and dipped water again and again to her thirsty mouth until she had her fill. She washed her face and neck and felt refreshed but hungry. As she made her way out the ridge, she paused beneath a giant chestnut and used a stone to beat the prickly burrs from a half dozen chestnuts. She stuck them in her pocket and ate as she walked. She bit through the brown leathery skin to reveal the soft yellow pulp meat inside. It appeared that this year's growth of chestnuts would be good. She loved them roasted. Her family frequently had them at Christmas time. Thinking pleasant thoughts had a calming effect on Becky.

She made good time and arrived at the ferry by mid-morning. As she approached the homestead her attention was drawn to the smoldering remnants of the barn. The house was intact along with the shop and granary. The towrope extended along the south bank of the Gauley like a great line drawn with a straight edge and pencil. The ferryboat was gone. Maude was tied to the rail fence near where the barn had been. She entered the house and her mother and father sat at the table talking. They both stood to greet her and the three silently wept arm in arm with their heads together. This continued for several minutes until Madison broke the silence.

"Becky, girl, are you all right?"

"I'm fine, Daddy. Federal soldiers captured John and me. We told them a yarn about us being married and me being with child. They let me go during a ruckus. They still have John, Daddy," replied Becky.

"How about Chris and the youngster? Did they get caught too?" he asked.

"I don't know. We got separated going up Pierson Hollow and I don't know what happened to them. There was quite a battle on that mountain yesterday. When I left this morning I heard the

When Gauley Ran Blood

cannons firing again. I guess things were heating up again," added Becky. "Did they burn the barn?"

"It appears as such. I guess we're lucky they didn't destroy the house. It was deserted this morning when we arrived. It looked as if they had treated their wounded here overnight. There were bloodstains on the floor and the bed sheets had been torn up for bandages. All the food is gone. They took everything out of the smokehouse. All the buildings, but the barn, appear in fair shape. Course the ferry is gone," Madison stated.

"How did you make out up the river? Did you have any problems? Did you find the sanctuary at Campbell's Branch accommodating?" she asked.

Becky knew her mother did not favor sleeping out of doors and was curious to see how she had fared. Mirriam appeared frazzled, but she had pluck. You could always depend on her in a pinch. Her years as a mid-wife had made her confident under pressure. She was accustomed to making decisions under duress.

"Now, Becky, you know I prefer my tick to a pile of hemlock boughs any day. Mad made us a pallet of branches and we tried to sleep, but I must confess you were on my mind most of the night. Then there was that screech owl that nearly scared the life from me. The beauty of that place with the water falls and everything is inspiring, but I'm just glad to be home again even in this mess," Mirriam stated.

"I want to get things cleaned up, fix something to eat, and then take myself a long nap. You didn't see your brother by any chance?" asked Mirriam.

"No, I didn't. We didn't make it all the way to the camp," said Becky.

She was shocked that her mother was not more rattled. Life there had been difficult at best over the past two weeks, and with the thousands of Federal troops in the area now, it could become even rougher. Maybe now was the time for her mother and father to visit their son Edward and his family in Ohio. Things would be safer there. He was a successful dentist there and would welcome them to his home. Her brother Virgil and his wife had gone just before the outbreak of the war and made a home there.

151

He also would welcome them. She could hold her thoughts no longer.

"Why don't you all pack up and go to Ohio before it snows? I'm afraid there is only going to be more grief around here before it gets better."

Madison swallowed hard as he spoke, "Your mother and I decided sitting right here this morning that we would stay put for the duration of this war or else. For years people have depended on your mother for delivering their little ones into this world and for me to fetch them back and forth across the river. We've endured plagues, floods, and five feet of snow and we're gonna endure this. The Good Lord mated us together and put us here, and He'll watch over us 'til he's good and ready for us to go somewhere else. If you're worried about this fighting, you know we wouldn't keep you here."

"No, Daddy, that is not what I want. I just want you and Mother to be safe. Don't you realize the danger you are in?"

"Maybe, but I don't fear them soldiers. The Bible says that the angel of the Lord camps around those that fear Him and that He will watch over them. I believe that Becky. Life will go on here. We will fear the Lord and trust Him to keep us safe. Right now, I'm going to dig us a few potatoes to go with our cabbage and corn for dinner. You want to help me?" asked Madison.

"Sure, Dad. I'll help you," Becky stated.

She wasn't sure she understood, but she trusted her father above all else. If his faith in God was that strong, she wanted hers to be the same. He had followed the Bible his entire life in word and deed. She now realized that it should not surprise her that he would take such a position.

"What are you gonna do about the ferry?" she asked.

"I'll build another flatboat. I'll even call it the 'Rebecca Jane' after you. But before that, we must prepare for other uninvited guests. We'll have to gather our scattered critters from the countryside. Then, we will hide all of the fowl and livestock beneath the cliffs and ledges, make a suitable lean-to and bed for us at the sanctuary, and store all our provisions in a safe storehouse. I know several ledges and cliffs that will accommodate supplies for an entire army. Even better than that, we

152

will hide our stores in a number of places. If one is discovered, we'll have others as standbys. We will take precautions that this does not happen again. We can't make it through the winter without food. We will have to prepare. Having faith in the Lord does not relieve one from making adequate provisions for his family. We must use our smarts as He gave them to us. We will be just fine, Becky, just fine."

Becky's thoughts now shifted to the fate of the southern men at Camp Gauley. She had no way of knowing in such a short time frame the outcome of the battle. She could hear the cannoning she had heard that morning still echoing in her mind like it had between the cliffs along the Gauley. What had happened to Chris and Johnny? Had Prott's unit escaped the Union forces as they marched through Summersville?

Chris' unit, the 22nd, maintained the rear guard of Floyd's retreat behind Prott's, the 36th. They traveled the Sunday road to its juncture with the James River and Kanawha Turnpike at Dogwood Gap. There they found Wise and his troops. The combined forces rested and spent the night at that location before leaving for safer grounds to the east.

Union General Cox was a persistent threat from Gauley Bridge and soon was pursuing the fleeing Southern army. Floyd kept a constant vigil of Rosecrans' position. Rosecrans appeared content to remain at Camp Scott near Cross Lanes. Floyd feared, with the resources available to the Union leader, that he might rebuild the Hughes Ferry and position large numbers of troops on the south side of the Gauley. He could then travel down the Wilderness Road and attack his forces at a point just east of the juncture of this road and the James River and Kanawha Turnpike near Meadow Bluff. Floyd was cautious not to allow Rosecrans to cut off his means of retreat. Wise insisted on staying a few miles west of the junction at a more defendable location known as Little Sewell Mountain. Both the Northern and Southern armies were consumed with establishing pickets and sending out scouting parties to locate the positions of the opposing troops.

General Robert E. Lee, who would take charge of the encamped southern troops, would soon visit the quarreling generals. As usual, this army lacked adequate scouts and horses.

When Gauley Ran Blood

Accustomed to making out with what they had, companies were asked for volunteers in the infantry willing to take on remote picket duty. Colonel Grogran and his cavalry had been out on the Wilderness Road for some time and had not encountered Federal troops. They had just returned to camp, but Floyd was not going to take any chances leaving the road unguarded for Rosecrans to attack from the direction of Hughes Ferry.

Private Chris Hughes was told, not asked, that he would again be headed for familiar country near Hughes Ferry. He did not object, not that it would have mattered, but he welcomed the chance of checking on his friends at the ferry. He hoped they would have some news of Captain John Halstead and Becky. He knew they had been captured and by now might be on their way to a Yankee prison camp. He hoped something more drastic had not happened to them. He had seen John's father, Mordecai, who had joined their ranks at Camp Gauley, but he too had received no word from John.

John's dad was an enthusiastic gentleman who believed in the preservation of Virginia. He was a tough old coot, but he was not fairing well in the damp weather.

Chris was now headed north on the Wilderness Road with four other soldiers on horseback. Two were regular cavalry and two were mounted infantry. The other infantryman was Private Prottman Hughes of the 36th. He was quite young, but he handled himself well and was very familiar with the territory. Chris was shocked to discover his new comrade. He recalled Mrs. Hughes mentioning her son, but he had not had time to seek him out for a "Howdy." Besides, the 36th had spent most of their time in Summersville rather than at Camp Gauley. They arrived there a short time before the battle.

The horses were at the point of exhaustion when they started and Chris feared they would give out at any time. As soon as they were out of sight of camp they agreed to stretch their legs and allow the horses a brief rest from their loads. The horses drank from a water filled wagon wheel rut. They drank readily from the murky pool. The soldiers talked as they walked the horses.

"Private Hughes, I have met nearly every member of your family but you. I've met your mother, father and Rebecca. Do you know Johnny Blizzard? I know he is from around here," asked Chris.

"Call me Prott. Sure, I know Johnny. He just joined the 36th at Camp Gauley. He and his dad are both in my unit. Why I grew up with him. We used to play together as children. His homeplace is just up the road here. How do you know him, and how is it that you know so much about my family?" asked Prott.

"It's a long story, but I met him at the ferry. Becky showed us the way to Carnifex Ferry. John Halstead was with us. I hate to be the one to tell you, but John and Becky got captured by the Yankees."

Chris spoke as he took a small birch twig out of his pocket and stuck it between his teeth and began gnawing on it.

"It happened just as we got to the fight. I couldn't help them. There must have been a hundred Yankees that surrounded them as they went up that hollow. I really felt helpless."

"Yea, Johnny told me about it. So you're the guy that was with them. He said all you could do was get them shot. I appreciate you not trying to be a hero and getting them killed. That Beck is a mustang. She's as wild as a whirlwind and windy as a Baptist preacher. I haven't seen any of my family for weeks. I got a note from Becky in Summersville, but with Rosecrans making his way south we didn't get any leave. I was hoping to see Mom, but I just couldn't get away. How did you meet Mom and Dad?"

"That's another long story, but let's just say I owe them one. I had picket duty at the ferry and they patched me up after a fall. Took real good care of me, they did. They're fine people. Your mother is a saint," replied Chris.

"You say you know John Halstead?" Prott asked. "He used to hang around our house all the time. He is older than I am, but I used to follow him and my brothers all over the place. My brothers got me caught in a rock pinch one time and John pulled me out. He looked after me a lot."

"He's my captain and a buddy of mine, " stated Chris. "I hope the Yankees are easy on him and Becky. You know, with all their plans and things."

"I don't understand. What do you mean plans and things?"

"They're getting married."

"You can't mean that. They were like family for years. Aw, they might have played a little, but that was kid stuff. Naw, you better rethink that," Prott said bewilderedly.

"Let me tell you, I wouldn't joke about something like that. I heard it from both their mouths. Kinda funny arrangement though. He's going to live at home and she is going to stay at the ferry. Do you do that often in these parts?" asked Chris.

"Chris, I'm telling you, you're barking up the wrong tree. I know both of them and that can never be. Trust me."

Soon the soldiers were on their way again in a light drizzling rain. Chris believed they could reach the ferry site before dark. They began pushing the horses as the evening wore on. They paused at a bend in the road when one of them saw riders through the trees ahead. They anxiously waited along side the road in the cover of a hemlock. They cocked their weapons as they waited for the approaching horsemen. As they came closer they could see that the two riders wore Confederate uniforms. They walked their horses onto the road and the riders pulled up after seeing that they were amid friends.

"Where you headed, fellars?" asked one of the riders.

"We're going on picket duty to Hughes Ferry," replied Prott.

"We just came from there. Not much is going on there. The boat is sunk. The ferryman or his family stir once in awhile. There's a little red head over there that looks mighty interesting," stated the picket.

"Maybe you ought to be looking for Rosey's troops instead of eyeing the locals," retorted Prott, taking exception to the mention of Becky as an "interesting red head". He obviously felt the honor of his sister was in question.

Chris intervened when he saw Prott's face turning red.

"How about troops? Have you seen any Yankees?"

"We saw Union pickets across the river on the Summersville side. They shelter under a rock cliff along the road at the first bend on the other side," replied one of the men.

"I'm surprised you had time to notice," Prott stated. "Sounds like you boys wage a pretty good war against the locals. You ever fight a real fight, or do you just like to hide in the weeds and watch?" Prott boldly challenged the honor of the riders; his own troops no less.

A rider responded, "You want to find out; just hop off that horse for a minute."

Chris looked at the two other cavalrymen in his group and they appeared to read one another's minds. They knew they had to get distance between Prott and the two pickets, or he was definitely going to create a problem.

Chris spouted, "Thanks, boys, you all have a safe trip. We gotta be getting on."

As he talked, he and the other men in his group positioned their horses between Prott and the picket he had challenged. Chris took his hat and slapped Prott's horse so that it bolted down the road. It took several seconds for him to regain control. He stopped and turned. Chris and company stayed between him and the pickets so that it was all but impossible for him to get through. The distraction provided enough time for the other riders to cover some distance and for Prott to reconsider his challenge.

"You at least know your sister is alive! She got away. That's good news. Maybe John escaped too. Come on, Prott, it's getting late and we need to get to the ferry. Do you know the cliff those guys were talking about?" asked Chris as both a sincere question and as another distraction for the frustrated youth.

"Yeah, I know it well. It's right along side the road. A man named Peter Simon lived there during the Revolution. He collected saltpeter from beneath the rock cliffs and made gunpowder. We always called it Simon's Cave, but it's not really a cave. It's a high cliff with enough space under it to hide a house. We used it for years as a barn before we built one. A whole company of men could shelter under that part of the cliffs and keep dry as powder."

"If you could show us when we get to the ferry I'd be obliged," said Chris.

It appeared he had been successful at distracting Prott long enough for his anger to subside. Prott's display of temper was the first time Chris had seen that trait displayed in any of the Hugheses. If he had gotten this upset at the casual mention of his sister, he feared the explosion that might result if he were to heat to full boil.

When Gauley Ran Blood

They continued their ride and reached the ferry in full light of day. They tied their horses at the base of a clump of small hemlock trees and climbed a sloping rock face that provided cover from enemies' sight across the river. The four men carefully watched for activity across the river. From their vantage point, they could see the green trees along the river on the other side of the river broken occasionally by the protruding white cliffs. They could see the road that disappeared into the Gauley at the ferry landing. Downstream from this, but up the hill a few yards, was the Hughes' house. There were a number of smaller buildings, but Prott noticed that the barn was gone. Burned by the Lincolnites, most likely.

Nothing stirred until right at dusk when riders were heard coming down the road along Salmons Creek from Summersville. As they rounded the final curve before the ferry, they veered to the left of the road and entered Simon's Cave just as the previous pickets had observed. There was not enough light to make out their uniforms, but the rebels knew they were Union soldiers. A few minutes later, six riders left the cave and made their way toward Summersville where they most likely were stationed. The night pickets had relieved those who had been on day duty. As the light faded, a bright fire from inside the overhang illuminated the rock cliff to half its height. The Union men could be heard making sport and laughing. They certainly knew that the Rebels were waiting just across the river, but they did not appear to be threatened by an enemy that had no means of crossing the Gauley. As long as they stayed out of the sharpshooter's sights, they had few fears.

The Confederates agreed that two of them would sleep while two kept watch. Chris and Prott took the first watch. They were to be relieved at midnight by their companions.

As the evening wore on and the conversation between the two men ended, they each retreated to the confines of their own minds thinking. Chris was relieved that Becky had made it back home. He was warm to the thought of being her friend and through the events of the day had noticed similarities between her and Prott. He wondered if her temper would match Prott's.

A faint light could be seen in the window of the Hughes' home. Prott thought of his family being so close, but yet so far away. He knew he could easily swim the river and be at home with his family, but he wouldn't dare place his family in jeopardy. If the Yankees captured him at his parents' house, they could make trouble for his family. Fraternizing with the sesech could be deadly for his family if the Yankees posted at Simon's Cave knew of it. He couldn't risk it regardless of his longing to see his folks. This was part of army life.

His family also missed him. Mirriam missed her baby boy although he was now a man. She wondered if he was getting enough to eat and if he had adequate clothing. It would be winter soon and she knew how he hated the cold. She had no way of getting him anything unless one of the men who had come home for a visit was willing to carry a package back to him at camp. She had heard that the southern boys did not have sufficient supplies and she had seen men at Camp Gauley with no shoes. How would the army supply and care for all those men?

The Confederate Army was not alone in its struggle to meet the needs of its fighting men. General Cox's pursuit of the southern armies was plagued by limited supplies, at least by Union standards. Supplies were brought by boat from the Ohio River up the Kanawha River to a point a few miles below the great falls at Gauley Bridge. From there they were taken by wagon train to Gauley Bridge and then to the front. There was a shortage of wagons at Gauley Bridge that made advance support of the fighting troops difficult.

Their counterparts in the Confederate Army suffered more severely from inadequate supplies. Staple foodstuffs were seldom available and often the men were forced to forage for food or starve. It was an unusually wet fall that added to the discomfort of both armies. Many men from both armies were sick with measles, dysentery, and camp fever. Many more died from these sicknesses than from enemy bullets.

The Union garrison in Summersville had been patrolling the ferry site since the Carnifex Battle. Little activity had been witnessed since the sinking of the ferryboat. The purpose of the Union pickets near the ferry was to guard against southern troops crossing in mass from the south and getting to the rear of Rosecrans' army. Enemy troops were also anticipated to be coming from General Lee's Camp Allegheny in the north, although they had no idea what route they might use for their approach. Another reason for the pickets was to cut off any detached bands of Rebel guerrillas that might be trying to join up with General Floyd. Rosecrans wanted to thin them out. He sent out a large scouting party from Camp Scott to assist in the potential roundup. It was led by Major Hayes and was comprised of four companies of the 23rd OVI, two companies of the 30th OVI, and a squadron of Schambeck's Cavalry. The cavalrymen had been at the ferry before when the flatboat had been sunk. They had had a man shot in the leg during the skirmish and were anxious for another encounter since they had been held in reserve during the Carnifex Ferry battle. They had been stung at Hughes Ferry and had yet to vent their frustrations. They had allowed some of the bushwhackers to escape and this added to their venom. They left camp early with a purpose.

It was an overcast morning at the ferry. Madison and Becky had been busy digging and gathering potatoes from one of their gardens along the river. In spite of the heavy rains, the potato crop had done well. The sandy soil along the river had helped drain the soil and allowed them to grow. Madison plowed them out of the ground with Maude's help, and Becky used a bucket to gather them. When her bucket was full, she would empty it onto the sled that was placed along the ferry road next to the garden. In only two hours she had gathered seven or eight bushels of potatoes. The sled had shallow sideboards and was now fully loaded. It would have to be emptied before any more potatoes could be collected. Madison knew they would have a good yield this year because he wasn't even half-finished with the plowing. He unhooked the plow and hooked Maude to the sled. As Maude pulled the sled, he and Becky walked alongside. They were going to dry the potatoes on the porch before hiding them at various stashes along the cliffs. They had just entered the gate at the site of the burned barn, making their way to the house. Becky heard it first; the clinkity-clank sound of canteens, tin cups, and plates striking each other as the infantry marched toward the ferry. They could also hear horseshoes striking the rocks in the road. As they looked up the hill at the road they saw three to four hundred infantrymen and mounted cavalry making their way to the ferry. In the lead were three mounted officers. The first of these was Major Hayes. A half dozen soldiers filed from Simon's Cave to greet the parade of men.

The Confederate soldier awakened Chris and Prott, who were lying beneath an overhanging rock. They were wrapped in their blankets on a pile of leaves the men had been using as a bed.

"We got Yankees, thousands of them," spit the excited soldier. "You better come and look."

They shed their blankets like cocoons and picked up their rifles. They joined the guard and peered across the river at the vast assemblage of Union soldiers. Prott quickly sighted his father and Becky in the barnyard. He had an empty feeling of despair in the pit of his stomach. The situation was not in his control. His family was being threatened and his small group could only look on. They would not dare challenge such a massive force. He wished his family had gone West to miss this conflict. He had talked to Madison about going to live in Ohio or Iowa with one of his other sons before he had signed up with McCauseland. He had only laughed and told him that running away would not solve his problems. Madison owned a choice piece of real estate, and to abandon it would destroy his livelihood. Well, where was his precious ferry now? If they had only gone west, they wouldn't be in this situation now.

They talked among themselves and agreed that two of them should ride to Meadow Bluff and inform Floyd of the advancing soldiers. They didn't know if this was the front guard of Rosecrans' main force or just a scouting party. If they tried to cross the Gauley, two of them would attempt to hold them up while the other two rode ahead to alert Floyd. Chris and Prott agreed to stay. If they needed a diversion, Prott knew the area and could lead the Union forces on a merry chase. He also wanted to keep an eye on his family and help them in any way that he could. Chris shared this interest with him. The other two soldiers waited with them to see if the Federals were going to cross the river.

The Southerners watched as the lead riders approached the sled and dismounted. The infantry swarmed the bank of the river and designated men in the various companies began filling canteens. Others dipped their tin cups or pressed their fingers together to form one and drank from the river. It was flowing clear in spite of the past night's light rainfall. The march from Camp Scott at Cross Lanes had started early that morning and they had marched without stopping to get to the ferry site. They had only taken hard tack and beef for breakfast and many of the men had grown hungry. The unpicked potatoes in the newly opened hills invited many of the Blueboys to help themselves to a fresh slice of raw potato. Others helped themselves and began filling their rucksacks with the fresh vegetables. The actions of these thieves either were unnoticed or ignored by the officers in charge. Prott took note and Chris had to stop him from taking aim on the pilfering Yankees.

Major Hayes walked toward Madison and Becky, leading his horse. Becky recognized him from the Carnifex battle. She immediately began stuffing the remaining tuffs of her hair into the base of her father's old felt hat that she was wearing. Her heartbeat quickened as thoughts of capture raced through her brain. She stepped behind her father and dipped her head so that the rim of her cap hid her face.

The officer spoke as he removed his dark blue hat and wiped his forehead with his handkerchief, "Good morning, sir. Major Rutherford B. Hayes, 23rd Ohio Volunteer Infantry, at your service, whom do I have the honor of addressing?"

"My name is Madison Hughes, and this is my daughter, Rebecca," stated the older gentleman.

"Pleasure to make your acquaintance, Mr. Hughes. Miss Hughes, have we met? Your face is familiar. I never forget a face. Little quirk I have," said the major.

Rebecca said nothing and dipped her head lower to hide her face completely from the officer. She positioned herself so that Madison was between the major and her.

"Sir, I would assume that you are the owner of this ferry."

"That's right, but your boys came through here a few days back and cut her in half. Set her right on the bottom just above the rapids there. All I can offer you right now is a poplar dug out."

"No sir, you don't understand. It is not my intent to cross the river today. I have come to deliver a message to you from General William S. Rosecrans. As you have stated, the United

When Gauley Ran Blood

States Army has found it necessary to temporarily close this vessel for the sake of the United States. I am told that at the proper hour the general has assured me that the flatboat will be replaced at no cost to you, sir," said the officer.

"Well, every day that boat sets at the bottom costs me money, Major Hayes. You have guards posted over there under the cliffs who are watching this place. People aren't going to use my ferry if they feel threatened. I can rebuild my ferry, but I'm not about to try and run off your soldiers. I'm not taking sides in this affair. I'm just trying to live my life, as God would have me here on this earth. I can build my own ferry, but I don't have an army to protect it."

"You must understand that you may not build your flatboat until the general approves it. This road must remain closed until the United States Army finds it in its favor to reopen it. Do you understand Mr. Hughes?" asked the major.

"My daddy got the patent for this place over 60 years ago from James Monroe who was the governor of Virginia at the time. He didn't put any strings on it. Now, you say you represent the United States and that they want the ferry closed. It appears to me that with all your talk about freedom you're first in line to take other people's rights away," stated Madison in a sarcastic tone.

"Mr. Hughes, I'm afraid you don't understand," muttered the major.

"I understand, major. The United States Army destroyed my ferry and closed my business. Does that mean my garden is also closed? If that is the case, you need to have your men return their contraband. I wouldn't want any of them to disobey the general's orders. If that is not the case, you will please ask them to stop filching my produce," requested Madison.

Major Hayes turned to witness the soldiers now actively digging the potatoes out of the ground with their bayonets and hands. His own horse had made its way to the sled and was actively munching on one of the large tubers. Major Hayes acted quickly out of embarrassment. He barked at one of the sergeants.

"Have the bugler sound call to arms. Let's get these men in their ranks. We have miles to go today."

When Gauley Ran Blood

Soon the call to arms was sounding and the Union soldiers slowly filed onto the ferry road and began forming into companies. The canteen brigades slowed the departure. Filling a canteen was a slow process because of the small openings in them. Many of the men filling them had to return to their units with only a handful of filled containers. The rows of infantrymen stretched from the ferry landing up the road past Simon's Cave and around the first bend.

"Sergeant, have two men hold the corners of a blanket and pass through the ranks. I would like that Mr. Hughes' potato crop be returned to him immediately," ordered Major Hayes.

"Privates Wood and McKinley, you heard the major. Pass through the ranks with your blanket and retrieve Mr. Hughes' potatoes," repeated the sergeant. "Any man holding even one potato after they pass will be punished."

Becky recognized that name and looked up to see the young soldier that had captured John and her. She was very uncomfortable and contemplated running for the house. With all the soldiers there, she realized she wouldn't have a chance and remained still.

As they passed through the ranks, the blanket began filling like a collection plate at a gospel camp meeting. The blanket was filled quickly and the men struggled to carry it. They made it to the sled and placed the blanket beside it.

"Use both your blankets," ordered the sergeant.

"Help them, Beck," instructed Madison to his daughter whose greatest desire at present was to become invisible before her former captor detected her.

Now she was holding the opposite corners of a blanket from him as they passed through the soldiers. His look indicated that he recognized her.

"I see you made it home safely," he spoke as he lifted his end of the blanket to start down a new row of soldiers.

"Yes, thanks to you. What happened to my husband?" asked Becky, attempting to continue the ruse with the private.

"The soldier you mean? I'm not so sure he was your husband. He didn't seem like the type of man that would jeopardize his family in such a frivolous manner. He is on his way to a war prison probably at Camp Chase, Ohio. I think that is where our prisoners were headed, " stated McKinley.

"I think you're a pretty good judge of people, but if you knew that, why did you let me go?" she asked.

"You didn't look much like a soldier, and I don't care to fight against women. I didn't think you could hurt us too badly. Was I wrong?"

"No. I'm no soldier, but John is a dear friend and I would die if any harm came to him. Are you going to turn me in?" Becky asked, knowing her life was again in this soldier's hands.

As they passed one of the soldiers in the 23rd, he asked loudly, "Hey, Billy, ain't that the woman we caught at Camp Gauley the day of the battle? What's she doing here? You and her setting up housekeeping?"

The private's face turned red. He looked at Becky and then at the outspoken soldier. He swallowed hard and tried to ignore the comment. The soldier was persistent.

"She get away from you Billy? You can get her now," muttered the soldier.

Major Hayes had remounted his horse and was waiting for the conclusion of the potato gathering when he overheard and asked, "What talk is this? Soldier, come forward. Private McKinley, escort Mr. Hughes' daughter this way."

As the trio approached the major, Becky dropped her corners of the blanket and fell into the private causing him to step backward upon the blanket that was full of potatoes. The potatoes like marbles caused not only the soldier to slip and fall, but in attempting to maintain his balance, slid his feet beneath McKinley's causing him to also fall on top of him. As the two soldiers regained their composure and stood to their feet over Becky, she discreetly placed a sizeable potato into the sleeping roll the soldier had draped over his left shoulder.

"Careful there, Miss Hughes," stated the Major.

"Private McKinley, is this true? Are you acquainted with this woman?" asked the Major.

"Well, major, to tell you the truth..." McKinley tried to speak and Becky interrupted.

When Gauley Ran Blood

"I don't even know this man's name. You dare come on our farm and accuse me of doing wrong. Mister, I would think you might examine your own before you start passing judgment on others. Your soldier there with the quick memory is no better than a thieving potato filcher himself. Just check his roll if you don't believe me."

After she spoke, she stepped toward the soldier and reached into his roll and pulled out the strategically placed vegetable. The soldier pushed Becky aside as he stepped forward to address the major. She fell backward over the sideboards of the sled and landed spread eagle atop the pile of potatoes.

Prott was watching intently from across the river. He could not hear the conversation but plainly saw what he thought was an attack on his sister. The perceived attack went beyond all he could stand. With reckless abandon for his father or sister, he lifted his rifle, took aim, and fired in the direction of the soldier.

The rifle discharged with a "boom". He missed the soldier but hit a rain barrel at the corner of the shop. The bullet struck in such a fashion so as to cause the water to leap into the air in a great plume. Splash from the barrel struck the major and his horse and caused the horse to rear into the air. He quickly regained control and surveyed the surroundings for the source of the attack. He was visibly shaken.

All of the soldiers jerked and twisted their heads wildly looking in all directions for smoke not knowing from where the shot was fired. They quickly took refuge behind the shop, fences along the road, trees, and any other solid object. Many of the soldiers near Simon's Cave made a mad dash inside for cover. Others ran up the road away from the river to escape the attack.

Chris and the rest of the southern boys joined Prott in his attack taking care not to aim at the house or in the direction of the civilians who scurried for the house. Their firing did not last as the Yankees saw the smoke from their rifles and returned fire with a massive blast of fire and smoke. The bullets struck the trees and rocks on the southern side of the river in waves. The Rebels dared not expose as much as a finger for fear of the nail being trimmed by lead from the Union guns. One of the soldiers was struck in the shin by a ricocheting bullet and determined it was time to warn

When Gauley Ran Blood

Floyd. Chris and Prott stayed put while the other two soldiers made their way to their horses and started the ride south on the Wilderness Road back to the main body of the Confederates.

Chris and Prott remained quiet and in a few minutes all of the firing ceased. Only the Rebel with the sore shin and Major Hayes would remember this day, the Rebel for his wound and the Major for his first accounting of being in direct fire from the Confederates.

Major Hayes, convinced that his troops had driven off the attackers, directed his men to form up at the first bend in the road and to prepare to move out. They had planned a long march north to Birch River before the end of the day.

The soldier who had made the claim against Becky and McKinley caught up with the major and walked along his side.

"What are you going to do, major? You're going to take care of this aren't you?" he asked.

"I believe you have said enough, " replied the major.

"Sergeant, see to it that this man is drawn and quartered when we arrive at camp this evening for disobeying my orders," added the major.

"But what about the girl? Are you just going to let her go?" objected the private.

"As I said before, we will leave this subject. Besides, these people have been through enough," added Major Hayes "let's get these men out of here."

"Major, Major Hayes," called Becky as she raced toward the mounted officer with a small parcel in her arms.

The officer stopped and turned on his horse.

Becky handed him the package of potatoes and said, "Daddy asked that I give these to you. He thought you might like them with your supper. He also said to tell you that you would always be welcomed at our house. Thank you."

The major took the package and placed it in his saddlebags. He wheeled his horse around in the direction of his troops and touched the rim of his hat with his hand in a partial salute and said as he rode off. "No, madame, it is I that thank you."

When Gauley Ran Blood

Chapter 10
Crossing Over

The Union scouting party headed north for Birch River and Becky breathed a sigh of relief. Her conscience was clear of any wrongdoing, but her life was complicated by this time of military operations. The intrusion into her life was without apology. The federal pickets now posted at the ferry kept a watchful eye on all the activities of the Hughes family who was now more aware of their observers. These uninvited federal troops, these invaders from the north, now controlled the very destiny of her family by brute force. She knew her father was crushed with the idea of not operating the ferry, but she also knew he was wise enough to know that defying the United States Army would be futile.

She sometimes thought if she were a man that she too would fight for the liberation of her now occupied state of Virginia. She thought the proposed new state of Kanawha was a farce. It's only a political name change. This is Virginia and regardless of its name it will always be Virginia. They bring in the army and scare away the people. Those that remain they intimidate or kill and accuse of being sesech because they own a rifle. This was not a war being fought by a foreign power against an enemy they despised. This was a war created by conflicting traditional and political ideologies of what the country was to become. Becky feared, regardless of who came out on top in the end, that the politicians would ultimately win. She knew her task. She had to keep her family alive and do her part in providing for them any way that she could.

There was no local commerce, so she began selling goods to the Union pickets at the ferry and moved on to the troops in

Summersville. She had traded with the Confederates and now it was the Federal's turn. She sold them fruits from the forest and field. Apples had done well this year, and she sold as many as Madison would allow. Pies brought top dollar and valuable trades. Vegetables were also saleable or tradable. She bargained them for everything from coffee to tobacco. Her best selling item was her corndodgers, but corn was getting scarce, and the family needed to conserve the balance of the remaining stores for the winter ahead. She and her mother even did sewing and knitting that the men sent home as presents for their loved ones. It was a time of dynamic economy; for wartime anyway. The greatest opponents were the plundering troops that took what they wanted. Anything and everything of value was hidden to keep it from the marauding soldiers. In keeping with Madison's strategy of keeping several stores of foodstuffs, the family kept busy like hoarding ground squirrels hiding their provisions in hollow trees, under rock cliffs, and in caves along the Gauley. They did what they had to do to survive.

The occupying army tried to make the best of what they considered a wild and dangerous country. There were no luxuries in this land, but the wonderful natural beauty of it befriended many of the boys in blue. For many it was the last joy they would experience. A bushwhacker's bullet waited for many unsuspecting men.

The soldiers' lives in Summersville consisted of hours of marching and drilling. They lived in houses abandoned by the former townspeople. Only a half dozen families remained in the town. When the winter weather came, the soldiers constructed large drilling barracks from milled lumber they cut with a steam saw mill that had been abandoned in the town. Scouting parties frequently were sent out from camp and would return with horses, cattle, or other farm stock. Local men were frequently arrested and accused of being secesh or friendly to the southern cause. Many of those arrested met their deaths on the return to camp when they would be shot in the back and accused of trying to escape. The soldiers, who were bored from lack of battle, fought their enemies one at a time in this most cowardly fashion.

When Gauley Ran Blood

Only the necessities of life were furnished by the army. Supplies were difficult to get in this out of the way little town. Sutlers, merchants who traveled with the army, seldom came this way, and when they did their wares were very expensive. Commerce was so scarce in the area that when the soldiers were paid they would have to buy change for their money to make local purchases. Many of the officers fared no better than the enlisted men, yet they coexisted in their displeasure and hoped for furloughs to visit their families at home.

Rosecrans made his headquarters at Camp Scott at Cross Lanes following the Carnifex Battle. He invited himself to occupy the Vaughn residence near the crossroads. Mrs. Vaughn was as hospitable as the situation permitted, and the congenial general obliged with ample stores from the Union quartermaster's supplies. The family's store had closed with the advent of the war and they were forced to make out, as best they could like everyone else. Vegetables from the garden and fruit from the orchards were a godsend. The provisions made available by the general were also very much appreciated.

In the evenings the general enjoyed walking in the garden and among the fruit trees. He had avoided the back porch since his unfortunate discovery of a large dark stain outside the kitchen door. Mrs. Vaughn explained about the unfortunate wounding and death of Colonel Dyer of the 9th OVI following the Cross Lanes battle. She was embarrassed by the stain and had tried in vain to scrub it away without success. General Rosecrans would often walk the short distance up the hill from the crossroads to Zoar Church where he had established a hospital. There he would visit his wounded and sick men. The sick most always outnumbered the wounded. As men recovered and were able, they would be sent back to their homes in Ohio or Illinois for recuperation if the circumstances so dictated. Many men unfortunately traveled to eternity through this church-hospital portal.

It was on one of his visits to the hospital that the general met a middle aged Mirriam Hughes. After initial treatment the surgeons would frequently rely on the local populace for post surgical or hospital care. Mirriam was a volunteer. One day each week, she and Virginia Halstead agreed to help at the hospital.

171

When Gauley Ran Blood

Their original intent was to serve the Southern boys, but it soon became apparent that pain and suffering came in both blue and gray. Mirriam had a marvelous talent of seeing suffering men and not blue or gray soldiers. Both were held at the hospital. Mirriam had a heart for the young men's suffering. She thought of her youngest son Prottman who had left home to fight in the war.

She often asked herself, "If he were in need, would there be someone there to provide love and care? " She hoped so.

She had been a mid-wife for over twenty years. Though there was no need of deliveries at the military hospital, there was a great need of people willing to deal with suffering and pain. Most of their duties involved general hospital tasks. Bathing the men and changing wound dressings was an endless and thankless job. Mirriam was more than an aide. She had a unique gift of being able to stop bleeding. When others had given up, they would call on Mirriam to do what she could. Observers witnessed her many times touching various wounds and then closing her eyes as if in prayer. More times than not the flow would be stopped. Some conjectured that she knew special holds that would allow the blood flow to stop and the wound to clot. Others said she was an instrument of God. "Aunt Mirriam", as she was affectionately called, would only reply, "It's just my special gift," when asked the source of her cures. The glow over her kind face and the twinkle in her eyes revealed that she derived her strength from a higher source than man.

Mirriam had been spending a great deal of her time with a young Union lad who had been injured by an exploding shell fragment at the joint of his hip. He lay on his opposite side with the wound exposed to the air. A saucer size piece of flesh had been torn away and the hip joint was exposed amid a black oozing cavity. Mirriam had carefully picked and washed out the maggots that had infested the wound. The boy, writhing in pain and being unable to raise his head due to being on his side, would move his head to and fro with his chin reaching his chest in his forward motion. She spent hours washing the wound and placing cloths on his fevered head. Attending to other duties, she thought the boy was asleep and paid him little attention. She returned to find his body cool to the touch. Her spirit hit bottom. As the tears swelled in her eyes, she closed them and prayed for the eternal destiny of the young man. He was so young to lose life she thought, about the age of Prottman.

It was her countenance and comments by others in his presence about her work that caused General Rosecrans to comment, "I am told that you have been a great service to the surgeons here at the hospital. I would like to attempt to repay you for some of your efforts. What might I do for you?"

Mirriam responded sharply without stopping to think, "End this damnedable war. End it quickly!"

She struck her fist against a washstand instinctively, and a pitcher and wash basin bounced into the air to make a loud clang. People in the room stopped what they were doing and looked up to listen to a normally quiet midwife deliver her request in exasperation to the ranking Union officer in western Virginia.

"I am sorry, general, I want this all to be over so much. I want the killing and hatred to stop. The two feed on each other, and they water the evil seed in people's hearts. I just want it to stop."

Margaret Halstead rushed to her aid and swept her aside to one side of the room out of fear of retribution by the powerful man.

Rosecrans froze momentarily. Her demeanor shocked him, but he had witnessed similar responses by women and men to what, for the most part, appeared as senseless slaughter and killing. He understood and knew the remark was not directed at him personally. It was obvious from this woman's actions that her intent was genuine to help stop the pain and suffering and to find an end to the conflict. She had only spoken from the heart. He continued his visit with his sick and wounded men going from cot to cot and many of them asked that he not be too severe with the outspoken woman. Her heart had comforted many of the young men there. He assured them that he understood her position.

"Sir, I am told she has a son in the Confederate Army," spoke one of the physicians in a soft tone of voice. " She has been a great deal of help to us here. She has an extraordinary gift, General Rosecrans."

The words, extraordinary gift, repeated again and again in Rosecrans' mind.

"What is her name?" He asked.

The physician replied. "Mrs. Mirriam Hughes. Her husband runs a ferry south of Summersville on the Wilderness Road."

"That's where I've heard that name, Hughes Ferry. My, I fear we destroyed the lady's family's livelihood the day of the Carnifex Battle. To circumvent a potential attack at our rear, we had to destroy the flatboat at that location. We would appear to have not been the best of neighbors. Unfortunately, I see no short-term remedy to that dilemma. The Wilderness Road must remain closed and protected. In time we shall see," stated the general.

The Federal pickets at Hughes Ferry provided assurance that the ferry would remain closed after the ultimatum Major Hayes had delivered. Madison was in such dire straights for lumber that when the time came for rebuilding the ferry he knew he would have to sacrifice the shop for materials. There was no lumber to be had, and the army controlled the sawmill in Summersville. All he could do for now was pass an occasional traveler across the river in his poplar dugout. That is all the pickets would allow. All of those that crossed had some type of business with the army anyway. Madison was satisfied to receive his rather inflated war time rate of ten cents. Of coarse, the rebels on the south side of the river didn't dare cross the Gauley, or did they?

Prott and Chris felt they had been forgotten and were not far from wrong. They had not eaten for two days and were starving. Their former companions had reported the visit of the sizeable Union force to General Floyd's staff and they believed Rosecrans was making his attack. Floyd sent out troops with axes to block the Wilderness Road as close to the ferry as possible. One of the parties actually made it to the southern picket's post. They informed them of the plan but offered them no food. Instead, they left them with additional cartridges and percussion caps. They told them that Floyd remained at Meadow Bluff and that Wise was still on Big Sewell west of him. Union General Cox was only a stone's throw from Wise's forces. They were preparing for an attack at any time and the Wilderness Road had to be blocked to prevent the rapid advance of Rosecrans' army to a position behind many of the Confederate troops. In reality, this was not the case, but Floyd's caution was understandable.

When Gauley Ran Blood

Prott informed Chris that he was going to cross the river tonight to visit his family and to secure food. He did not want to swim, but now he was desperate. Prott had attempted to get his father's attention on a number of occasions in the past since he and Chris had arrived at the ferry but to no avail. He couldn't call out too loudly for fear of being heard by the Union pickets and Madison didn't hear well anyway. When darkness came he would be on his way.

Wearing only his underwear, the young soldier eased himself into the cool water and swam like a frog toward the north shore of the Gauley. His heart raced as he slowly lifted himself from the stream atop a large flat rock submerged along the shore. He carefully jumped into the grass from the submerged rock to avoid leaving any trace of his arrival. He ran to the west side of the house in the darkness. No light was on in the window and from all appearances the family had gone to bed. He lifted the latch on the door and slowly pushed it open. Just when it was open far enough for him to enter, a loud metallic clang was heard. Prott didn't know what had happened, but he could hear the man of the house engaged in conversation with others.

He began calling out, "Dad, Mom, it's me. Dad it's me, Prott. Can you hear me?"

He walked toward the bedroom continuing to call out. He heard the floorboards squeak as he walked and paused monetarily, but the squeak continued. Someone, in addition to him, was moving inside the house.

He continued to call out, "Becky, is that you? It's me, Prottman. Why don't you answer me?"

He could make out the outline of a person against the window and approached the form determined to solicit a response. He was ready to throw his arms around the person when he heard a voice.

"Issac Prottman, Issac Prottman Hughes, is that you?"

He turned to hear the voice behind him and was met on the chin with a hard blow. He was out instantly with a loud thud to the floor. His shoulder contacted the table as he fell, and the legs of the table scooted along the floor making a high pitched squeal.

"Prottman, is that you?" the voice continued, but received no response.

Madison had heard enough. He grasped an old ax handle beside the bed that he kept for just such a purpose, and made his way to the main room of the house. As he entered the room, there was a commotion at the door and it opened and closed with a bang. Madison stirred a kindling stick in the ashes of the fireplace and a single flame lit the darkness. He used the burning stick to light the wick of the lamp. He replaced the globe and slowly approached the pile of humanity on his floor. He knelt on the floor with the lamp in one hand and the axe handle in the other. He set the lamp down and reached for the form. The form was wet as Madison rolled it over and discovered his son, unconscious.

"Mother, it's Prottman!" he yelled in an excited voice.

Soon Mirriam and Becky were making over him asking numerous silly questions that women ask at times like this. Mirriam placed a damp cloth on his forehead and he awoke shaking his head.

"What was that about? What did you hit me for?" he asked.

The mother and daughter were so overcome that he was alive that they made much to do over him. He explained how he had been on picket duty across the river for several days and had been unsuccessful in contacting them with the Union pickets so near. He told them that Chris was with him and that they had been without food for two days and that his hunger had prompted him to swim the river to secure food. He was immediately presented with bread and butter, potatoes, and cabbage from the family's evening meal. He ate heartily.

Madison looked at the door and saw a rifle lying along the wall. It was a Springfield rifle, like some of the Yankees were using. The family put their heads together, and concluded that Prott had interrupted a pilfering soldier, and then met with his unexpected wrath. When he entered the house, he had leaned his weapon against the door, and when Prott entered, he had knocked it down. He had struck Prott to make good his escape, but in his haste forgotten to retrieve his weapon.

"Do you think he will return with the others?" asked Becky. She was becoming more frantic as she spoke anticipating another capture.

"We must not take any chances. Son, you will have to leave as soon as you have eaten," stated Madison.

"Mad, the boy just got here. How can you shun him?" Mirriam asked.

Madison responded, "I am not shunning him. You must understand that we cannot risk that soldier returning with others to reclaim his rifle and capturing Prottman. We will have to meet at a later time. Prottman, can you make it tomorrow?"

"Sure, but how about Chris?"

"Bring him. I will meet you opposite the upper end of Beaver Island in the dugout at dawn. We will cross over and meet the ladies at the falls of Campbells Branch. I think we'll be safe at the sanctuary if no one follows us," instructed Madison.

Mirriam filled a quart jar with cooked potatoes and cabbage and another with bread, butter, and dried apples. She placed a heavy rubber gasket on each jar and then folded the metal fastener until it snapped the lid closed to provide a watertight seal. She tied the two jars together with a leather throng and handed them to Prott.

"See that Chris gets something to eat, too. He must be starving," Mirriam said as she handed the jars to Prott, "I love you, son. Please be careful."

"See you tomorrow," said Becky as she kissed the cheek of her younger brother.

Prott was out the door and headed for the Gauley. As he slowly closed the door, he could hear the scurrying and whispering of men coming from the direction of the ferry road. He crept to the opposite side of the house and made his way to the old log barn in the back. This building had not seen much use since they had built the new barn that the Yankees had burned. The building was barely standing due to its age and lack of maintenance. Prott leaned his back against the logs as he looked over his shoulder around the corner. He wanted to see that his family wasn't harmed before he left. He could see four or five soldiers making their way toward the front of the house and then he heard them call out.

"Open the door. We know you have a sesech bushwhacker in there. Send him out, or we'll burn the house down," yelled one of the Union pickets who had been on guard at his post near Simon's Cave watching the ferry site.

Madison answered as he stood behind the door in his nightshirt, "hold your horses; I'm opening the door."

"Where is he?" asked the first soldier through the door. "Check the house, men."

The men began looking in corners and under the beds. Mirriam and Becky sat at the table. Becky held a cloth to her cheek and lightly moaned as if in deep pain.

The third soldier that entered the house had no weapon. Madison thought it odd and asked if the Springfield rifle now lying on the table belonged to him. He quickly took it up and proceeded to join the others in searching the house. They soon found that only the three Hughes in the kitchen were present.

"We know something funny is going on here and rest assured that we will be keeping a closer eye on you people," stated the lead soldier.

Madison responded, "You men have a lot of nerve. Someone breaks into my home and strikes my sleepwalking daughter and you accuse us of funny business. It would appear that someone here needs to apologize, or I may well have to speak to the general."

Madison stood behind Becky and patted her on the shoulder as if to comfort her.

Three of the soldiers stared with their eyes squinted at the soldier who had misplaced his weapon. He could only smile and then look at the floor.

One of the soldiers started to speak, "Sir, we regret..."

The deafening bawl of a wild river creature was heard near the house. There was a quiet lull and then another deafening moan. The soldiers quickly left the house to investigate.

Prott had been watching the house from the corner of the old barn when, much to his surprise, the tentacle of a monstrous night beast wrapped its slimy wet tentacle around his head and onto his ear. It pulled his head against the logs. He shuddered with fright until he realized it was not a tentacle, but the tongue of Bessy, the family's milk cow, searching for the cooked cabbage he had eaten moments earlier. With the loss of the barn, Madison was forced to place her in the old log structure to keep her from running into a Yankee bullet and cooking pot. She had stuck her head out between two logs that had lost their chinking during past years.

As Prott slid his back along the wall of the old barn in an attempt to keep an eye on the house and yet escape the exploring tongue of the creature, the cow followed along and its neck became jammed between the logs. In her pursuit of food, Bessy had not noticed the unleveled floor in the old building and the rising gap in the logs. She had lost her footing and was now hanging by her head choking to death between two of the logs. Her labored bellows for help resonated between the cliffs and created a heinous sound.

Prott ran from the barn to a brushy swale near Salmons Creek where he hid. The soldiers had made their way, with cocked weapons, in the direction of the old barn. They cautiously approached the structure. The lead soldier held a lantern high into the air. Poor Bessy, in her last fleeting reach for life and with her eyes glowing in the lantern light, gave one great final bawl that startled the soldiers and provoked them to empty their guns in her direction. One of the bullets struck her and she cried no more. Not knowing what had occurred, the Hughes family was struck with fear of the potential harm to their Prott.

The soldiers, having discovered the error of their targeting, were quick to offer payment for the lost cow. Madison agreed to sell them half of the family's milk producer for beef, providing an apology was offered to his seemingly wronged daughter. He hated the loss of his cow but was glad it had not been his son.

With his family now safe, Prott made his way down the creek to the Gauley. The night air had the threat of winter in it, and the water felt warm as he entered for his return trip. He placed the string over his neck and had a jar hanging on each side of his chest as he dog paddled his way back to the south side of the river. Chris greeted him as he stepped from the water.

"Boy, am I glad to see you. How's the family?" asked Chris.

"They're good. You'll get to see them tomorrow, " replied Prott. "Mom sent you something to eat. Here you go."

When Gauley Ran Blood

He handed the jars to Chris who opened one and began stuffing his mouth with pinches of bread and butter and an occasional taste of dried apple. The two sat and ate by trading the jars back and forth. In a short time all of the food was eaten, and Prott was telling Chris what had happened and explaining the plan for the family get together the next day. Neither man slept during the night in anticipation of the coming reunion.

Both men were up before light, and Prott became frustrated with Chris' insistence over bathing before they left for the half-mile walk up river to the meeting point. He finally consented.

Chris went to the spot where he had first seen Becky below the Big Chute falls and felt his way in the darkness through the rocks that guarded the little sandy beach. He removed his clothes and stepped into the water. The cool water made his shoulders shake. He used the sand as soap as he had seen Becky do some weeks before. He finished quickly and returned to put his clothes back on. It was then that he realized the odor emanating from his clothing would insult a hog, but there was nothing he could do about it now. There just wasn't time.

Chris and Prott made their way up the south side of the river to their rendezvous point. The trip through the jungle of huge boulders and laurel thickets was made easier by Prott's knowledge of the area. This area was his boyhood playground. He knew every nook and cranny. The river was wide and slowly flowing at this point, except in the middle where the current moved noticeably swifter. A great eddy stretched from the ferry upstream to Beaver Island, but a gentle bend in the river obstructed a clear view of the entire reach. The island sat to the left side of the river as you traveled upstream. Both the Joe Branch and Campbells Branch emptied into the river along the narrow waterway on the north side of Beaver Island.

They waited only a few minutes until they saw Madison in the large dugout canoe appear from behind the upstream end of Beaver Island and start across the river toward them. The island was a haven for beavers that frequently dammed up the narrow waterway between the island and the north shore of the Gauley and built their lodges. Floods would strip the dams in the springtime and the beavers would begin again. The heavy rainfall of this year had prematurely removed the dams and the waterway was open from one end to the other.

Madison paddled from behind the island into the main body of the river. He headed the canoe upstream and guided it into the current. As the current caught the small boat, Madison used the oar as a rudder, and headed for the two soldiers as they stood on the south bank of the river. He landed the canoe and Chris stepped aboard. Prott pushed the canoe off the bank and jumped aboard. The older man stroked the water and the two soldiers sat in the bottom of the canoe with their rifles lying across the boat. The boat crossed the river and pulled into the narrow stretch between the island and the north bank. Madison guided the boat down the channel a short distance and then into a "V" shaped depression in the bank where Campbells Branch entered. The three men departed the canoe and walked a short distance up the wooded hillside to the cliffs that lined the river. They followed the cliffs to the point where Campbells Branch plummeted from above, and found the two ladies waiting at a nearby rock.

Mirriam and Becky hugged and kissed Prott. Mirriam hugged Chris and kissed him on the cheek. Becky hugged Chris but felt awkward and did not offer a kiss. The two parted after the hug and looked at each other with sober faces. Becky rolled her nose as if she smelled something dead. Chris caught her discomfort and quickly apologized for his stench. Mirriam put him at ease when she said that she had brought soap for doing laundry. They could do that during the heat of that September day and it would allow time for Prott's and his clothing to dry.

Mirriam had spent most of the night preparing food for the day. Bessy's demise did have its benefits and also offered the family a reason for being up much of the night. She had prepared beef with parsnips, pone with butter and honey, and apple pie. Condiments included canned pickles, cabbage salad, and the last tomatoes of the season. It was a feast by anyone's standards. They would eat, but first the laundry had to be done for the sake of those not in the military. Men in camp grew accustomed to the odors emanating from their comrades, but the ladies found them totally unacceptable. Mirriam did not want these foul smells spoiling the aroma of the meal she had spent most of the night preparing.

When Gauley Ran Blood

The party made its way along the cliffs a short distance from the falls to the hidden entrance of the sanctuary. The ladies placed their food and blankets beneath the towering hemlock on a bed of pine needles that had accumulated over the eons. When everything was in its place Mirriam announced that it was bath time.

Chris felt at ease and comfortable with the Hugheses. He felt like one of the family but he was uneasy about his feelings for Becky. He would not betray the trust of his dear friend John Halstead, but he was going to have a good time this day. A day to forget about his circumstances. A day to forget about the war. A picnic that reminded him of home and days from his youth, when his family, like this one, would take lunch along the banks of Johns Creek or slip over to his Grandpa Francisco's on Craig Creek. His thoughts of home made him feel a bit melancholy, but he was going to make the most of this day.

Madison cut the soap block into four pieces with his knife. The ladies took their pieces and walked downstream. He gave Prott and Chris each a piece and they began bathing at the base of Campbells Branch falls. Madison carried their clothing around a bend in the stream and left it with the women. The stream followed the base of the cliffs for a short distance and then turned abruptly toward the river and followed a rocky and tumbling course into the river. The ladies selected a pool where a flat rock gently sloped into the stream as a place to launder the soiled clothing of the young men. With six men in the family this had always been a routine chore for the ladies of the house. They lathered and rinsed each garment as clean as they could and then spread them over dead branches in a downed tree in the soft morning sun to dry. The rising sun held promise of a warm autumn day and with the gentle blowing breeze the clothes would dry quickly.

The soldiers felt as if they had rubbed the outer layers of their skin off and the cool falling water they used to rinse with chased any thoughts of sleep from them. They dried with their blankets and wrapped up in them. They made their way back to the sanctuary and were soon joined by Madison and the women. The sun was now shining and its rays fought to penetrate the heavy canopy of the giant hemlock and the surrounding cliffs. Light beams shined brightly on the group in a surreal scene as they sat talking and getting caught up with the news. Prott and Chris, dressed in their blankets and growing their stubby beards, looked like the biblical characters Moses and Aaron waiting on instructions from God. The sun felt extraordinarily good on their faces, as if God had chosen them as His favorites for the day. Soon, steam could be seen rising from the moss blankets that covered the sides of the sanctuary walls. It would rise gently in the protected stone room and then disappear in a wisp of wind when it reached the top of the majestic rock faces. The giant hemlock quietly and gracefully stood in the room as if keeping vigil over the family's activities.

The time went quickly and they all took turns telling the stories that had impacted their lives in recent months. They were elated that the next to the oldest son, Jeremiah, had felt God's calling to become a minister. They laughed when they talked of how ornery he had been as a youth. They pondered what a marked change had occurred when, in his teen years, he had made a decision to receive Christ into his life. His attitude toward life had changed. He became interested in other people's lives and their well being. He spent long periods reading and studying the Bible. As they reminisced, they concluded that his calling did appear in line with his interests and deeds.

Mirriam asked if they had seen Mordecai Halstead. Chris informed her he had seen him and he had survived the battle, but that his arthritis was troubling him.

Becky told them about her and John's capture and that she believed John was a prisoner at the Union prison near Camp Chase, Ohio. The ladies at the hospital had heard that some of the Campbell and Dotson boys had also been sent there.

Mirriam wept as she related the stories she had been told about the deaths of the soldiers at the Carnifex Ferry battle. She had seen first hand in the Zoar Church hospital the devastation that had been done to the wounded soldier's bodies. War was an instrument of death. The war that had been so distant and impersonal was now fully upon them. It was like the odor of a dead rat in a wall. Its vileness came from all directions. Blood was now even being spilled upon their land at the ferry.

When Gauley Ran Blood

Prott held Becky as she cried when she informed him of the murder of Nick Ramsey that had occurred a few days after the Carnifex battle. His wife, Amanda, was Becky's dear friend. Mirriam had heard at the hospital that while Amanda was carrying Nick's young son in her arms, she had discovered his rotting corpse near their house after he had not returned home for several days. People speculated that he had been killed by the sesech because of his father's loyalties to the Union. Others said he was mistaken for a sesech bushwhacker and murdered by Union soldiers on patrol as retribution for the Yankees who had been killed at the recent battle. Becky owed Nick her life. He was gone now. Becky thought of how Amanda must have been suffering. She would have to try and visit her.

Chris thought of how similar this sounded to the death of his young comrade on his first scout of the ferry. As conversation of the wounded and dead continued, each member of the group spoke softer and less frequently until no one spoke at all. They all sat as if in a deep trance like state with their eyes open yet seeing nothing.

The silence was broken when Prott's stomach growled and everybody laughed simultaneously, as if looking for a release from the seriousness of their circumstances. The soldier had received his body's call for lunch. He and Chris found their cleaned and aired clothing. They dressed and rejoined the family for lunch. Becky commented that the air was much fresher with the clean change of clothing.

Madison removed his hat and blessed the food. Mirriam had outdone herself and the family enjoyed the meal. The soldier boys ate much more than their equal shares and yet there was food left over. Mirriam had planned it that way. She wanted something for the boys to take with them.

Following the picnic Becky, Prott, and Chris climbed upon a rock that provided a view of the river yet kept them from direct view. They sat in the early afternoon sun and talked. The scene of the two young soldiers in their uniforms and the attractive woman in her dress overlooking the great green valley of the Gauley was fit for an artist's brush. They conversed as they enjoyed the warmth of the day. Becky removed her bonnet and allowed her auburn hair to rest on her shoulders.

"So you and John are getting married are you?" asked Prott.

"You've been in the sun too long," replied Becky.

Chris jerked to attention and stared at the two siblings.

"Where did you ever get that idea?" inquired the smiling young woman. She pursed her lips and dropped her eyebrows while speaking.

"Chris, you want to explain this?" inquired Prott.

"Why Chris, what ever gave you the idea John Halstead and I would ever get married? We never really even courted," said Becky.

"Mrs. Halstead made some comments that day at Camp Gauley after the parade. You talked about where the two of you were going to live the day you led us to Carnifex Ferry and..."

Becky interrupted, "You asked where we were going to live and I told you that John would live with his parents at Gad and that I would live with my parents at the ferry. Do you think I wouldn't stay with my husband? I even told you that he was marrying Ginny Dotson just as soon as the war was over."

Chris sheepishly continued, "I must have misunderstood. It made sense to me. You and John were always together. I thought John was the luckiest man in the world."

"You did?" responded Becky as she heard Chris say more than he may have intended.

Becky had noticed the young soldier before, but had always been preoccupied with other things that were happening. In the beauty of this day she found his comment quaint and welcomed it in any form.

He cleaned up well and his stocky and muscular build was pleasing to her eye, not that she normally noticed such things. She pondered what was under that light beard of his, but satisfied herself with the fact that he was handsome regardless.

"Prott, I saw Verna Campbell and she was asking all kinds of questions about you. Where you were and how the military was treating you. I do believe she is sweet on you," said Becky so that her younger brother could join their troupe of love bitten sojourners.

"Really?" asked Prott. He had never given much thought to women, but he and Verna had shared a pie at last summer's church picnic.

"Maybe I'll write her. Yea, I'll do that," he added.

"Look," said Chris, as he pointed toward the Gauley in the direction of the main channel opposite Beaver Island. Three deer were swimming the river. Only their heads could be seen above the surface of the water.

"Let's pet them," said Prott at a mischievous whim.

The three were racing off for the river. Down the hillside and toward the dugout canoe they scrambled, like school children playing a game of hide and seek. Prott quickly jumped to the front of the canoe. Chris waited for Becky at the bank and helped her into the craft. She needed no help, but took advantage of the circumstances to allow Chris to display his gentlemanly qualities toward her. She liked them.

He held her hand and steadied the canoe as she entered the bulky canoe. She gathered her dress in one hand and held it above the calves of her legs. With her other hand, she took a firm but delicate hold of Chris' hand and stepped into the canoe. He was embarrassed that he actually saw her ankle at her shoe tops. She smiled. He pushed the boat off the shore and paddled vigorously for the main stream of the Gauley. Becky and Prott encouraged him on as he stroked toward the deer that had changed directions and were now headed downstream and for the southern side of the river. When the trio reached the swiftly flowing center of the Gauley, they approached the deer rapidly. Recent rains were helping the river along.

Chris guided the canoe down the Gauley and steered into the slower moving water of the eddy near the south bank. Prott and Becky coaxed Chris to hurry before the deer exited the river but they were too late. The deer walked from the river with their antlers dripping water. They scurried up the bank and Prott pretended to shoot at them with an imaginary rifle since they had not brought along their guns on the joy ride.

"Pow, pow, pow. I got all three of them, " exclaimed Prott as he boasted about his imaginary kill, as the fleeing deer ran from sight across a rise below the cliffs on the south side of the river.

When Gauley Ran Blood

A loud pow, pow, that delayed too long for an echo, was heard a few seconds after the deer ran from the sight of the joy riders. Prott and Chris looked at each other as if to ask, what have we done? They both hoped that a local hunter had bagged his buck. Chris began backpaddling away from the shore so that they could see who had fired the shots. They saw two men in civilian clothes on horseback approaching the area where they had last seen the deer. Chris turned the canoe and began paddling back upstream. He wanted to put as much distance as he could between them and the unidentified men. He entered the current and the canoe shot downstream at an angle. Chris used the current to increase his speed as he steered away from the strangers. He headed for Beaver Island because he could now see the ferry site downstream and was afraid that the Union pickets might spot them. Little did he know that their presence was insignificant in comparison to the force that was rapidly approaching on the south side of the river.

There was another series of shots and Prott slumped over the side of the canoe and fell into the water. The canoe rocked back and forth following his exit.

"Oh, what's wrong?" Becky spoke excitedly as she reached for her brother as he floated by the canoe.

"Take the paddle," Chris replied as he leaned from the boat and grabbed the unconscious Prott by the arm.

Chris could see the blood flowing from the side of his head, leaving a crimson line in the water.

"Is he dead?" asked Becky.

"I don't think so," replied Chris as he struggled to raise Prott's body into the canoe. The heavy canoe nearly upset with his efforts so he stopped and held tightly to his friend.

"Look, Chris," said Becky, as she motioned with her tilted head while paddling furiously toward the north side of the Gauley.

He looked up to see the two men taking aim at them. At a distance, between small breaks in the trees along the Wilderness Road, he could see a column of blue clad soldiers making double-quick speed toward the two men. He heard the rifles fire and saw the smoke roll from the barrels. One bullet danced along the top of the water making little circles in its path and the other struck the rear of the canoe in the thickest wood with a thud.

When Gauley Ran Blood

He realized they were firing at their Confederate uniforms and Becky's gray dress. He pulled hard on the body he was holding and the canoe rolled onto its side emptying Becky and him into the moving water. He held on to the side of the canoe with one hand and to Prott with the other. Becky grabbed the edge of the boat and held on. They were at the swiftest point in Gauley along the ferry eddy. The water swirled in different directions and looked to be boiling from the center of the earth. They were now only about a hundred yards above the ferry site.

Chris couldn't believe what he saw next. The Union soldiers on the south side of the river were so numerous that the green sides of the river were now blue and the soldiers were joining in firing on the canoe. The sounds of the rifle discharges echoed in the river canyon with a multiplying effect that made them sound like they numbered in the thousands. Lead struck the surface of the water as if it were raining. Thuds and thumps were heard when the bullets struck the canoe in various places. He observed men on horseback, most likely officers, approaching from down river.

A handful of Union pickets on the north shore were now standing at the ferry landing looking on the action, but confused as to what was actually happening. They took shelter when the bullets began striking rocks and trees along the water's edge in front of them. It appeared that their fellow soldiers on the south bank were now firing upon them, but they were really only shooting at the side of the poplar dugout.

As the trio floated past the ferry site, the south landing filled with Yankees firing on the old boat in order to take out their vengeance on it from the battle of Carnifex Ferry. They appeared anxious for a fight. This enemy could not fire back. Chris held Prott's head out of the water with the bend of his elbow. Becky held to the side of the canoe and slid back to where Chris and Prott were located. Her movement in the current caused the boat to turn sideways and to expose them to the fire from the south bank. She quickly pulled herself back to the front of the boat and it resumed its position parallel to the shore, providing cover to them from the south.

When Gauley Ran Blood

One of the officers rode his horse into the Gauley firing his pistol at them. He got to within twenty yards of them and then turned back when his horse was forced to swim and the current threatened to carry him into the falls below.

Chris saw the falls known as the Big Chute and realized their canoe trip would end at that point. He knew if they survived the fall that the Yankee soldiers would gladly spill their blood into the river. There was really no other hope. Wait, maybe there was one other chance. Many soldiers in battle, when faced with their greatest fears called out to the one who patiently waited to console them. Chris had the presence of mind to ask God for help.

He spoke in his mind to God, "God, if you're real, if you're really who you claim to be, help us! Please, help us! Do this and I'll follow you to the end. If you won't do it for me, at least do it for Becky."

He could hear the roar of the falls only moments downstream and waves were starting to splash against the side of the boat, but a peace came over him. He couldn't explain it. He knew that regardless of the outcome he would be all right.

Chris yelled to Becky, "Do you want to try to make it to shore? Go."

She responded in a forceful voice, "No. I know this water. When we get to the bottom, follow me if you can. I'll try to help you with Prott."

When Becky spoke his name, Prott's head jerked and he moaned as though he recognized her voice. Chris knew he at least was alive.

Chris didn't know what she was talking about, but he prayed that he would get the opportunity to find out. Their speed picked up as they neared the falls and the roar from below was now deafening. The additional rainfall of the season caused the throat of the Big Chute to raise so that the dugout carried over the falls without touching a rock. The three, along with their craft, plunged into the watery abyss. The canoe entered the water nearly vertical and almost completely submerged, before the buoyant log shot back into the air, and then continued on its side down the river. The three bodies fell directly below the falls and the force of the water held Chris and Prott below the surface for several seconds. When they reached the surface, Becky called out to Chris to follow her. He swam on his side with Prott trailing behind in his grip. Chris thought how absurd that they should survive the spill from the waterfall and be picked off by a Yankee bullet now that they no longer had the dugout for protection.

The soldiers had followed the boat to the falls and continued to shoot at it, but the terrain had thinned their ranks. The giant rock boulders and trees that lined the shore of the river caused the soldiers to form groups and fall behind others to wait for their turn to pass through or around them. They would spread out after passing around the rocks and seek the best position for another shot. They truly were eager to seek vengeance for the deaths of their comrades at Cross Lanes and Carnifex Ferry.

Prott began coughing as Chris followed Becky in the swirling water. He began thrashing about in the water and was trying to regain consciousness. He only made Chris' job harder. Becky was headed for a large rock that was located at the lower end of the pool.

As they approached the rock she yelled to Chris, "There's an air pocket under this overhanging rock. Maybe we can hold up there until these Yankees go their way. Let me help you with him."

Chris and Becky looked at one another as they held Prott between them. They each took several breaths of air and then sank beneath the water. As they disappeared into the water Union soldiers made their way onto the top of the large rock that sat in the Gauley in the hole just below the Big Chute. Becky felt her way beneath the sandstone monolith. Chris was uncertain of this ploy, but he had spent sufficient time with Becky to know that she exercised good judgment and that she could be trusted to the uttermost. He wanted to swim back to the edge for air, but then his hand felt air in place of the rock atop his head. When his hand again touched the rock, his head was well out of the water, and he was able to breathe again. He took a giant gasp of air when he surfaced in the cavity beneath the rock.

Prott was coughing as Chris lifted his head as far out of the water as he could. He began striking the water as he attempted to swim. Becky led them to a rock face that had a series of ledges along its height. The uppermost ledge was at the intersection of the wall and ceiling of the overhang and provided a good handhold so that they could rest from swimming. A lower ledge was wide enough that they could get a foothold and partially stand. The light was dim in the space beneath the rock where they were sheltering, but the water and rock edges below were illuminated by the light of day and took on a light green hue. They could make out each other's face in the scarce light.

Prott spoke, "Why did you hit me with the paddle?"

"You were shot," answered Becky.

"I think the ball grazed your skull and knocked you out. You bled like a stuck hog," added Chris.

"What are we doing at the Big Chute?" asked the dazed soldier.

Chris responded, "We had us one wild deer chase and canoe ride. The scouts we saw that shot at our deer took a crack at us. They hit you and the army they were leading decided to start target practicing on the little gray ducks in the dugout canoe. Good grief, there must have been a complete regiment of Yankees behind those scouts. We're fortunate to be alive and this thing ain't over yet. I just hope we can fool then into thinking we're dead by staying under here until they go."

"Sounds like its going to be a long afternoon. My head is killing me. Feels like a mule kicked me," stated Prott.

"Chris saved your life, Prott. You would have drowned back there for certain if he hadn't kept a hold on you," said Becky.

The three survivors made the most of their afternoon with chit chat and actually laughed a couple of times when they talked about their ride over the Big Chute. They chuckled when Chris told Prott that he was probably the first person to ever be asleep while coming over the falls.

The Union soldiers followed the dugout a quarter of a mile down the raging river. They continued to shoot at the boat until it finally stopped. It had cruised through a small falls and hung up on a driftwood jam on the north shore. The chase was over. They thought this group was only the remnants of a larger scouting party or post of pickets that had run at the sight of the massive Union force. It was apparent to all that the barrage of gunfire had taken care of the confederate vermin. Their dead bodies were most likely lodged under rocks in the numerous rapids in this stretch of the river. Their bloated bodies would surface at Carnifex Ferry in a day or two. The officers of the unit began collecting their men and getting them into their ranks. Colonel Smith of the 13th Ohio Volunteer Infantry, who was in charge of the expedition, gave orders for the column to form and move out. The bugle sounded and the soldiers began their long march back to Camp Scott.

Nearly a thousand men had left Camp Scott the previous day and crossed at Carnifex Ferry and traveled up the south side of the river on the scouting mission. Their goal had been to make it to Hughes Ferry and catch the bushwhacking cavalry and scouts who had been reported earlier by Major Hayes. They also explored the viability of the Wilderness Road for advancing troops toward Floyd's position at Meadow Bluff. They made no significant advances on this road; perhaps because of the earlier efforts Floyd had taken to block it.

The Federal troops were advancing on the southern route. Major Hines was leading the Union advance guard in front of Cox on the James River and Kanawha Turnpike. He reported that the Rebels had withdrawn from the west side of Sewell Mountain to the east. The Confederates feared massive Union troop movements and reports had been made that a significant crossing had been made at Hughes Ferry. He also said that Sewell Mountain would provide a militarily adequate fortification for General Rosecrans' entourage if they desired to move forward from Camp Scott. Following the receipt of one of his daily reports, General Rosecrans responded to Cox, who was positioned a few miles west of the mountain at Camp Lookout.

SEPTEMBER 20, 1861.

Brig. Gen. J. D. COX,
Camp Lookout:

Major Hines' report makes me think a report we started yesterday worked well. It was stated that we intended to cross Hughes' Ferry if Gauley ran blood. Three companies of the Twelfth and 600 men of the Thirteenth did cross over and go up that road nine miles. The birds had all flown, but the effects of the scout have been salutary. As to your advance under my former instructions as to care about position, you are authorized to do so. Let the advanced guard on Sewell examine and choose a strongly defensible position, and allow no passings whatever.

W. S. ROSECRANS.

The general knew they hadn't crossed and couldn't cross at the Hughes Ferry because they had cut the flatboat in half and sunk it several days earlier. They had, however, scouted the south side of the Gauley from Carnifex Ferry to Hughes Ferry. Their maneuvers had placed additional concerns in the lap of Floyd who was convinced that Federal troops were advancing along the Wilderness Road from Hughes Ferry. Gauley had drawn its share of blood from both sides, but three additional souls were hanging onto life beneath an overhanging rock in its current.

Hours passed and the water turned dark as night came. The stranded trio knew it was time for their exit. Chris told the two siblings to wait and he would see where the Yankees had gone. He took a large gulp of air and pulled himself along the rock that was above his head. He paddled his legs in the water that were now stiff from standing on the rock ledge in the air pocket beneath the overhang. He made his way to the edge of the overhang and then to the surface of the water where he slowly stuck his head into the fresh air. It was dark now and he could not see anything. The only sound that he heard was that of the falling water passing through the Big Chute. He dog paddled his way to the bank and slowly crawled onto the sandy beach. His eyes stared into the darkness as he scanned the riverbank by turning his head to the left and then to the right. There was not a sign of a soldier. He stood to his feet and climbed to the top of a rock that overlooked the river. He could not see a fire or even a light except for a dim glow through the window from the Hughes' house in the distance. Thank God, the Yankee scouting party was gone.

Chris returned to the water and swam back to his friends.

"It's clear now; they have gone. I saw a light in the house," he said.

"Good, let's get out of here," said Prott.

Becky spoke, "If we cross the river here it is only a short walk back to the house."

"OK, we can cross here, but we can't go back to the house. They will be watching for us. We will have to get our guns and go. Dad may have brought our gear back with him from Campbells Branch. We will have to cross Gauley again so that we can report back to our regiments, " added Prott.

They were off into the dark water. Prott took the lead. Becky and then Chris followed him. They swam from the relatively calm water above the rock overhang into the center of the stream. Chris waited for Becky who appeared to be slowing the further she journeyed. In the middle of the river where the current was at its peak she started down river.

"Becky," cried Chris. "What are you doing?"

"I can't help it. It is my dress. The current has caught my dress and is pulling me down river. I don't think I can make it," she screamed.

The distance between them widened. There was an increasing roar coming from down river. Another set of falls awaited them. Chris could not see her now, but he heard her gasping for air. She was really struggling to make any progress across the river. He swam as quickly as he could to her aid.

Prott was oblivious to what was happening and thought they were behind him. He could now stand up in the water on the other side and turned to see where they were. All he could see in the darkness was white splashes, but he heard Chris call out again to his sister.

Chris yelled to be heard above the crashing water down river, "Get on my back; we can make it together."

He approached the young woman from behind and she grasped for his neck. She found his shoulders and pulled herself close to his back and he momentarily submerged. He resurfaced with a renewed strength and his legs and arms plowed through the swiftly flowing water. With his mighty reaching arms stretching into the torrent his hand contacted a boulder. His hand only scraped across it, but with his next stroke he held fast and pulled both of them atop it. The top was just below the surface of the water, but its size caused the current to part and provided a resting spot for the weary swimmers. They held on for their lives. Staring into the dimly lit night, he thought he could make out a hazy shoreline ahead. He stood on their sandstone island and dove along the surface for the shore. Much to his surprise the water was now only chest high and the current was waning. He called out again to her and she dove into the water in the direction of his voice. He grasped her outreached hands and pulled her into his arms. She clung to him as he helped her to shore. Before she stepped out of the water she paused, turned, and stood trembling in his arms. They held each other for a brief moment before they joined Prott and started toward the house.

The two Rebels waited on Becky's return in scant moonlight at a shelter rock that was part of the cliffs, a short distance down river from the Hughes' home. While they waited, Chris thought about the promise he had made to God before going over the falls. He reflected on what the preacher had said a few days earlier at Camp Gauley about Jesus Christ dying for his sins so that he could be justified before God by believing on what His Son had done. God loved him that much. Aw -ha! It was similar to what he had just done for Prott and Becky. He was willing to sacrifice his life that they might live. Huh? He had never thought about religion like that before. He thought he understood now. His salvation was not based upon what he could or could not do. It was based upon his faith in the one sacrificed in his place. Prott and Becky were helpless to save themselves. He had interceded for them, out of his love for them, and saved them from death. Is this how God works? Wow, how simple it seemed to him now. Too simple, he thought? I'll have to think more about this when I have more time.

Madison, Mirriam, and Becky joined them near the cliffs after collecting the men's weapons and accouterments. The couple was relieved to see the forlorn youths again. They spotted the

When Gauley Ran Blood

Union troops a short while after they became curious about the whereabouts of the trio. When they saw all that blue they knew the boys would go into hiding, but they couldn't believe they hid under a rock in the middle of the Gauley. Mirriam had prepared food for them from the leftovers they had enjoyed at lunch. They said their good-byes and Madison shook their hands. Mirriam hugged and kissed each of the young men. In the process of kissing Prott, she touched the fresh bullet wound that appeared as a dark thick line above his temple. He jumped and let out a soft cry.

"Issac Prottman, why you're wounded son. Won't you let me put something on that?" she asked. A small trickle of blood stopped as she touched his head on examination.

"Mother, we have to get back. We are soldiers you know. They will need us when Rosecrans makes his move against Floyd."

As Becky hugged her sibling she said, "My dear little brother, I love you. Keep your head down. At the rate you're going you need all the luck you can get."

Then, in the grayness of the night, she stood in front of Chris and embraced him and as she softly touched her lips to his cheek she whispered, "Please, be careful."

The soldiers made their way to the river with their rifles in hand and their gear gathered into a ball. They each freed a log from a catch of driftwood. After placing their rifles atop the log with their other paraphernalia and pushing off the bank into the Gauley, they disappeared into the night.

Mirriam stood on the bank and mouthed the words, "God be with you boys."

Becky felt a torrent of tears rolling down her cheeks as she stared across the river into the darkness. No one knew what lay ahead for the two men again crossing the Gauley.

Madison heard the sobs of his daughter and took her face between his rough hands and asked, "Are you all right? Are you all right?"

Chapter 11
Ferry Christmas

"Are you all right? Are you? Grandma Becky, are you all right? "asked Anna as she stood beside the elderly woman and gently placed her soft white hands on each of her cheeks.

"You have been sitting in your chair and haven't eaten a bite. You've been just staring out that window at that swing and not saying one word. When I do that momma says I'm getting sick. Are you getting sick, Grandma Becky?"

"No, honey, I'm not sick. I'm just an old woman who daydreams too much," replied Becky. "Did you get enough to eat?"

"I had plenty. I even had cookies. I knew you wouldn't mind. Are we going to bake Thanksgiving and Christmas cookies again this year? Gingerbread is my favorite kind. Can we bake gingerbread? Please?" asked the granddaughter.

"Sure, honey, if that's what you want. Don't you want a Christmas tree?" asked Becky in a soft voice, as she dozed back into a mid afternoon's slumber. Her thoughts passed quickly back through the years.

⊷⊛⊶ — — ⊷⊛⊶

Becky watched the project from the house. The soldiers talked a lot about whether or not they would be home for Christmas, as they worked on a raft in mid December of 1861. Some of the men thought they would be going back to their homes in Ohio, and others thought they would be going to General Rosecran's winter camp at Gauley Bridge. The wet and the cold, in addition to being away from their families, put many of the men in sore spirits.

197

When Gauley Ran Blood

They had been working on the raft for four days cutting the logs and fastening them together. They had refused Madison's advice about building a flatboat rather than a raft, but were determined to see that a craft would be available for crossing Gauley. General Crook, the Union commander in Summersville, wanted access to the south side of the river for scouting purposes. Madison told them that rafts are top heavy and can become unstable if there is much current. With a flatboat the weight is lower and thus more stable. The sergeant in charge told him he could handle things just fine without his help.

Madison was anxious to have his ferry back in operation, but the United States Army had other plans. At least until it was to their advantage to have passage over the Gauley to the Wilderness Road. It had been over two months now since they had sunk the ferry, and traffic on the Wilderness Road to Summersville had stopped. The Union pickets at the ferry kept a constant vigil to prevent enemy crossings of any kind.

The family came to know many of the Ohio men. They would take turns on duty coming from the Union garrison at Summersville. Mirriam nursed the sick and often fed the hungry. Her charity knew no colors. She would take no payment for her services. The men, with gifts of coffee, sugar, salt, rice, pickled beef, and other items of endearment, rewarded her efforts. One soldier brought her a looking glass. It was only the second one she had ever owned, and it meant much to her. The soldiers also brought in Cincinnati newspapers. Although six or eight weeks old, they told the story of the early war. Aside from the returning soldiers' stories, these were their only sources of outside news. Letters were few, but now and then they would hear from their sons, Jeremiah and Edward in Iowa and Ohio. They had not heard from Prott since the picnic. It was probably better that way. His life and the lives of the rest of the Confederate contingency had been cold, wet, and miserable that fall. Winter conditions made it worse.

He and Chris had made it back to Meadow Bluff only to find that their units had moved out to Sewell Mountain with General Robert E. Lee to oppose General Rosecrans' forces stationed there. Hungry and tired, they eventually made it to their regiments who were also hungry and tired. They became faceless soldiers in the Confederate Army. They were tallies on the sergeant's muster roll. Supplies were scarce and forage for the animals was nearly gone. It had rained almost every day. When there was no rain, there was sleet or snow. The camp was full of sick soldiers as was most every home and church in the vicinity of Sewell Mountain. The hospitals back in Lewisburg were also full of soldiers suffering from ague, measles, diarrhea and camp fever.

The bickering between Generals Floyd and Wise was an ever-present distraction and nuisance to General Lee until the arrogant Wise was ordered to Richmond. This lowered the mental aggravation of the general, but with the extreme survival conditions the mild tempered leader's hair began to gray. He, like most of the men, also grew a beard. To this time in his life he had been clean shaven. Perhaps the only good to come from his duty in western Virginia was the purchase of a horse from one of his majors. He had seen the horse while on Sewell Mountain and later bought him. The general named the horse Traveller and they spent the remainder of the war together.

In the fall of the year the normally awe-inspiring view of the leaf covered western Virginia mountains took on a dismal tone in the wet and cold weather. It was a war of waiting. Each side sent out scouts and skirmishers to ascertain the strength and position of their opponents. Although a few men were killed, none of the skirmishes resulted in a full-scale conflict. With the horrendous weather conditions and continuing supply problems, General Rosecrans elected to withdraw his army to Gauley Bridge in early October 1861, but not before plundering and burning much of the village of Fayette Court House. He and one of Cox's regiments occupied the Tompkins farm known as Gauley Mount. The wife of Colonel Tompkins of the 22nd was the hostess to the uninvited general at their farm. This put Chris' dear commander under great duress. Rosecrans, however, was a man of honor and eventually allowed Mrs. Tompkins to seek asylum in Richmond.

Lee's army followed after Rosecrans' as best they could. The James River and Kanawha Turnpike was virtually impassable. The Confederate Army attempted to drain and repair the road in places. They filled in the holes with logs and rocks in a somewhat puncheon style. It was not uncommon for wagons to become so stuck in the large mud holes that they would have to be unloaded and abandoned. Exhausted horses were shot beside them.

Rosecrans was not seeking a fight under the prevailing conditions. In light of this, Lee felt the crisis had passed for the time being. Other concerns of the war drew Lee away from the area in late October, but Floyd continued to antagonize Rosecrans from a mountaintop called Cotton Hill across the New River from his position. Floyd established a new post near Cotton Hill called Camp Dickerson.

For nearly a week Floyd pounded the Federal position at Gauley Bridge with cannon fire that could be heard as far away as Summersville. The overall result was a dozen Union soldiers killed or wounded. The 22nd was kept busy positioning cannons and anticipating counter attacks from the Federals. Floyd even ordered bombardment of Colonel Tompkin's Gauley Mount estate for his amusement. Tompkin's wife and children continued to reside there under the protection of General Rosecrans. With the cannoning of his property jeopardizing his family's lives, the colonel had no choice but to resign his commission. He had had enough of the militarily inept Floyd

Floyd's commanders were so concerned about the vulnerability of their position on Cotton Hill that they all signed a petition asking him to withdraw. They pointed out that the Yankees, who were in vast superior numbers, could cross the river and flank the Confederate position. Floyd again revealed his military incompetence and rather than withdrawing, he sent additional troops and cannons to harass the Union position. His zeal was soon spoiled by his nemesis.

Rosecrans, who had been slowed by the rain-swollen rivers, had also had enough of Floyd's harassment. He ordered one of his generals, who had been positioned down stream on the Kanawha River guarding his right, to advance toward the southern position. The movement of this force of 3,000 had been masked by small skirmishes during the previous week's engagement. The troops crossed the Kanawha River on flatboats constructed of wagon bodies with canvas tarpaulins stretched across their bottoms and sides to provide a watertight skin. They lashed the boats together with bed cords for stability and sent the troops across. Other crossings also took place near the mouth of Gauley River and the Union advance was under way. Floyd's command of Cotton Hill was over. The Union Army was again on the move.

The southern troops began their withdrawal with the 22nd and 36th Virginia Infantry Regiments again in the rear. The rear guard was a dangerous place to be, but there were advantages that day. In the haste of retreat, the first Rebels out were forced to abandon much of their gear in the camp and along the roads. They left behind everything from barrels of flour to frying pans. Entire wagonloads of supplies that had become stuck in the soupy mire were left behind. This was a hay day for the boys of the 22nd. Many of the men in the unit were totally destitute to the point of being barefooted. With their feet swollen and bleeding, they gleaned the supplies left by their comrades with eager expectations. Many of them acquired much needed clothing and some exchanged their old muskets for Enfield rifles that had been left behind. Twelve wagons were left at one spot in a sea of mud. The horses that pulled them appeared as if drowned, but in reality, they had been shot when they became inextricable in seas of mud. The toll of war in the western mountains of Virginia continued to climb.

General Floyd did not stop his retreat until he reached Dublin Station, Virginia, on the Virginia and Tennessee Railroad some three weeks later. The end of 1861 saw Floyd and all of his troops but the 22nd bound for Kentucky. The 22nd, which had started the year with almost a thousand men, was down to under 500 due to deaths, wounds, sickness, and desertions. The 22nd was headed for Lewisburg, which was only 15 miles from Meadow Bluff and where they had started in September. Lewisburg was to be their post for the remainder of the winter. They would be spending Christmas in Lewisburg.

Christmas that year was just another cold, snowy day for Private Christopher Columbus Hughes. He wrote a letter to his mother and one to Becky. Both were short because he knew his labor could be in vain as deliveries of mail were sporadic at best. He spent much of his time thinking about Becky and her family.

When Gauley Ran Blood

With no significant concentration of Confederates to fight in western Virginia, Rosecrans' Union troops at Gauley Bridge were dispersed to locations in Kentucky and in Virginia near Washington. They were also sent to many outposts in the towns and villages in the mountains where they had traveled earlier that fall. Summersville was occupied by the 36th Ohio Volunteer Infantry who was commanded by Colonel George Crook. He had received orders to make a scouting expedition to Meadow Bluff to ascertain the strength of the rebel forces there. The Union soldiers building the raft at Hughes Ferry were under his orders.

They had cut large poplar trees from Madison's woods along the Joe Branch and dragged them to the ferry site. Madison was successful in convincing them to allow him to use one of the logs for the construction of a new dugout canoe to replace the one he told them bandits had stolen some weeks earlier. Fortunately, they believed him or felt that his wife was due a favor for her charitable deeds. In any event, he now had a new canoe.

Madison again attempted to convince the sergeant in charge of construction to build a flatboat, rather than a raft, but it was to no avail. He wouldn't hear of it. He had built many rafts back home on the Ohio River and he was confident this one would get them across the river. The poplar logs were strapped together with boards across the top. He had not carried horses before, but how difficult could that be? He was soon to find out.

The weather was damp and cold as the soldiers secured the ferry rope to the raft and led the six horses onto the craft that had been constructed. The horses didn't like the gaps in the logs and were unsettled and agitated as the first load of soldiers started for the south landing. The soldiers tugged on the towline and the raft began its voyage across the river. As they neared the center of the river where the current was the strongest, one of the horses shifted its weight, stumbled, and stepped to the side onto a soldier's foot. The man called out in pain and spooked the other horses. The scream created a movement among the horses that shifted them in unison to the down river side of the raft. The dismounted riders, in an attempt to correct for the weight shift, pulled the bridles of the horses to the opposite side of the raft. As they steered them, the horses' hooves and legs became tangled amidst the logs and strapping. Some fell and others tripped over the fallen ones. The men did their best to calm the animals, but it was of little help. Aided by the river current, the raft tilted to its side and two of the massive animals fell into the icy water accompanied by their dismounted riders. When the raft shifted from the loss of the two horses to the other side, it threw two more off the opposite end along with the four infantrymen.

The men remaining on the raft called out to the ones in the icy water to grab hold of the horses and let them take them to shore. The cold water nearly took away the breath of the now freezing soldiers. Two of them were quickly pulled back aboard the raft and the rest managed to grab hold of the horses. The animals snorted through their giant nostrils as they swam and blew a watery mist in their foggy breath across the river. The raft, horses, and men managed to get back to the shore and the river crossing was postponed for another time. The freezing men were taken to a guard shack that had been constructed near the ferry landing. They were allowed to warm and dry their clothing by the fire in the picket house before they had to report back to the remainder of the garrison at Summersville. They were most fortunate that the Gauley had not claimed other lives that day.

When Colonel Crook reported via telegraph the events of the day to General Rosecrans, he was given in reply an order and a message. The order was issued to Colonel Crook and the message was for the Hugheses. The order was to be carried out at sunrise the following day and the message delivered simultaneously. The morning would prove to be very interesting.

Becky awoke to the sound of her mother humming a hymn as she flipped the fried mush in the skillet on the fire. There was something different about her demeanor on that cold December morning. She sensed there was something in the wind this day. Why was her mother so cheerful?

She quickly dressed and went to the living room where Madison sat reading his Bible. He held the book awkwardly directly in front of his face so that Becky could not see him. He was pretending to hide. In the corner of the room set a beautiful holly tree. It was the deepest green she had ever seen. It had hundreds of bright red berries as big as marbles sprinkled across it.

They had not had such a fine Christmas tree in her life. She was, admittedly, a bit too old for the childish traditions the family tried to observe each year as they celebrated the birth of the Christ child, but the spirit of the season warmed her heart. In an instant she recalled the sounds and smells and tastes of Christmas. She was reminded of the gifts her brothers showered upon her at this time of year. After all, she was their little sister, their only sister. She was given a whistle, a blue ribbon, a sock doll, and of course Prott's bird nest. This gift today, the berry covered holly tree, was her best ever. At a time when the boys were all gone, she really needed this moment. Her parents always knew how to please and they did it liberally.

"Daddy, you're wonderful," she said as she pushed the book down from in front of his face and bent to kiss his forehead beneath his graying hair.

"Mother, did you have anything to do with this?"

"Who, me? Why, I haven't any idea of what you're talking about, " responded Mirriam with a sheepish smirk on her face.

There was a quiet moment and then they all laughed aloud. The laughter was interrupted by a knock at the front door. Becky answered it. When she opened the door she could see a wagon loaded with boards at the ferry landing. Her curiosity was again stirred.

"Major Andrews would like a word with Mr. Hughes, please? " inquired the Union captain.

"Tell them to come in from the cold, Becky," said Madison.

The major entered followed by two of his officers. They removed their hats and the two of lower rank looked at Becky and then at each other and smiled. She caught their smiles but looked away, and then walked to the fireplace and pretended to fix the fire by adjusting the position of the logs.

Madison recognized one of the officers as the sergeant who had built the raft. He wondered what part this one would have in their visit. Was he there to put the blame for the failure of the raft on the aging ferryman? He had honestly told them what he thought was best, but had been ignored. He did not want any more of their insolence.

When Gauley Ran Blood

The major spoke, "Mr. Hughes, General Rosecrans has asked if he might conduct some business with you? He is aware that you are without the use of your ferry. He would like to make the following offer. If you would be willing to supervise the construction of a new flatboat to be used as a ferryboat, the general has agreed to allow you to use the boat for your own purposes when it is no longer required by the United States Army."

Madison looked at his wife, who was drying her hands in her apron, and winked. She smiled in return and shook her head as if to indicate yes.

"I think we could agree to those arrangements," stated the surprised but elated Madison. "When would you want to start?"

"Immediately, if possible. We have a wagon loaded with lumber we brought from the mill in Summersville this morning. The best carpenters from our regiment await your instructions," stated the major.

"Yes, we can do that; we can begin first thing today, " Madison added.

As the soldiers were leaving the major paused in the doorway and stated, "Oh, I almost forgot. The general asked that I personally present you with this telegram Mrs. Hughes. You are Mirriam Hughes?"

"Yes, I'm Mirriam," she said as she stepped toward the major and was handed a piece of paper.

The soldiers left and Mirriam closed the door. Madison and Becky crowded the woman and they read the message from the general together.

DECEMBER 14, 1861.

Mrs. Mirriam Hughes,
Hughes Ferry:

I regret any inconvenience the loss of your ferry has caused you and your family. If your husband has accepted our offer, please receive as a gift the materials and labor for the construction of a new flatboat. If he has rejected our invitation to assist, I

205

assure you I intend no offence, I beg you please accept the new boat as a small token of our appreciation for your labor in our service showing mercy to our boys in the hospital. I wish you and your family Christmas tidings and will forever remain in your debt. Your obedient servant.

W. S. ROSECRANS.

Mirriam blushed at the honor bestowed upon her. Madison and Becky had watched her age many years during the past few months and knew the price she had paid for the respect shown her. Neither could deny that what the general had done was certainly noble and that he too understood the personal cost the war was extracting from the aging woman. Unfortunately, prices were about to rise.

Chapter 12
Long Hard Wait

In mid December 1861, Madison helped the soldiers build the new flatboat. Ten soldiers were placed under his direction. It took them three days to construct the boat. It was nearly identical to the one they had destroyed nearly four months earlier but a little longer. The length of the boat would easily accommodate a wagon and four-horse team. It was beautiful. The cream-colored poplar boards had purple streaks in their centers where the heartwood of the log had been penetrated. The workmen would place the boards side by side and then saw down the crack between them. After several passes were made, the boards would fit snugly together and only a little hemp was required to caulk the gaps. Only the corners required heavy caulking and coal tar to make the craft watertight. The wide boards made for quick framing of the sturdy skeleton built from 6" by 6" timbers. The deck of the flatboat was constructed of the same wide boards, but a double layer was used where the wagon wheels would run and cause it to wear.

Colonel Crook, the Union commander in Summersville, wanted to use the new ferry immediately. Late in December under his orders, Major Andrews, with a wagonload of supplies and 150 men, crossed the Gauley and made an expedition along the Wilderness Road to Meadow Bluff. Their goal was to ascertain the strength of the Rebel forces in that area and to check on the conditions of the roads to see if they would support troop movements. There was a light snow on the ground, just enough to make out a man's footprints around the boat landing. Madison had been out early that morning to make a final check of his handiwork. It was a fine craft.

The anxieties of the men who had attempted the raft crossing a few days earlier were peaking. The first load across was

207

a dozen infantrymen. The ones, who had been spilled from the raft, paced along the length of the boat nervously. The flatboat rode atop the water surface as carefree as a wind blown duck's feather in a water hole. The flatboat returned to the north shore and two dozen men were carried across. Again, the ferry operated flawlessly, but Madison interrupted the proceedings to drive a piece of hemp into a small fountain that spouted between two of the sideboards. The soldiers, who were dressed in heavy blue wool coats, were in no mood for an icy early morning swim. The flowing water interior of the flatboat caused no little alarm. In moments, however, the craft was again ready for use.

Now was the time for the real test. Four horses, along with ten men, were placed on the flatboat. The boat lowered significantly in the Gauley. One of the captains asked the major if he thought the boat would hold. The major looked away as if not to hear the question. Madison gave the order to shove off. Several of the soldiers on the landing used their feet and legs and pushed the craft along its way. A wave of water splashed along the bow of the boat and it rocked to and fro, but then it steadied itself. The men on board pulled the towrope and in short order the boat returned for its biggest load.

They led the four-horse team, followed by the large freight wagon, onto the craft. The top of the boat nearest the shore nearly dipped into the water as the second team of horses cleared the landing onto the craft. The horses' shoes struck the planking and made a sound similar to that of a drummer in a firing squad. The keel of the boat squeezed mud to both sides as it struck the bottom of the river. A cloud of muddy water appeared to swallow the sides of the flatboat. Two soldiers at the opposite end of the boat were thrown into the air but landed on the deck. They had to scuttle to get out of the way of the teams that were pulling the wagon aboard. As the wagon cleared the landing, it traveled smoothly onto the flatboat trailing the horses whose weight had helped balance its entrance. In spite of the cold weather, the major was seen wiping sweat from his brow. There was but six inches of freeboard along the sides of the craft as it was pulled across the Gauley. If the men pulled too hard, a wave of water would break across the bow and they would have to stop pulling and allow the boat to become still again in the water. Then, with a softer pull, they would continue their voyage until they were safely across. Madison was in his glory and the Union troops were on their way to Meadow Bluff.

Riley Ramsey joined the group as a guide soon after they crossed the river. Riley was a Nicholas County man and had always been loyal to the Union. Since the murder of his son, Nick Ramsey, reportedly by Confederate bushwhackers, Riley had pursued by every means available to him to put an end to the conflict. Many people wondered if his zeal was not motivated by his desire to avenge the death of his son. His brother had also been taken prisoner and sent to Libby Prison in Richmond. It was believed that men were not treated well there. It was a long hard wait for the poor men confined in the old warehouse. His imprisonment only added fuel to the kindled fire burning in Riley's chest.

He was always anxious to take any suspected sesech sympathizer prisoner. He had been a friend of Captain John Halstead before the war, but their relationship was now strained because of their choice of flags. John was often heard to say that Riley was as sly as a red fox. Perhaps if John had had more of his cunning, he would not have been a prisoner at a Camp Chase, Ohio, prison. John, too, had a long hard wait.

Major Andrews' entourage traveled south along the Wilderness Road clearing it of the Rebel's blockages as they went. While some of the soldiers made camp near Hominy Falls, Riley Ramsey and others made raids on homes believed to be havens to the sesech. Any family with a gun, and almost all the families had hunting rifles, was fair game to be accused of harboring secessionists. The list of families whose homes were searched was long, but some of the older established families in the area were surprised to have Union soldiers searching their homes by candlelight that evening. Odell, Props, McClung, Nutter, Amick, the list went on. In some instances, the man of the house was gone, but any weapon and ammunition found in the house, along with the livestock, would be taken. For the less fortunate, the man would be found and taken prisoner. For the least fortunate, especially if any resistance was offered by the accused, the man would be shot attempting to escape. Some said the Federals had learned this method of disposing of prisoners from the Rebels. Many wives were left widows when their husbands were only taken for questioning but reportedly attempted to escape and were shot multiple times in the back of the head. Many of the wives had long hard waits throughout the war sometimes for husbands who did not return home.

When the party arrived at Meadow Bluff, they found the camp deserted. There were 110 log cabins some with puncheon floors. They put the torch to all of them and started their return trip with their guerilla prisoners: 17 horses, 4 mules, 5 oxen, 90 fat cattle, 112 fat sheep, 23 rifles and guns, and one heavy oxen wagon. The only resistance they met was from a small band of Confederate cavalry out of Lewisburg.

The livestock slowed their return. It took them two hours to cross Hughes Ferry with all their spoil. The cattle made quite a mess on the new flatboat and Madison was very upset with the major, but it was not his ferry again, yet. He would have a long hard wait before he could call it his own.

The jockeying of the armies for control of western Virginia appeared endless. As the war raged on during the years of 1862, 1863 and 1864, much of the warfare utilized in western Virginia was quick hitting raids into enemy controlled territories. Each side felt the need to make a statement about the vulnerability of western Virginia by striking the often unprotected and treacherous mountainous regions.

The Rebels, like the Yankees, conducted raids into western Virginia collecting booty. With Union forces occupying most of the Trans-Allegheny section of Virginia, southern leaders encouraged Confederate harassment of the newly created state of West Virginia. Elections held in western Virginia in October of 1862 for statehood were overseen by Union troops which discouraged mountain people sympathetic to the southern cause from voting. A great deal of controversy surrounded the election.

Colonel Crook, who had spent the previous winter in Summersville, had routed the Confederates, under General Heth, from Lewisburg in May of 1862. Later that year, troops under Confederate General Loring were successful in driving the Federals out of Fayetteville and much of the Kanawha Valley. It was a short-lived occupation and the Union again seized control of the valley in October of 1862. Chris' 22nd Virginia Infantry spent an uneventful winter near Lewisburg.

In the spring of 1863, Confederate General John Imboden and General W. E. Jones began a raid into western Virginia. Imboden had 3,400 men and Jones had 2,100. While 700 cavalry were mounted, many others were on foot. They were hoping to secure horses enroute. The generals were intent on destroying portions of the B & O Railroad in the north central part of the new state near Grafton and threatening the newly established Unionist Virginia government in Wheeling. The plan also included defeating scattered Union garrisons along the way, collecting foraged supplies for the army, and enlisting manpower for the Confederacy.

Imboden started from Staunton, Virginia on April 20, 1863. Jones left the following day from Lacey Springs, Virginia intent on a more northern route. The two planned to rendezvous latter in their raid.

The 22nd Virginia Infantry, under the command of Colonel George S. Patton, left Lewisburg and met Imboden at Hightown after a seven-day march through mud, snow, and frozen rivers. They continued north with Imboden to Beverly where they drove off 900 Federals in a hard fought battle. The garrison moved on to Buckhannon where it joined forces with Jones.

Jones' cavalry had made a sweep through Oakland, Maryland, and then to Fairmont via Rowlesburg, Kingwood, and Morgantown. At Fairmont, he succeeded in destroying a large iron railroad bridge. He then moved on to Philippi and then to Buckhannon. His troops fought numerous skirmishes during their raid and were able to successfully turn back their foes.

On May 3, 1863, Jones and Imboden joined forces and marched on Weston to find the Yankees had fled. While occupying that town, several skirmishes were fought in surrounding neighborhoods including Simpson Creek and Jane Lew. By the time the generals were to leave Weston, Imboden's troops were down to 2,300 men. Aside from the troops that had been sent back south with herds of livestock, many were left along the way sick or wounded. Others deserted.

Jones started toward Parkersburg, but hearing of numerous Federal troops in the area, he chose instead to attack smaller targets on his route in West Union and Cairo. He was successful in destroying the oil refinery and burning 150,000 barrels of oil at Burning Springs. He then headed for Summersville.

Imboden also traveled south to Summersville via Sutton struggling in the cold and mud. Heavy rains had plagued them through most of the raid. He successfully defeated a small squad of Federals as they abandoned Summersville. He was able to capture two dozen men, nearly 30 supply wagons, and over 150 mules with harnesses.

Before the Union pickets had left Hughes Ferry, as they retreated from Summersville, they had received orders to scuttle the flatboat. Hearing of a large Rebel force headed south, the soldiers hastily chopped a hole in the flatboat and allowed it to sink. They left the landing headed for Gauley Bridge blocking the road behind them with fallen trees. Mirriam and Becky had to restrain Madison from attempting to defend his ferryboat against the Yankees. He would have been no match for them and the result could have been disastrous.

Generals Jones and Imboden were again together. They considered a run through the Kanawha Valley but decided against it considering the weary condition of the men. Perhaps they had done enough, after all, their combined spoils totaled 4,100 head of cattle, 1,350 horses and mules, and numerous wagons and small arms. It had been rumored that General Lee was contemplating a campaign into Pennsylvania and the supplies gained on this raid would prove most helpful in that effort.

They had killed more than 30 of the enemy while wounding many more. Almost 700 Yankees had been taken prisoner. Although their primary objective had not been achieved, they had destroyed more than two dozen railroad bridges, one railroad tunnel, two trains, and burned 150,000 barrels of oil. What they accomplished was not bad for a month's work, but the men had paid dearly. Not withstanding the other units that had accompanied them, the 22nd had been hit hard. They had marched 24 out of 35 days and more than 40 of them did so barefooted. Nearly 70 of the 22nd had been left ill along the wayside. It was said you could have traced the trail of the 22nd by following the birch trees which had been stripped of their bark for food. They now stuffed themselves with the provisions that had been left behind by the Federals in Summersville.

While Jones' and Imboden's troops were camped at Summersville, advance riders had discovered the sunken ferryboat at Hughes Ferry. Having made the raid with General Imboden, Private Christopher Columbus Hughes was now in Summersville with the 22nd. He wanted to slip away to the ferry to see Becky but could not get away. When he heard that the Yankees had sunk the boat and that his regiment would most likely be taking another route to Lewisburg, he was very disappointed. He had not seen her since the night Prott and he had crossed the river after being fired at by the Union regiment the day of the picnic. It had been a long hard wait.

He had become acquainted with several men of the 22nd who were originally from Summersville. Most of them knew the Hughes family and held them in high esteem. He took quite a ribbing when he mentioned his interest in Becky. The men said that she was but a young girl and that he should be ashamed for robbing the cradle. He would respond that his intentions were honorable, and that he did not want to listen to coarse talk. His temper flared on more than one occasion when the talk grew salacious. They also teased that if they had a girl whose boat was sunk, they would raise it and sail away on it with her. Chris laughed at their jest, but the more he thought of what they said, the more reasonable it sounded, or at least the part about raising the flatboat. With all the men, horses, cattle, mules, wagons, and cannons the garrison had to transport across the mountains, the more practical and attractive the crossing at Hughes Ferry sounded.

The Wilderness Road route, though not easy, was far superior to the unplotted Cold Knob Mountain alternate route that some said the generals were considering. Chris decided to sow some ideas among his comrades and the officers of the 22nd. When the rumors finally reached Colonel Patton, he commented in jest that it would take 100 horses to raise that boat. All the horses that belonged to them and the ones they had acquired were at the point of exhaustion. Their ribs showed through their sides like staves in a corncrib. He laughed beneath his breath for only moments when he realized that they had just captured 168 fresh mules with harnesses from the Federals. Would that not equate to 100 horses? Maybe it would be worth a try.

Colonel Patton, being one who was not afraid of trying new tactics, casually mentioned the topic of raising the ferryboat to General Jones. His efforts were reinforced by rumors that large bands of Union forces were on their way to Summersville from Clarksburg in the north and from the Kanawha Valley to the west. Jones diplomatically agreed that it might not be a bad idea, but his concern was the recent heavy rains that might cause the Gauley to be in high tide. Patton quickly pointed out that the rain in the Yew Mountains to the east would have not only the Gauley in the brush, but its upstream tributaries raging. The Cold Knob route would take them through the Cranberry and Cherry Tree Rivers, both tributaries of the Gauley. Patton's argument was well made. At this point, Jones asked Patton to send out a reconnaissance envoy to the ferry to assess the situation and to report back by midday.

When Chris' captain asked for volunteers for the mission that morning, he was first in line. Little did he know that Colonel Patton, who had heard about his horsemanship during the retreat from Carnifex Ferry, had requested his assistance. Chris was given a horse and he rode off with Colonel Patton and six other soldiers toward the ferry. It began raining immediately after they left camp.

They reached Hughes Ferry after a ride of thirty minutes. It continued to rain as they dismounted and walked to the north landing of the ferry. Chris had a gum blanket around his shoulders, but he gave it up when he realized he was soaked to the skin already. He wrapped his rifle in the blanket and carried it under his arm.

A figure could be seen coming from the Hughes house toward the ferry landing. Madison made his way through the barnyard and joined the soldiers at the ferry.

"Mr. Hughes?" asked Colonel Patton.

When Gauley Ran Blood

"Yes," replied Madison. He saw a familiar face in Chris and nodded a greeting.

"My name is George Patton. I'm with the 22nd Virginia," stated the colonel.

"We have come here to survey the possible use of your ferry to cross a sizeable garrison of equipment and soldiers. Do you think it is possible to salvage your flatboat?" asked the colonel.

Madison wiped the rain from his face and spoke, "You can't tell it now because of the muddy water, but the boat is only about twenty feet from the shore. It's in about eight feet of water. The Yanks pulled off one side of the wheel boards so that they could chop through the keel. They cut out a board roughly two feet wide and four feet long and then gave the boat a shove into the river. It didn't make it very far."

"But, do you think the boat is salvageable?" asked the colonel again.

"Oh, sure, when the water goes down we can hook to it and pull it to shore and patch it," replied Madison.

"How long would that take?"

"I could patch it in a couple hours. If it doesn't rain any more, we could probably get to the boat in two or three days after the water goes down and drag it on shore," stated the ferryman.

"Oh, no, we can't wait that long. Our troops are exhausted after an extended march and the horses are near death. We have reason to believe that Union forces are approaching us from the north and west. We have a day at best to evacuate Summersville. Part of our contingency will most likely leave there today by another route. No, we don't dare wait for the river to go down. We do not have that luxury. We will have to take the alternate route with General Imboden," sighed the disappointed Patton.

"Sorry, Mr. Patton, I don't control this river. The Good Lord is the only one with any authority over it. I sometimes wonder if even He doesn't get disgusted with it at times," said Madison.

The colonel, who was himself nearly exhausted, ignored the ferryman's attempt at humor and kicked a channel into the soft mud that quickly filled with rainwater. He stared at the ground as he thought. He feared he would lose the remainder of his regiment to the rough terrain if he were forced to travel over Cold Knob Mountain. His men were tough, but their vinegar had been thinned by their exploits over the past thirty days. He loved those men and they knew it. Every one of them, without asking, would gladly die for this man. There was but one choice remaining now. They would have to continue with Imboden and risk losing it all.

Imboden planned a return route crossing Gauley several miles upstream from Hughes Ferry. He would lead his troops up Cherry River and over Cold Knob Mountain to return to Warm Springs. O.K. for him, but he had not walked 400 miles like the 22nd. Jones, who was now burdened with prisoners, livestock, and wagons, desired a gentler trek to safer territory. He wanted to cross Gauley at Hughes Ferry and to return to Lewisburg via the Wilderness Road and James River and Kanawha Turnpike. It did not appear that this would now be an option. The 22nd would have another 100 miles of the most difficult topography yet to crawl over to get to safety. He dreaded the long hard wait for his men to cross the swollen streams and steep rocky hillsides.

"Thank you, Mr. Hughes," said Colonel Patton as he turned and started for his horse.

"Colonel, sir, may I speak?" asked Chris as he stepped toward the officer.

"Go ahead."

"Colonel Patton, I think we can get that flatboat out of the river. If you would just give us a chance, " stated the bearded soldier.

The officer stopped momentarily.

"Private, I know you're tired of walking, but that's a whole lot better than drowning. You'll get yourself killed in all that water," replied the colonel.

"Son, remember when you move the boat off the bottom the current will catch it and put up an awful drag. That is, if you can get it off the bottom. It may be stuck fast in the mud. You may need half the horses in Nicholas County to pull it up," added Madison.

"We have lots of mules," said Patton with a mischievous grin.

When Gauley Ran Blood

The sun appeared from behind a cloud, but a light rain continued to fall. The officer may have taken it as a positive sign.

He stopped his advance toward his horse and turned to the private. He folded his arms in front of him, tilted his head back, and squinted his eyes as if in deep thought and asked, "Do you really want to try this?"

"You bet, Colonel," Chris replied enthusiastically.

"How can I help you?" asked the convinced colonel.

"When you get back to camp, ask those Summersville boys in the 22nd if they care to lend a hand. We will need mules and harnesses. Oh, yeah, and some strong rope," requested Chris.

"I have spare ferry rope," Madison said.

"That ought to work," said the soldier.

Patton asked, "How many mules, soldier?"

"I think ten teams would be handy. Best to have more than we need," Chris answered.

"I'll get them back here as soon as I can. You men, help him if you can, " said the colonel as he mounted his horse and started for town.

Madison took the opportunity to extend his joy in seeing his soldier boy again.

"How you doing, Chris? I haven't seen you for at least a year and a half. How is the war treating you?" asked Madison.

"O.K., Mr. Hughes, I can't complain. This last march has been one of the longest and hardest since I joined up. Seems we do a lot more marching than fighting," responded Chris.

"Ah, how's Becky?" he asked.

"We almost lost her back in the winter to pneumonia, but she stuck it out and is fit as a fiddle now," stated Madison. "She is up to the house if you want to see her."

"Yes, I would like that, but we must get this boat out of the water first. You said you had a rope?" the determined private asked.

Madison made a short trip to the shop and returned with two ropes. One was egg size in diameter and the smaller one was the width of a man's little finger. As he returned to the landing the sun shined through the clouds and the day began to clear.

Chris asked, "I know what the big rope is for, but what's with the little one?"

Madison explained that he needed to attach the larger rope to the inside frame on the front of the ferryboat. The smaller rope would have to be attached to his waist and used as a safety line. Chris removed all of his clothes except his trousers. The other soldiers manned the ropes as he waded into the water. It was cool but bearable. As he slowly walked chest high into the coffee brown torrent, a voice called from the fence near the shop.

"Good luck, soldier boy," shouted the young woman who was accompanied by her mother.

The soldier looked over his shoulder to see the woman who had occupied much of his thought life over the past two years. A warm rush passed through his body in spite of the cold mountain stream that engulfed him. What he beheld was far superior to any thought he had had of her in his mind. The sun shined on her hair and it glowed like firelight. She smiled and his heart stopped, but in front of the other soldiers he could not let on.

"Thanks, I'll need it. Say a little prayer for me," he asked.

"Be careful," Becky added.

Chris cleared the rope that was around his waist over a mooring post at the landing and took a mighty gulp of air. He vanished into the river and the soldiers slowly allowed the guideline to be pulled into the river. The heavy rope, that was held in Chris' hand, was periodically jerked along in three-foot segments. All at once, the ropes tightened and they quickly slid along the soldiers' hands. In moments, Chris reappeared several yards downstream on top of the water in a heavy current. The soldiers pulled him to shore.

Chris was breathing heavily as he spoke, "The current is too strong ... and I can't stay down. I need ... to add an anchor ... to me someway."

Madison thought for a moment and then said, "How about an old sharpening stone. There is one in the shop. My son, Mathew, wore it out years ago. It must weigh 45 or 50 pounds."

Madison and one of the soldiers fetched the round stone with a hole in the middle which had been used as a grinding wheel in Mathew's blacksmith shop. Madison tied a length of rope to the stone and then secured it to Chris' waist. He looked like a murder victim from a dime novel ready for disposal. The stone was tied to his waist and his safety line was tied above it, just under his arms.

This time he started into the water up stream of the landing. He struggled in the mud for a moment with the weighty stone suspended between his legs. Soon he was free. When he was neck deep, he again took a giant breath of air and disappeared into the water. The rope fed into the water following him.

Becky could not help but hold her breath as Chris entered the water. She thought she might use that as a gauge of how long he should remain underwater. She held until she thought her lungs would burst and then blew out a mighty gust as she struggled for air.

"He's been under too long. Pull him up!" she cried.

The soldiers were dumbfounded but could not disagree. They quickly pulled on his rope and it began to come in. Then it became fast. They pulled as hard as they might, but the rope would not budge. Becky sensed there was a problem and ran toward the landing. Just as she arrived, the rope gave way and the men continued their pull. Then the rope skimmed along the top of the water. Chris was not to be found.

"Oh, you've pulled him in two!" shouted Becky.

One of the soldiers barked, "Lets try the big rope."

They pulled it in only a few feet and it became stuck. They pulled as hard as they might, but it would not budge. Madison and the men stood helpless looking at one another.

"Help him, daddy!" screamed Becky.

There was nothing he could do. Chris had known the risks and willfully accepted his mission. Maybe the current was just too swift. Had the Gauley taken another good man? Madison shook his head. Becky began to weep. Mirriam prayed to God. Dead silence set upon the place. Even the Gauley seemed to pause its incessant roar in the distance. It was a long hard wait.

The silence was broken by the great sucking inhale of an oxygen deprived private as he shot several feet into the air a short distance downstream of the landing. Chris sucked air through his lips and made a loud whistling sound.

All of the people on the shore also breathed again.

Mirriam spoke aloud, "Praise the Lord!"

"I got it! I got it!" shouted the excited private. "We're hooked to the keel."

Chris swam to shore and was greeted by the soldiers and Becky. He explained that he had been successful in attaching the large towrope to the boat frame, but just as he finished he had been pulled away, and his stone weight had become lodged in the frame. He had no choice but to slide out of his rope. Then he had to untie the stone and that nearly cost him his life, but as his lungs burned and he thought he would have to submit to the great river, the stone broke in half. He didn't have words to explain it. It just broke into two pieces and he sprang off the bottom of the boat, headed for air at the surface, like a Chinese rocket.

The crew was invited to Madison's for lunch. Madison found a change of clothes for Chris, and he and Becky got to visit. Mirriam only had dried beans and cornbread, but the men ate heartily. She also served wild leaks or ramps as they called them. They grew wild in the sandy bottoms along the Gauley and were one of the first plants to show their green shoots in the spring of the year. They were considered by many to be a type of spring tonic. They could be eaten raw or cooked similar to collards or spinach. Some people preferred them to green onions, but their pungent aroma would linger on the breath and body oils of those who ate them for days afterward. For some reason, Chris chose not to partake of the wild onions. Becky followed suit.

Before noon, the four soldiers left the house thanking Mirriam for her hospitality as they exited. She and Madison followed them outside, since the sun was now shining leaving only Chris and Becky in the house. The couple stood facing each other unsure of what the other would say.

"I missed..." Chris started to speak as did Becky at the same moment. He excused himself and allowed her to speak.

"I missed... I missed you too. Have you seen Prott?" Becky asked.

"I ran into him in camp at Charleston in September of 1862. We were under the same leader then, Colonel McCauseland. He appeared fine and dandy. Has he not written?" asked the young suitor.

"We received one letter from him. It was written when he was in Fayetteville. He sounded homesick," stated Becky.

"That's just part of soldiering. Everybody gets the blues now and then. They miss their family or their sweetheart. In camp you wait and wait and wait and get really bored. You do too much thinking. Then you're called out to march and then to fight and everything gets crazy. Then you don't have time to think," said Chris.

"Oh, did you hear that John Halstead got released at Vicksburg? " he added.

"That's good news, Margaret and Ginny will be tickled. I got the letters you wrote me from Lewisburg and Charleston. I wrote six times. Did you get mine?" she asked.

"I got one in Lewisburg, but that is all. It's the one where you told me about the Yankees building the raft. That was funny. We were so close, but when you can't leave because of military duty you might as well be a thousand miles away. When we were in Monroe County, which is just next to Craig County, I slipped over the hill to see mother one evening for a spell. I got in all kinds of trouble for that. They said I deserted. They liked to shoot me for it, but Colonel Patton took my part and wouldn't let them. I wasn't leaving for good. I got a letter from my sister, Sarah, and she said mother had been sick and I feared she might die before I saw her again. I wasn't gone that long, but I assure you I won't be doing that again," he replied.

A mule brayed in the distance.

"Becky, there's something I ... I wanted ...to ask..." Chris cleared his throat and started to speak, but the door flew open and a soldier stepped in.

"Hughes, men are coming with the mules. You better come on," he said.

"Well, maybe I'll get to see you again before I leave. We have to get that boat out of the river now," Chris said.

"I hope so. I wanted..." Becky was interrupted.

"Come on, Hughes. The captain is going to be fit to be tied. Those new boys said the Yankees were headed this way," stated the soldier.

When Gauley Ran Blood

Chris met the boys from Summersville he had requested at the landing. They gave him a great deal of grief about his private conversation with Becky. Although they were kidding in fun, Chris felt the pressure of the task before him and was in no mood for their joking. He was also frustrated that he had not had the talk he intended with Becky. There was just too much going on. There were now ten soldiers and ten teams of mules ready to attempt to raise the boat. Madison looked on along with the captain in charge. Madison suggested that they place runners beneath the flatboat to "ride" on as they pulled it from the river.

The soldiers took their axes and entered the woods. Soon they returned with two long poplar poles as round as a man's leg and twice as long as the flatboat. The tall lean young poplars made excellent runners. They carried the poles to the water's edge and dropped them. The water had risen until it was knee deep at the ferry landing which to Madison meant the flatboat was in approximately 10 feet of water.

Madison instructed the soldiers where he wanted the runners placed, so they would intercept the boat when it was pulled toward the shore. Chris instructed the rest of the men how he wanted the mules harnessed and the pulling line attached.

"Captain, we are ready to give it a try, " said Chris.

He had attached each team of mules to a knotted loop in a long length of ferry towrope. The rope ran between the animals and attached to the harness at each pair. The harness rope was then attached to the line Chris had tied to the keel of the boat. The runners the soldiers had placed in front of the boat were not visible because of the muddy water. Chris' plan was to pull the boat onto the runners only inches out of the water and then stop to allow whatever water was above the river surface to drain down through the hole in the bottom. By doing this, the teams did not have to raise a boatload of water which would weigh tons and most likely destroy the boat in the process. They would slowly raise the boat and allow time for it to drain.

"Get up! Hay-ya! Hay-ya!" shouted Chris to the mules and the men stationed alongside each pair of mules.

The men coaxed their teams along, and as the slack in the load rope was taken up by each preceding team, their movement would cease and only the mules not under the load continued to move forward up the ferry road. When the fourth team came under the load their harness snapped and they ran into the team in front of them. Their driver ran for cover. As the mules plowed into the team in front of them, the other driver lost control of his team, and they tried to escape what they must have sensed as danger from behind. They started sharply to the left, with the load rope in tow, and when the rope became taut one of the animals stumbled across it and another fell upon the first.

The soldiers and Chris all shouted, "Whoa! Whoa boys! Whoa!"

The pulling was stopped and the teams were quieted. The mule that had fallen had sustained a broken leg when the animal behind it had landed on it. The soldiers scurried to free the struggling animal. They unhooked the team with the lame mule from the load rope and replaced it with the team that had broken its harness load chain. They used the chain from the lame team to attach the replacement team and positioned all of the mules in line again along the load rope. There was now a gap where the team had been moved up the line.

Blooming daffodils paid tribute beside the innocent fallen animal. The captain drew his revolver and shot the mule in the head where it lay. Chris was explaining to the soldiers to keep the rope tight when he was startled by the gunshot. The mules flinched in unison.

When all were in place, Chris again barked his commands and the mules began tightening the rope. This time each team advanced slowly until all of the animals were in tow. The load rope tightened and the column of teams straightened into a distinct straight line. The rope sliced into the riverbank beside the ferry landing. The flatboat did not budge.

"Get up! Hay-ya! Hay-ya! Get up!" again shouted Chris to the mules and the men stationed alongside each pair of mules.

Mirriam and Becky stood by the shop observing every action of the soldiers. Mirriam commented that she had never seen anything like this in her entire life. Becky had her experience at pulling the ferry from the river, but the flatboat had not fully sunk when she dragged it to the bank. It was obvious that this boat was stuck to the mud on the bottom of the river. Under the load, the mules would briefly stagger to one side, lower their backs and then find their footing anew and strain their huge legs trying to pull the load. They struggled.

A rider approached the ferry at full gallop. He dismounted and approached the captain.

"Sir, Colonel Patton asks to be informed that if the ferry is to be salvaged, when might he expect the boat to be ready?" asked the rider.

"Private, this boat may be a goner. We ought to know in about fifteen minutes if you got the time," replied the captain.

"I have the time, but the colonel says Union scouts were seen down on Peters Creek. They don't know how much time we have until the Yankees will be here raising cane. If you can't make it work, he needs to know so that General Jones can accompany General Imboden over Cold Knob," continued the private.

Chris had heard the private's inquiry and his patience had plum worn out. The mules, pull as they might, could not move the boat.

Chris stopped the attempt. Now flustered and with nothing to lose, he directed the men to back up their teams several steps. He yelled out the commands again, and the mules ran forward until the slack pulled from the load rope. When the line was in full load, the mules stopped for a moment, and then they began slowly moving forward. They had broken the boat free from the suction of the muddy bottom and were gradually moving forward.

Mirriam and Becky both clapped their hands at the successful attempt. Madison breathed a sigh of relief. Now, if they could just get it on the runners. It was a blind shot at the poles, but the mules kept moving and Madison soon saw the front of the flatboat emerge from the water beside the landing. Chris continued to drive the teams until the side rails of the flatboat were visible. The boat caught the end of one of the runners, and it slid along in front of it until it protruded toward the bank from the water like a giant fishing pole. Pulling the boat at an angle to the bank helped drain some of the water from it. When it had been pulled to the point that water was spilling over the sides; it gave a loud screech. Madison motioned to Chris to stop the pull. To continue up the bank with a boatload of water would most certainly pull the craft apart. Now they needed to go very slowly. If they had to, at this point they could patch the hole in the bottom and bail out the water to float the flatboat.

Things were looking up for the young private. It had been a long hard wait. The captain asked why he had not become a teamster to begin with, and he replied that, admittedly, he liked horses and mules but not enough to live with them. All the men laughed at his comment.

The captain told the waiting private that the boat would be ready by late afternoon. The private mounted and was off with the message for Summersville. Word of the successful salvage was welcome news to Colonel Patton and General Jones. It had been a long hard wait.

The Confederate contingency had 1,700 men, 800 horses, 164 mules, 1,100 head of cattle, and 25 wagons to cross. They knew the Federals were headed their way, and that way was toward the ferry. They did not have a clue how this large band would cross the rain swollen Gauley before the Federals arrived.

The soldiers worked diligently at the ferry. They slowly pulled the boat forward and allowed it to drain. When they had half of the boat out of the water, Madison said he could get to the hole well enough to fix it. Once the hole was repaired with a new board spliced across the bottom of the boat, the men would have to bail the water out with buckets. After thirty minutes of filling and dumping buckets, the flatboat began a sluggish float still filled with considerable water. Another hour was consumed before all of the water had been emptied and the boat sat high in the water.

A general feeling of relief was felt among everyone who had participated in the operation. Tensions again rose when Colonel Patton, who had ridden ahead of his regiment, questioned the captain about how soon the crossing could commence. There was hardly two hours of daylight remaining. It was obvious that their crossing would have to be at night. Their cadre, men, and accouterments would take hours to cross. What about the booty desperately needed by the army marching north in the Shenandoah Valley? Would they have to leave it behind?

Madison overheard the confab and offered a suggestion.

When Gauley Ran Blood

"A flying bridge. You need a flying bridge," stated the elder Hughes.

Colonel Patton looked at the man as if he had lost his marbles. He asked, "Care to explain what a "flying bridge" might be?"

Madison gladly volunteered, "With the river this high, you use the current to your advantage. We will lengthen the towline of the ferry and move the landing upstream. When we send a boatload into that current, it will shoot downstream and across Gauley as if it were flying across a bridge. We can pull the empty boat back upstream with little effort because it will be on top of the water. We'll have you across in a few hours."

Madison had no idea of the size of the Confederate contingency that had to cross the river. Getting them across the Gauley would be the largest undertaking of his life.

The colonel understood the plan and ordered that Madison's directives be followed. The entourage began arriving before the boat was in its new mooring. They quickly attached a retrieval rope through a pulley wheel that was anchored to a tree. One end of the rope was attached to two teams of mules and the other to the same tree as the guide pulley. The rope passed through another pulley that was fastened to the front of the flatboat. This pulley arrangement would mechanically double the effort of the mules that would be used to control the crossing of the craft. When it was all hooked up, the colonel suggested that two teams of mules be used as passengers for an experimental crossing. A heavy door from the old barn served as a gangplank and the animals were soon on board and headed for the other side. A soldier walked beside each of the mule teams slowly allowing the rope to feed through the guide pulley to the load pulley on the ferryboat sailing down river with the strong pull of the current.

Privates Hypes and Campbell volunteered to steady the teams as they made the trip across the river. White caps licked the sides of the boat as it made its way past midstream. Beyond this, the ride was smooth and without incident. The current caused the boat to drift down stream of the south landing. Madison corrected this on the second trip by tightening the ferry rope. The next load of eight cows traveled across in less than twelve minutes and then twelve more in fewer than ten minutes. With each trip the men gained additional knowledge to streamline the passage. Some suggested swimming the horses and cows across, but the current would have swept them downstream and over the falls to a certain death.

Two great bonfires were lit, one on each side of the river. The soldiers worked feverishly through the night, and just past midnight all of the cattle but two had been safely passed to the other side. A pair of rambunctious steers had miraculously climbed the railing on the flatboat. When it gave way they plunged into the water, but made their way to the south side of the river and were retrieved. One was butchered on the spot and cooked by the bonfire for camp meat. The captain saw that Madison's family received a portion of the beef for their assistance.

The horses followed the cattle and it was noon the next day before all of them were across. They were followed by a steady procession of wagons and men who by now were anxious to cross. The anticipated Yankees had not attacked. It had been a long hard wait.

After raising the boat, Chris worked the crossing mules many hours and then found a spot by the fire where he managed a few hours sleep. He again worked the crossing mules during most of the day for hundreds of trips but did manage a rest when he crossed over with Madison to check the ferry tow rope. Following their check of the rope, they sat down on a rock on the riverbank and talked of hunting and fishing and things of life. Chris liked this man and the feeling was mutual. He was uncomfortable and Madison sensed the uneasiness in his spirit.

"Is there a problem, Chris?"

"Would you permit me to marry your daughter?" Chris blurted out.

"I wouldn't object, but I think that would be between you and the girl. Becky has her own mind about such things. As her father, I never expect her to wed being the independent sort that she is. Yep, you will have to take that up with her," replied the ferryman.

"That is fair, sir. Thank you."

Madison had really given him something to ponder.

When Gauley Ran Blood

Just before 9:00 PM, the last stragglers loaded the ferryboat by firelight and Colonel Patton expressed his appreciation to Madison for his assistance. The colonel was uncomfortable with his next request.

"Mr. Hughes, I have expressed my sincere regard for the assistance you have graciously rendered the Confederacy but regret that I must ask you to remove your ferry from service after our crossing. Can you make it so?" asked the colonel.

Madison responded, "Colonel, I will move the ferry to the north landing and remove the board that was covering the hole made by the Yankees two days ago. It should sink in about twenty minutes."

"I am sure you understand our position. We must be given time to make our way to Meadow Bluff. Our men are worn out but still have a long march ahead of them. Please take the remaining mule team as payment for our crossing. Good night, sir," added Colonel Patton as he stoked the fire for the last time.

Chris also shook Madison's hand and bid him farewell as he jumped aboard the ferryboat. He had not had the opportunity to speak with Becky, but with the war and all, it was probably better this way. He could make a widow out of her. The knot in his stomach was not getting any smaller either.

Becky agreed with her parents that it was best if she stayed out of sight of the soldiers. They were friendly, but young women had the knack of bringing out the animal in the best of men under such dire straights. She stayed in the house during most of their crossing. She wanted to see Chris, but it just wasn't prudent under the circumstances.

It was now nightfall and she had only seen Chris through the house window leading the mule teams back and forth. She and her mother were determined to have some fresh air after being penned up. They walked to the landing to see her father who was leading a mule team that was passing the last boatload of soldiers.

As the women walked past the fire, the boat was at mid stream, but Chris made out Becky's form and his heart raced. He thought to himself, should I do this or not?

"Becky?" he called out in the darkness.

"Chris? Is that you?" she responded.

When Gauley Ran Blood

"Will you wait for me?" he asked.

"Yes, I'll wave to you," she responded with an enthusiastic waving of her hand not having understood him clearly.

"No. I said will you wait, wait for me?" he desperately shouted above the roar of the Gauley.

There was a lengthy pause. It was a long hard wait for Chris. It seemed an eternity. Had she not heard him?

The ferryboat was almost to the opposite bank when a faint response was heard.

"Yes."

A great cheer went up from all the soldiers on the boat. Chris thought of how foolish his request had been under the circumstances and admittedly was quite embarrassed. He did not hear clearly. The cheer confused him. He was frustrated.

"What did she say?" he asked.

Colonel Patton turned to Chris and spoke, "She said, "Yes," private. Good job, soldier."

Becky was in store for a long hard wait.

The war dragged on during 1863 while Becky waited. Chris' 22nd Virginia Infantry, under Colonel George Patton, fought a two-day battle along side other regiments in late August against Union General William Averell at White Sulphur Springs. It was a significant victory for Patton as they managed to turn back Averell to the north. The troops spent time that fall savoring this victory while resting, drilling, and working on local farms in the Lewisburg area.

Their rest was interrupted in November at Droop Mountain when Averell returned to drive them from Lewisburg. Confederate General Echols' troops, including the 22nd, were routed by General Averell's forces and driven in disarray into the forest. The Confederate losses were heavy. Patton's boys regrouped near Frankfort seven miles north of Lewisburg. The next day they attempted to establish a defense of Lewisburg but were forced to flee again, leaving their "colors" to be taken by the Federal troops.

When Gauley Ran Blood

For nearly a month the 22nd scrambled from camp to camp until they were reunited at Salt Sulphur Springs near Union.

Chris took the opportunity to visit his mother and family across Peters Mountain on Johns Creek. He told his mother, Mary, about Becky and her family, and she was excited about her son's new friend. She sounded like quite a gal and she looked forward to meeting the hillbilly girl in the future. His visit was short, but his mother was able to relay an amusing story about his cousins, James and William Francisco, before he had to leave. His mother had had a long hard wait to see him since his last visit, and he felt the least he could do was hear her story. Chris had played with these cousins in his youth but had not seen them for years.

Their father, Christopher Francisco, and Chris' namesake, had moved to Tennessee in the 1850s. When the war started, James joined the Union, but William was conscripted, against his will, by the Confederacy. During a battle, William was taken prisoner by Federal troops and forced to ride, sitting backward on his horse. In camp one evening, James just happened to observe his younger brother, who had just been brought into camp, being taunted by the Union soldiers and in danger of being shot. He was prepared to defend his brother, but in the end, did not have to intercede. James and William were able to convince the commander that he had deserted his company and was looking for a Union regiment to join when he was taken prisoner. He swore an allegiance to the Union and was now in the Federal army. Chris laughed at the amusing story, but he hoped he would not have to take up arms against his cousins. He had not seen them for years, but they had been great chums as children. He thought that sounded like something William would get caught up in. He was always into some type of mischief. Chris returned to the 22nd the following day after bidding his mother and siblings farewell.

The 22nd moved to Caldwell, near Lewisburg, and established their winter camp. They called it Camp Gauley like the one at Carnifex Ferry. No one knew why. It was at this camp that Christopher Columbus Hughes began his journal. Several of the officers kept diaries, and on occasion, they would take them out and reminisce the numerous battles they had fought in. It helped them remember the details more clearly, and he thought it might be interesting in the future - especially if he were wounded or killed. At least Becky would have some idea of a private's life. He knew it would be a long hard wait until he saw her again and figured the diary might help pass some of the boring hours in a private's life. Little did Chris know that 1864 would not allow the idle hours his previous service afforded him.

When Gauley Ran Blood

Chapter 13
Journal of Private C. C. Hughes

January 9, 1864

Bought a paper book in Lewisburg today and have decided to keep a record of army life. Helped some of the men finish a church building near the camp on Dry Creek. Invited me to come there on Sabbath, tomorrow.

January 10

Cold and snowy. Went to church at Dry Creek. Colonel Patton said that they would continue to fast (not eat) and pray that God would bless this army. I did not know that he was so religious. They said he never missed a service.

January 14

Sat by fire in hut today until 4PM. Wrote letter to Becky. Hope to send it with some of the boys going to Nicholas County on furlough. Picket duty on Greenbrier River tonight.

January 16

Nothing new today. Bad cough last night and today. Started reading on a dime novel, *The Indian Wife of the White Hunter*.

January 24

Helped break up a fight last night among the boys in Company D. They had been in Lewisburg and got a hold of some sour apple wine. One of them shot his .58 Enfield across their hut and nearly took off another one's ear. They shook hands in church this morning. Colonel Patton was there again. He read from the book of John, chapter 3, and verse 16. No fire in church, very cold.

Boys from Nicholas returned the other day with Federal prisoners. The Yankees had captured them in Clay County, but turned the tide on them, and brought them here as prisoners. Ha-ha. They had crossed in a dugout at Hughes Ferry, but there was no sight of a ferry. Mr. Hughes was given Becky's letter.

January 27

Grub is scarce. Dug acorns from beneath snow and roasted today. Crackers are all the food we get, Yankee's hardtack.

January 29

Worked today for a local farmer. He gave me a chicken. I shared it with boys in my hut. We had chicken and gravy with dumplings. We watered it down, but it was still good. Rumors are that we are headed for Richmond

February 1

Drilled today in snow. They said there are nearly 650 of us in 22nd, over 2,000 in brigade.

February 4

Sawed firewood all day yesterday. Arms sore. Snowed 2 feet. Read book all day.

February 24

Nothing new today. Drilled all day.

February 26

News that some of the Kanawha boys left for home, surrendered and gave oath to Lincoln.

February 28

Went to church. Message from book of Revelations. God will spew the lukewarm from his mouth. Colonel Patton insisted that 22nd be present.

March 1

Got new underwear today. Bored in camp.

TWO PAGES MISSING

April 5

Arrived in Union, Virginia, after 3 day march. Rained and wet all day.

When Gauley Ran Blood

April 12

Shot turkey on picket duty today. We cooked him and every man got a bite.

April 15

Rain and sleet all day. Cooked and ate ramps. Men would not let me sleep in hut. I bedded down in leaves near camp.

April 30

Told that General John Breckenridge is in charge of Army of Western Virginia. He was a senator and a vice president at one time they tell me.

May 6

Sunny and warm today. Drilled for General Echols today. First beef to eat in two weeks.

May 7

Camped at the Hughes farm (no relation) on road to Staunton.

May 8

Camped near Covington, Virginia. My shoes are nearly gone. I have sewed patches across soles and they work good. Did not get relieved from guard duty last night.

May 9

Marching in mud. Tired.

May 10

Marched last two days. Camp tonight at Crawford Springs near Staunton.

May 12

Colonel Patton had 22nd go to Presbyterian Church in Staunton and it is not even Sabbath. Reverend Wilson preached. Beef in camp.

May 14

Marched down the valley to near New Market today. Trees are turning green in Shenandoah Valley. Many farms we pass are burned. This was beautiful country.

May 15

Fought against Union General Sigel at New Market. Rained all day. We were stationed on the east side of the Valley Pike with the 23rd. Wharton and Heth were across the road. Poor Cadets from Virginia Military Acadamy came along side and helped with the fight. We gave them a mighty cheer. A dozen of the poor lads were killed. They fought fearlessly and bravely.

The Federal Cavalry charged our position and we wheeled right while the 23rd wheeled left and we caught them in a horrible crossfire. We shot the horses or anyone or anything else we could hit. That started their withdrawal. Sigel withdrew all the way to Strasburg. I am told that 540 of the 4,100 brave men that fought became casualties. Some said because we fought on the Sabbath. The north had to have lost 8-900 of their 8,000 men. We sure ran them off.

May 16

Had services and buried dead. My friend, poor Dan Bushong was among the dead. His body was a mess.

May 18

Camped near Staunton, Virginia. We had a visitor today. It was the Presbyterian Church's preacher's boy. I engaged him in conversation today. His name is Woodrow Wilson and he is sharp as a tack at no more than 8 years. He invited me to church. I showed him how to make a pop gun from a sumac sapling.

May 19

Marched in the mud to Staunton and then rode the railroad to Hanover Junction north of Richmond. I nearly fell off as we passed through Charlottesville. The wind blew my hat off to the side of the car, and when I caught it, I lost my balance. John Nidy caught me. He was helping me work on my shoes. Heard we are headed for Richmond to help General Lee.

May 22

Received rations of bacon and hardtack. I made gravy from the grease and some of the crackers. I scooped it up and ate it with the balance of my crackers. We camped near the South Anna River.

May 26

Heard cannoning yesterday. We are happy to have received a tobacco ration today. Finished all my bacon this morning.

When Gauley Ran Blood

May 27

Left the railroad today and camped west of Richmond.

May 29

Weary march to Atlee's Station yesterday. We stood guard in the breast works near Totopotomoy Creek last night and all day today. After noon a few Yankees fired on us, but they ran and didn't put up a fight. I bought John Finch's tobacco ration for $5 Confederate.

June 1

Cannoning yesterday caused us great worry. One shell landed near us, but didn't explode. One of our men threw it from the earthworks and it exploded when it landed. I was on picket duty today and we had a skirmish and ran the Bluecoats off. Some of the boys got overrun, but pretended to be dead until the Yanks passed through, and then they returned to their company. I must remember that one.

June 3

Yesterday we were fed bacon again and marched through a swamp to this place. Its called Cold Harbor, but it's anything but cold. It's hot as thunder and there are thousands of Lincolnites across the way. They're thick as the mosquitoes here. We fought all day along side of General Lee. We tried to dig earthworks, but all we had were our bayonets and bare hands. The soil is sandy, but the tree roots make it hard to dig. Where it is not hot and buggy, it is wet and muddy. My shoes gave out today and I am tired of trying to fix them. I must find another pair of brogans somewhere. We are a miserable lot.

Today we fought hard and killed many Yankees. They line up by the thousands and we shoot them. If we had not been relieved by Finegan's Battalion, we surely would have been overrun. We are here in the trenches tonight with nothing to eat. Death will probably take us tomorrow. Al Rowan was shot through the head.

June 4

Can't write, under constant fire. Ammunition is getting low. Nothing to drink all day.

June 6

Been here at Gaines Mill for last two days. Found a pair of brogans yesterday on a dead Yankee. They fit a little big, but they are better than being barefooted. I didn't think he would mind. Tobacco is all gone. No good birch trees here to chew.

June 8

Yesterday we got on a train in Richmond. What a beautiful city it is. Some of the roads even have cobbles to walk on. I want to visit there when the war is over. It is the biggest city I have ever seen.

Now we are camped near a railroad tunnel. I heard a Union General Hunter is making problems in the Valley. We are going to help defend Lynchburg.

June 10

Camped at Waynesboro. No action today.

June 16

Marched in rain and mud to here. Rubber blanket leaked a little on my paper book. Camped near Lynchburg. General Jubal Early rode past me today. Saw some of the boys from McCausland's 36th. They said General Hunter had whipped them at a place near Staunton called Piedmont on the 5th. General Jones was killed. They said they thought Sergeant Prottman Hughes was wounded. I must check on him and give him the dickens for getting hurt. I can't believe that boy made sergeant. Becky will be so proud.

June 17

Oh, dear. Prott is dead. I found some of the boys from the 36th that were at the Piedmont Battle and they said he was leading his men to safety when he was blown in half by a shell. Why, Prott, after all you have been through. My soul aches for him. I tried to pray today, but nothing came out. I must write Becky if I can muster the strength.

June 20

Last two nights I spent writing Becky about her brother. Boys from 36th filled me in on what happened to him. If I could somehow take the pain of the news for her I would do it.

June 23

We are camped near Buchanan not far from the James River. We had a fight with Hunter in Lynchburg a few days ago. He headed for Lewisburg. My friend Al Lypes was killed. He was just a boy. I can't take much more of this. I want to take off. I don't want to write. Everybody is getting killed or shot up.

June 30

New Market. They claim there are about 15,000 of us now. We passed General Stonewall Jackson's grave 4 or 5 days ago back in Lexington and paid him tribute. Patton said Stonewall was a Christian. Prayed every day with his men. I was taken back when they said he had a little table that he used for studying his Bible. He carried it with him. Wouldn't do him any good in the grave. Many of the boys are barefooted. They will kill Yankees for their shoes and food.

July 4

Camped at a place called Bunker Hill. Found a mess of turnips at a farm. Had a fight with a few Yankees. A bullet broke the stock on my Enfield.

We are to cross the Potomac River tomorrow near Shepherdstown. They said we were headed to Washington to whip Mr. Lincoln. Maybe that will end this war.

July 9

General Early had a fight with the Yanks under General Wallace today. We guarded the train at Monocacy Junction. The sun was scorching today. Many of the boys are tuckered-out but they got shoes day before yesterday and feel good about that. Patton said if we had not had to stop here and fight that we coulda eaten dinner with Mr. Lincoln in a couple of days. Could it be that they have saved their capitol by this fight? Got another Enfield today.

When Gauley Ran Blood

July 11

Outside Washington. We can almost see the capitol building. Five weeks ago we were in Richmond. We are waiting for orders to attack. The boys are anxious to end this. I hate this waiting. I would rather fight than have to wait. I got the trots from some bad beef. Other boys got it too. Makes it that much harder. You never know when you have to go, and if you go, you know they may come, and then you may have to go, and then you can't go.

July 14

Tonight we are camped at Leesburg. Crossed the Potomac at Whites Ferry. The boys are mighty disappointed that we pulled out of Washington without much of a fight. We all wanted it to end. Runs are better today.

July 17

Had a skirmish with General Thoburn's Union boys yesterday at Purcellville. Bullet hit my bayonet and bent it. Patton said we were headed for Snickers Gap in the Blue Ridge Mountains. Saw a pretty girl today selling beans along the way. She reminded me of Becky.

July 18

Crossed the Shenandoah River today. Had a fight at Castlemans Ferry. Reminded me of Hughes Ferry and Becky. No rations today. I tried to snare some suckers in the river, but didn't have any luck.

July 21

Camped at Fishers Hill near Strasburg. Patton had us dig earthworks. We got dough and beef tonight. Cooked the dough wrapped around sticks in the fire. Noticed the beef was moving on another stick in the fire. It was maggots working out of it. I cooked it good and done and ate it anyway.

July 22

Went to Strasburg. Sick.

July 31

Rejoined the 22nd in camp north of Winchester. Spent the last week in hospital in Winchester. I was awful sick with runs. Bad meat most likely. Lady in hospital asked me if I knew Jesus. Told her I heard of him. Boys had a fight with General Crook at Kernstown. Several good boys got killed.

August 10

Camped near Winchester. We just marched our butts off. I am too tired for words. We crossed the Potomac at Shephardstown and then went up to Willamsport and crossed back over it again. We are running in circles. Poor old boy was shot for desertion this evening. The way we're marching I don't blame him. I would like to leave. If it weren't for Colonel Patton I probably would.

August 14

Camped at Fishers Hill. Patton had a little church service this morning. Poorly attended. He asked if we were ready to meet God? He said if we weren't we were headed for Hell. One of the boys spoke up and said the 22nd would run the Devil out of Hell. Patton did not care for the man's remark and rebuked him. I think the man was wrong. His brother, Jubal Early, wouldn't let us run him out. We would torment him just running him around in circles like we are doing now.

August 31

Past two weeks we have been up and down the Valley twice. We are chasing General Sheridan. They call him Little Phil. We had a good fight with him at Charles Town about a week ago. All we do is shoot and then run. Shoot and then run. Boys are downhearted. Got nice shoes this morning. Bacon in camp.

September 8

Picket duty near Brucetown. Fought at Berryville last week. We crossed Opequon Creek and then came here.

September 18

Camped near Winchester. Expecting attack any time. I hate this waiting. Can't even think of Becky. She has forgotten me. Not one letter.

September 20

Camped at Fishers Hill. Horrible battle in Winchester yesterday. The smell of death was everywhere. We fought hard, but there were so many Yankees. They were like ants, everywhere. Heard there was 55,000 men ready for battle. They tried to sweep in on us from the north and east. All we could do was go back up the Valley to here. Patton was wounded in the leg and captured by Federals. What will we do without him? Had no water yesterday.

As we made our way up the pike there were dead horses along the way in such a state of putrefaction that the odor would take your breath. We attempted to pull some of them from the way with horses and they pulled in two. We had to give it up and make paths around them.

September 23

Driven from Fishers Hill yesterday by Sheridan. They call us "Patton's Brigade" now. They broke through a gap in the line and we couldn't hold them. That devil General Crook swept around us. Had to run or die. Had to leave my canteen and bedroll. Low on bullets. Feasted on wild grapes today. That is all we had to eat. Our regiment is down to about 150 men. We had almost 700 at the first of the year. Expect another fight today. Tried to write Becky. No use, she wouldn't get it anyway.

September 24

Pushed back from Mt. Jackson yesterday. Tin cup may have saved my life. Yankee bullet stopped by handle. Cal Lucas got shot in the leg. He's not doing any good. I tried to comfort him last night. He may lose his leg. He ate some crackers today. He needs ...

September 25

Couldn't hold the centerline at Rude's Hill yesterday. We passed through New Market and are taking a rest break here at Port Republic. Prott was killed at Piedmont a few miles south of here. I would like to visit his grave. When we are not marching we are running. Our regiment is in battered shape. Men are thin and look like ghosts. Today I got a jacket with only one hole in it and hardly any blood. The boy won't need it anymore.

When Gauley Ran Blood

September 27

Today we wrestled with a small group of Yankees at a place called Weyer's Cave. Camping again at Port Republic.

September 29

In camp near Waynesboro. Spent a few moments with Prott yesterday. I wanted to get him moved home, but there is no one around interested and I don't have the money to have it done anyway. Maybe Becky has gotten my letter by now and Madison can send for him or come and get him. His grave is well marked and I put a border of rocks around it in case his marker gets torn down.

October 6

We have moved to Harrisonburg. We were told three days ago that Colonel Patton has died. All is now lost. There is but a few over a 100 left of us today. We started in January with nearly 700 of us. Our brigade had gone from 2000 men to less than 300. I am at the point that I no longer care if I live or die. If I depart this world I desire to go quickly.

October 9

Some of the cavalry came in tonight and said they had confronted two divisions of Union cavalry at Toms Brook and were chased up the valley through Woodstock by a long blond haired cavalryman. Said his name was General George Custer. A wild man they say.

October 13

Today we drove back the Yanks from Cedar Creek. We are camped on a hill near Strasburg called Fishers Hill. We fought Sheridan here about a month ago. I bathed this evening in a little creek that runs south of this place. It is peaceful here when the guns are silent. The leaves are turning. Their beauty appears immune from the ravages of this evil affair, like my Becky. I live for her.

October 19

Tonight we rest at New Market. Early this morning we attacked Sheridan at Cedar Creek. Hell came to the surface as we attacked in the morning light. The Yanks ran like scared pups and we helped ourselves to their vittles. Some of us had not eaten for days. We gorged till we could eat no more and then the Yanks came back and drove us out of the camp. Word had it that old General Sheridan had made a mad rush back from Winchester and had put a burr under the saddle of his men.

Many of our men gathered up the Yanks blue clothing, in anticipation of the coming winter, and when they were dressed, it was hard to tell which was Union and which was Confederate, except the Confederates were running South. Poor Captain Dickenson was shot and lost a lot of blood. I doctored him as best I could and had to leave him in a barn at a place called Belle Grove Plantation. I don't know what happened to him after that.

October 22

Today I passed by where we fought some days ago and some of the bodies were still there. Funny how the Yanks swell up all blue and twice their size and the Rebs stay white as can be and hardly swell at all. Doc said it was the food we eat or rather the food we don't eat that keeps us small. Early this evening I was invited to a meeting in camp tomorrow by a Negro teamster, named Joel, I helped with a horse. He has no last name. He said his master wouldn't have it. I asked him how it was being a slave and he said it was like this war, but there was 'no lull 'tween the battles, jes one big struggle.' He said he put his trust in 'the Lawd and took each day as it come.'

October 23

Went to church service in camp. Preacher said we could not earn our way to Heaven. He said in the book of Ufeshions it says that ' By grace you are saved through faith and not by doing good. It is a gift of God and not of works cause then you could brag.' I have tried to be good and I just can't. If this fella is right, all I have to do is place my faith in Jesus and what he did for me and it is a done deal. All this time I thought I was walking toward God, but I have been walking away from Him. He is the one who has been coming to me. Like old Joel said,' there has been no lull between the battles, just one big struggle.' I am tired of the struggle. I am tired of being a slave to sin. I will let Jesus do it now. I have decided to follow Jesus, wherever he takes me. I am at peace, but yet there are tears in my eyes. There is a lot I don't understand about this Jesus.

October 30

Camped at New Market tonight. There was no fighting today. Today I got a testament from Captain Johns. I am going to read it all. I read some to Joel this evening. He said it was ' a balm to his soul.' I like the way he puts things.

October 31

In camp at New Market all day. Cold wind blew this morning. I get put out at the coarse talk by the troops. They talk like hooligans.

November 13

No services today. Cold and rainy. On the move early to get away from General Sheridan. We are headed back up the valley. We had a short prayer service and prayed for a quick end to the war.

November 20

Camped at New Market. Light snow last night. There is not a piece of meat in camp. Horses are next. Caught two Jesse Scouts and hung them yesterday. General Early said that would make them think twice about masquerading as Confederate soldiers.

PAGES MISSING

December 18

Camped near Harrisonburg. It was cold and rainy last night. Hear we are headed for Waynesboro for winter camp. We ate a scrawny sheep last night.

December 25

Today we had a fine service in camp. We sang hymns and carols for two hours to celebrate Jesus' birthday.

December 29

Camp near Waynesboro. Cold and snowy. Had 30 inches snow last night and this morning. There was a man killed in his sleep last night by soldiers felling a tree for firewood. Heard that General Stoneman passed through Marion , Wytheville and Saltville. He destroyed the salt-works and wells at Saltville. The cause cannot live without salt.

PAGES MISSING

January 30, 1865

Camp at Red Sulphur Springs. Slipped over the hill late yesterday and saw mom. She is alright but she has not heard from my brother Lewis for over a year. She fears he has joined the Confederacy and has been killed. She heard my Bluecoat cousins James and William Francisco were travelling with General Stoneman when he attacked Saltville. Neither of them got hurt in the battle. Mother and I prayed together for the first time since I was a child. Sisters Sarah and Mary Virginia were in high spirits as usual. They sure are growing up. They have become young women since I left.

February 28

Camp at Red Sulphur Springs. Hear we are headed for Richmond to help Lee again. Some of the men have given up and gone home. I can't say I blame them.

March 8

Camped at Union. Light snow last night. Sick with runs and coughing. I fear pneumonia. If I should die in my sleep I leave all my worldly possessions to my little brother Sidney.

March 12

Feeling much better today. Ate solid food and sat in the sun for a spell. The sun felt good on my face. Word spread that General Stoneman was headed for Saltville again. I hope I won't have to face James and William in battle. It would kill mother to know her son had to fight his name sakes boys.

When Gauley Ran Blood

March 15

We are headed for Richmond again. This time we go on foot. The men are tough, but most are in rags and worn out. Several finished the winter with no shoes. An army can't march without shoes.

March 30

Camped near Abingdon. My greatest fear is coming true. We are headed to Saltville to drive away Stoneman. May God protect James and William.

April 1

What a great day for fools. We made it to Saltville, but Stoneman had already flown the coop.

April 6

Camp near Wytheville. Had a scrape with General Stoneman. I didn't see James or William.

April 9

Meeting in camp. We prayed hard for an end to the war. Everyone admits to having enough. We pray that God will be merciful and end the killing. Saw a single daffodil blooming this Palm Sunday. I take this as a good sign.

April 10

Praise God Almighty! Lee has surrendered at Appomattox Court House to General Grant. It is finished.

April 15

I am headed home to Johns Creek. I can't believe the war is really over. I wonder if brother Lewis made it back home. What am I going to do now? I wonder if Becky is still there? She never did write. She probably found herself a younger fellow. Maybe I can work at grandpaw's mill. Uncle Lew can't run the place by himself. Lord, I need your help. Help me to know what to do.

NO FURTHER ENTRIES

When Gauley Ran Blood

Chapter 14
Glory

Life at the ferry was becoming normal - if there was such a thing as normal in that time. The real estate around Summersville and the ferry was controlled by the Federal troops during most of 1863 and 1864 with a few exceptions. For most of this time, pickets, who were stationed out of Summersville, heavily guarded the ferry. Bushwhackers were an ever-present threat, but as fortune would have it, their vengeance was not meted out again at the Hugheses. The family was soon, however, to discover its greatest sacrifice.

Becky continued her trading with the Union troops in Summersville and managed to secure salt, sugar, coffee, and newspapers on a sporadic basis. Many of the farms in areas surrounding Summersville lay fallow because of the war. Farmers were tired of working their fields and livestock, only to have marauding bands of foraging soldiers steal their produce. Many of the refugees friendly to the Union relocated to Ohio. Those friendly to the southern cause relocated to Greenbrier County to the east or to Monroe County to the south.

Contact with the refugees was limited primarily to personal visits, but mail did find its target occasionally. Sending mail during the war was always "ify." Couriers found the ferry to be a godsend when it wasn't out of service. It saved them a cold dip in the winter and from certain drowning death in the summer if the Gauley was in the brush.

A story circulated in many of the Union camps that a special military courier, who had come from a western state and was new to western Virginia, made a trip south from Clarksburg carrying a large Federal payroll intended for Union troops serving in southwest Virginia. He traveled alone so as not to attract attention from bushwhackers or other civilians. He had made a short stop in Summersville and left the soldier's pay for those stationed there before starting again toward Meadow Bluff. The poor fellow was never seen again. Pickets found his horse a few days later wandering around near the Hughes Ferry landing. He was gone and the saddlebags were missing, but his rifle was still in the saddle holster. Most of the soldiers believed he had hidden the money in one of the many cracks or caves in the cliffs along the Gauley River and then had a spill from his horse or been waylaid by bushwhackers. Some questioned the robbery theory because his rifle apparently had never been drawn. Who would ever know? Such were the many perils of carrying the mail.

The Hugheses did receive letters from their son Edward in Ohio and from Jeremiah in Iowa. Edward's dental practice was flourishing and he had helped his brothers, Mathew and Virgil, find work on a friend's farm. Mathew was pleased to continue his blacksmith trade when the farmer's blacksmith joined the Union Army. They periodically received news about Summersville from Ohio soldiers that were returning home following their turn of service or that were home on furlough. They longed to return to the mountains they loved, but they felt it best for their families that they stay in less dangerous territories.

Jeremiah found himself in Iowa. He had found a pretty young woman named Amy Newton and made her his wife. He continued to pursue his calling into the ministry and was actively involved in starting new churches. He wrote his mother that he was a circuit walker not a circuit rider because of his form of travel. Mirriam proudly smiled and then giggled as she thought of her preacher boy.

Madison strutted like a peacock when Jeremiah revealed that he was granddaddy to two new Hugheses, Eva and Willie. Both had been born during the war. Jerry, as they called him, wanted to visit his parents, but he didn't dare return to enter the no man's land of the new state of West Virginia. His parents longed to see their son and his new family. They understood his circumstances and held fast to their position of riding out the war at the ferry. Maybe they could visit Iowa after the war.

When Gauley Ran Blood

Then there was Prott. Issac Prottman Hughes was the baby of the family. He was the "attention getter" of the family. He wrote only one letter during the war and that was to his sister. From his youth, he was always getting into hot water. Poor Prott was made the focus of every practical joke his older brothers could conceive. Many times Becky had to take his part in the heated debates that often followed when his brothers' ruse was discovered. Bloody noses were common place; unfortunately, they were usually Prott's. When Becky jumped into the fray, her older brothers always backed down. They certainly could have man handled the wiry young girl, but Madison forbid touching a hair on her head. Becky knew it and used it at every opportunity to gain an advantage over her ever-conspiring older brothers.

She and Prott became allies at an early age against a common foe, their brothers. Sibling rivalries, as harmless as they were, stirred the competitive spirit in these two. As a united team, they were invincible, but as opponents, they were like spit on a hot griddle. As babies they fought tooth and nail. As they matured and their bodies changed, they realized their wrestling days were over, but the mental gymnastics they utilized against one another would have confounded Socrates. They exercised this cunning against one another and they used this keen wit to deliver a cup of poison hemlock to their older brothers on many occasions.

One such occasion found Virgil, as a teenager, working at a neighboring farm after his chores were done at home. He slowly began accumulating a small stash of money. Becky and Prott in harmony plotted how they might share in his riches. With their plan conceived, they set out to fleece their hard working but gullible brother.

For weeks Becky and Prott talked of their good fortune of having eaten "fruit" at the Odells at Hominy Falls. This so-called "fruit" was in their opinion the true nectar of the gods. At every opportunity they rolled their eyes and licked their lips as they discussed how delectable this "fruit" was that they had partaken. Poor Virgil, whose spirit was sweet but also vulnerable, took the bait and asked how he might also experience this utopian delight. They explained that it could be arranged for him to have a portion of this "fruit" for a mere dollar. He balked at the price but in a few

251

days returned with renewed interest in this ambrosia. He passed them his hard-earned dollar. They made arrangements for him to have dinner with their relatives, the Odells. Following the disappointing event, Madison had to separate Virgil and Prott and Becky to avoid a major altercation. When he determined to find the root of the problem, Madison queried just exactly what this "fruit" was?

Virgil abruptly responded, "it wasn't nothin' but blamed old apple sauce."

Becky and Prott laughed with reserve for fear of their father, but when he, too, could no longer hold his composure and was forced to wipe a broad smile off his face, they all cackled together. Even Virgil joined in the choir realizing he had truly been snookered.

When the laughter halted, the younger Hugheses vowed they had not lied in any fashion, but Madison saw through their ruse and made them return their brother's hard-earned cash. Virgil agreed there was no harm done. Such was the shared cunning of this brother and sister team. Afterwards, the two sat on a rock in the middle of the Gauley River and laughed at their nearly perfect but mischievous plan.

It was times like this that made reading the letter extremely difficult for Becky. It was as if her spirit had left her. The fire in her heart dimmed the day she received the letter from Chris. Sorrow filled her soul as it did for so many during the war. It was truly a gray day.

June 18, 1864
Waynesboro, Virginia

My dearest Rebecca,

I write you this night, not as a suitor, but as a friend in mourning. I regret that I must be the one to tell you that Prott is dead. An exploding shell struck him as he attempted to lead his men to safety during a battle. Becky, Prott had been promoted to sergeant and I don't think you all knew of it. I have enclosed his picture in his stripes with this letter. I knew you would want to have it. Some of the boys he had been with a few days earlier in Lynchburg said he had the picture taken there.

My unit came from Richmond to Lynchburg and joined with Prott's unit there under the command of General Jubal Early. It was then that I learned of his death.

His men said he only lived a short time after the shell exploded, but that he had requested that they get a message to a Verna Campbell and to you. He said to thank her for the nice letter and that he had intended to write her, but hadn't. He asked that they tell Verna that she need not wait on him. He would remember her affectionately and would be obliged if she would do the same for him. He also wanted them to tell "Carrot Top" not to take any wooden nickels. I guess that would be you. You know that Prott; he was always joking about something. He also said to tell his maw he loved her.

Tell Madison that Prott, with the 36th Virginia and five other regiments and some home guards, had come from the battle of Cloyd's Mountain to meet Union General Hunter at Piedmont, east of Staunton, in the Shenandoah Valley. It was the morning of June 5 that Prott's company was on the left flank of General W. E. Jones line on a bluff overlooking the Middle River. The Confederate line ran from the bluff to a road at the top of a ridge that the general thought he would be able to defend. They said there were 6,000 Rebs with about 14 cannons, but there were at least twice as many Bluecoats with twice as many heavy guns.

Prott's men had built a rail pen breastwork out of fence rails that lined the road at the top of the hill. It provided protection from the Yankee bullets but was useless against the cannon shells that began exploding directly in front of their position. Prott began withdrawing his men from the certain slaughter toward the bluff overlooking the river and out of cannon range. One group on the left had not heard the command to pull back and he had gone back to summon them. Just as he returned to the rail pen, a shell exploded, and he fell wounded amidst a heap of splintered rails. His men bravely carried him to safety, but he died a short time later. They buried him in a shallow grave with the intent of seeing that his remains are returned home as soon as practical. He died a hero's death leading his men.

When Gauley Ran Blood

He was respected among his men and the other officers. His captain said he had heard his Christian testimony on numerous occasions at camp meetings. They said it would comfort you to know that he is now in the presence of the God he served.

The Yankees started back momentarily but returned shouting, "New Market, New Market " remembering their rout a few weeks earlier at that location and seeking vengeance. General Jones was forced to withdraw several hundred yards to another road intersection before our boys could take up the fight again. It was not long after that he too was struck in the head by a Yankee bullet and fell from his horse to rise no more. With the brave and fearless leader gone, our boys had to flee the field or be massacred. Many of the men did not understand why the cavalry was on hand, but was never called into the action. Surely they would have made a great difference. Whatever the cause, the day was a loss for the south. The blood of many brave Confederate boys and their beloved general had stained that hilltop that day. May God have mercy on their souls.

General Jones was the one at the ferry the last time I saw you there. You know when we crossed all the troops, horses, and cattle on the ferry. He was the one we nicknamed "Grumble".

Becky, you know I share your sorrow and regret that I cannot be there to comfort you and your family. I hope this letter makes it to you and I think it will. One of the boys from Summersville that is injured and unable to fight for awhile is coming your way and I trust that he will deliver it.

If I get the chance, I will visit Prott and see that his grave is well marked so that appropriate arrangements can be made. I would send him home, but I have not been paid for months and currently have only the clothing on my back.

I have written you several times, but I have not had one letter from you. I understand if you do not want to wait for me until the end of the war. I do understand. This war seems to be going on forever and you are too nice of a girl to be lonely so long.

Please give your parents my deepest regrets and sympathy about your brother. I will never be able to repay the kindness shown me by your family. I trust that you will pray for the victory of Virginia and I shall forever remain

When Gauley Ran Blood

Your affectionate servant,

C.C. Hughes
Pvt. 22nd Virginia Infantry

The letter was delivered by one of the Dotson boys who had come home to Summersville to allow his wounds to heal. He had many other letters in his possession for other families in the area. Most of which carried similar bad news.

The family read the letter and wept together. They tried to comfort one another.

"God's will be done. God's will be done, " said Madison with his tear soaked eyes.

Mirriam was never quite the same. She carried the photo on her person the remainder of her life. For some time she questioned how God could take her baby boy especially after all the soldier boys she had doctored.

Becky wept uncontrollably for days. She made a trip to the Long Point and spent most of her time talking with God. She reasoned that God knew what was best for her brother, but she knew she would miss him. She knew that part of her had passed with him into the grave.

She lifted her head to the heavens and felt the warm evening sun on her face. She spoke her last words to her brother.

"Prott, my dearest brother. I find that the tears cannot wash you from my mind. Your sight and smell and touch will be with me forever. Oh, if I could but see you one more time. I would take back all the mean words I said to you when you picked on me in our youth. Oh, but what fun we had. I remember you took the blame for me when I set the broom sage field on fire after we found the clay pipe and tried to smoke the corn silk in it. When daddy took you to the barn for your punishment that was rightfully due me, I told myself, from that day forward I would die for you if you asked me to. Mother and daddy hurt so much. They don't speak aloud of you. If we speak your name, mom has to leave the room. She misses you as I do. I try to comfort her, but the pain is so deep. She sits for hours looking at your picture in your uniform.

When Gauley Ran Blood

What should be pride is remorse. Before you left us she worked a day a week in the hospital. Now she works most every day. It was difficult when Mordecai Halstead was killed in 1863. Poor Virginia liked to die, and mother with her. But that was nothing compared to your passing. Oh, don't get me wrong; daddy suffers too. He is skilled at hiding it. Remember daddy telling about when your namesake, his brother Issac Hughes, was seen leaving on that steamboat at Charleston never to be heard from again. Everyone expected to see him come home someday and he never did. Now you have gone away and aren't coming home. Daddy thinks it's strange. Shoot! We all think it's strange. He doesn't smile like he used to. He tries to cheer up mother and me, but he is often left with no words to say. He chops a lot of wood. We have three cords in, and it isn't even winter. I don't wear your clothes anymore. When they looked at me I knew they hoped it was you coming home after a bad mistake. Hoping that you really weren't gone - just a mistaken identity. Verna Campbell is doing better. She was sick to death when she got word about you. I wish you all could have been together. Your youngins would have been beautiful. Their Aunt Becky would have spoiled them rotten. I will miss you, Prott, but I know I will see you again as you wait for me beside the Crystal Sea. I'll look forward to it. I love you so."

"...And God, please don't send me a letter like that with Chris' name in it. Please!"

Chapter 15
The Last Strand

The fiddler played a lively tune and Chris danced with his sisters, Mary Virginia and Sarah Jane. His mother, Mary, happily looked on but did not believe in dancing. She had been taught in her youth that it was of the devil, but she was the first to admit that sometimes it seemed right for the young ones.

The service had been solemn as they paid tribute to the war dead, but the event that followed was a celebration of survival and the end of the conflict. Many of the Rebel boys slowly had made their way back to their homes on Craig, Sinking, and even Johns Creeks. Some had been shot up and were still healing. Some were ill with diseases they had contracted in northern prison camps. Some would live, and others, well, they were all happy to be home again.

Union scouts continued to look for Rebels in out of the way places in Arkansas, Virginia, Texas, and West Virginia. Unruly homeguards and vagabond military units, unwilling to accept the Confederate defeat, were still troubling many locations. This was not the scene at this homecoming celebration given by Chris' uncle, Lewis Francisco. Lew, they called him.

It was a grand turnout for a county affair. Lew had done things up right. People came for miles to the "Soldier's Shindig" as he called it. The sun was out and it had been a beautiful day. The rhododendron along Craig Creek had contributed its magnificent blooming flowers to the setting in the picturesque bottom beside the mill. Some of its pink blossoms adorned the tables constructed of sawhorses and sawn lumber. The tender green spring plants carpeted the pasture and dandelions dotted the field.

The women had made the most with what little they had. Wild game was the favorite of the day. Venison, boar, turkey and

257

groundhog were prepared in a sundry of ways. Dried apple and canned berry pies were consumed as though recently invented. Bread and pones were scarce, but there was enough to go around.

The ladies and gentleman of the community feasted and danced as they never had before. The crowd was sparse of men, as one would expect following a war. The young ladies were out in force to show off their new dresses with fancy sleeves and collars and to attract the men. Some of the young women wore hoop petticoats that filled out their dresses. The older ladies pointed and discussed them with whispers. There were flowered bonnets that demanded attention. These were the order of the day.

The people congregated in little family groups standing together and sitting on blankets spread on the ground. As the day wore on the family groups dissolved and the whole field became one gigantic mass of people visiting. No one had seen anything like it since before the war.

Chris finished a dance with Sarah Jane. He walked, followed by his sisters, to the punch crock for a glass of sassafras tea. His uncle Lew intercepted him.

"Where's your brother, Lewis? How come he didn't make it today?" asked his uncle and Lewis' namesake.

"He has gone into West Virginia looking for work. He heard they were doing a lot of timbering there and felt he might get on as a logger. You know he helped Russell Stover saw before the war. He is a good hand at that."

"He had asked me about helping with the mill and I told him I wouldn't need any help until the late summer or early fall. I didn't know he was going to leave this part of the country," stated Lew.

"Lewis has always been unsettled; you know that Uncle Lew. He likes to keep moving," said Chris.

"Oh, I see," acknowledged Lew.

"Chris, boy, looks to me like you have your pick of gals today. Which one is for you?" asked Lew.

"Aw, Uncle Lew, you know me. I'm no lady's man. I dance a little now and then, but those girls don't want anything to do with an old fellow like me. I'm past thirty," replied Chris.

When Gauley Ran Blood

"Chris, I know for a fact that Mary Jane Huffman has had an eye on you ever since you come back home, " interjected Sarah.

"Julia Champ said she would just die if you were to ask her to dance," added Mary Virginia.

"I'm not interested in Julia or Mary Jane. They are nice girls, but they aren't for me. I'm just not interested, " stated Chris.

"You're not still sweet on that hillbilly girl, are you, Christopher?" asked Mary Virginia.

"Why don't all of you just mind your own business. Let me alone," snapped Chris as he walked away in a huff. Mary Virginia had hit a nerve.

His family had not intended to injure his pride, but it appeared that was the case. They only wanted to see him settle down and start a family like some of the other returning soldiers.

Chris left the event and began the long walk over Huckleberry Ridge back to his home. The girls and his mother could bring the wagon. He needed some time alone. He needed time to think. His thoughts rambled from events of the war to his childhood. He remembered walking this same steep trail over the mountains when he was a boy returning from his grandfather's mill. It was the same one Uncle Lew was operating now. He would work all day bagging meal and in the late evening his grandpa would give him a small sack of corn meal and start him home over the mountain. His mother would make him corncakes with jam for breakfast the next morning. He loved those corncakes. He remembered making hoecakes in a spider during the war. He would never forget the breakfast Mirriam Hughes had made for him the day he left her care there at the ferry. What a great lady she was. What a great family they were; Madison, Mirriam, Prott, and Becky. Poor Prott was gone. Becky Hughes came to mind, what about Becky Hughes? Why had he not heard from her? She was constantly on his mind. She had not been out of his thoughts for over three years. His heart was tender. As he walked, he wiped a tear from the corner of his eye. He knew she was one issue that he needed to resolve for his peace of mind if for no other reason.

Months passed and Chris grew restless. He enjoyed being home with his family, but the war had changed him. He seldom slept more than a few hours at a time. He was irritable and easily angered. He was unusually jumpy when unknowingly approached by someone from the side or rear. His sisters and mother had developed a routine of daily life during the war that he was not a part. He felt out of place. They meant no injury to him, but his four years of Confederate Army service had removed him from the house and the patterns of living that had been established there. No men had lived in the house for a significant period of time since his father had passed away some years earlier.

Chris had become acclimated to the life of a soldier. He was up early demanding breakfast and continued issuing orders throughout the day. His infrequent bathing was particularly troubling to his sisters. They did their best to cope, but on occasion, he would be reminded of his personal hygiene by awakening to a wash tub at the side of his bed. He loved his family, but he just didn't fit there anymore.

He helped his Uncle Lew at the mill on Craig Creek for a few weeks in the fall. He enjoyed the hard work, but it soon became apparent that his uncle had created a job for him. Farms were slow to get back into production that first year after the war and there just wasn't that much grain to grind. Again, Chris felt out of place.

He often daydreamed about the Hugheses and their farm along the Gauley River. He pictured Becky as he had last seen her standing beside the ferry. He wondered if she was still there and if she thought of him.

Through the remainder of the fall and during the winter, Chris helped a local farmer on a part time basis and did miscellaneous carpentry work. With the advent of spring, Chris' uneasiness grew unbearable. It was time for him to move on. It was a stroke of fortune when his mother finally received a letter from his brother Lewis. Mary read the letter as the family listened intently.

Lewis explained he had migrated north down the New River. Upon reaching Gauley Bridge, he learned of a man who was timbering nearby at a place called Panther Mountain. The locals said he was harvesting giant tulip poplars used for flooring in Charleston, Pittsburgh, and Cincinnati. He eventually located the man's operation and was successful at securing employment for room and board. The lumberman promised to pay him wages in the future if things took off like he planned. They camped in the woods for months at a time, and he had not had an opportunity to correspond with them. Because the operation was small, Lewis did everything from felling trees to building log rafts. The lumberman had told Lewis that he had ordered a portable steam mill. That meant he would soon need additional help.

This was just the ticket for Chris. He had a line on work and he was going to go for it. The postmark on the letter was Keslers Cross Lanes, West Virginia. That's not far from the Hugheses... and Becky, he thought. Next morning, Chris was packed and off for his appointment with destiny.

It was a long walk to Gauley Bridge. By the time he covered the ten miles from Johns Creek to Pearisburg he had already grown tired of walking. Chris had a plan. He knew that the New River flowed downstream all the way to Gauley Bridge. He reasoned that if he had a raft he could float the entire distance in only two or three days. He was unsuccessful at getting a raft, but he did manage an older dugout that was in fair condition considering its age. Chris was aware that there were many dangerous falls and rapids on the torturous New River. His plan was to portage around the falls and to float the big eddys. The huge dugout was much too heavy to carry, so Chris reasoned that he could just let the dugout go and catch it below the falls. His was a great plan... in theory.

After a good night's rest, Chris was off at daybreak in his dugout. He had an oak paddle and a ten-foot boat pole. It felt good to be on the move again. He felt really alive for the first time in a long while. Things were looking up. His plan worked great until he reached the first rapids. When he exited the craft to walk around the rapids, the dugout cleared the whitewater and could not be found for over a mile and a half downstream where it washed up on a sand bar. So much for that experience, Chris thought. At the next falls, he fashioned an anchor from a large rock and secured it to the boat with a length of sturdy grapevine. He set the boat adrift with the anchor trailing the boat floating on a much smaller log raft. He had constructed it by tying two driftwood logs together. He figured that when the two went over the falls, the anchor would fall from its float and get caught on the bottom after reaching the foot of the falls. He could then more readily retrieve his dugout. This option worked quite well except that he had to swim to the base of falls to free the anchor. The details of his float trip were beginning to make walking look more attractive as time went on. The final straw came when he, being greedy for gaining as much float time as possible, misjudged the current and was unable to escape it and plowed boat, clothing and all into the foaming chasm below one of the falls. As he thrashed about in the water trying to locate the dugout, he thought of his trip over the falls with Becky and Prott. What a wild day that was.

Having retrieved his possessions, he pushed the dugout into the current and set out on foot again. Chris laughed to himself that he would certainly not seek employment as a steamboat captain having nearly drowned three times in his one-day voyage. Exhausted from his nautical escapade, he made camp on a long sandbar near a large rock and slept.

Chris spent the next five days making his way to Gauley Bridge. His journey was as difficult as only Satan could conceive. He was in the river to avoid vast expanses of rhododendron and in rhododendron to avoid rapids. It became obvious to Chris, that wherever he was he needed to be somewhere else. If he were fortunate enough to arrive alive, he would not utilize this route again.

From Gauley Bridge, he was directed to Keslars Cross Lanes, which they said was in the direction of Summersville. He knew it was close to Summersville and Hughes Ferry. A long day's journey found Chris near his destination. The next morning he arrived at Vaughn's Store at the intersection of two roadways.

Chris read the new small sign below the store sign. It read, *U. S. Post Office, Keslers Cross Lanes, West Virginia.* He wiped the sweat from his forehead with his handkerchief and another sign caught his eye. *Summersville 7* and, below it, *Hughes Ferry 4* were scrawled on a board and tacked to a fence post. It was almost as if he were being called home when he read the Hughes Ferry sign. He put his hat back on and had taken only a few steps toward the ferry when someone called to him.

When Gauley Ran Blood

"Can I help you, mister?" asked a man with a soiled apron around his waist. He spoke through a small crack in the open door.

Chris whirled and quickly responded, "Panther Mountain, I'm looking for Panther Mountain."

The storeowner directed him back about three or four miles in the direction he had come. The grocer laughed when he told Chris, "You walked over that mountain yesterday."

It was apparent to the man that Chris was worn to a frazzle. He introduced himself as John Vaughn and asked the traveler to join him for lunch. Chris eagerly accepted. They walked to a two-story house beside the shop and the man asked his wife to prepare an early lunch.

While they ate, Mrs. Vaughn explained how General Rosecrans had been a houseguest there during the war. He had been there after the battle of Carnifex Ferry. She explained that, although she did not favor the Union, he had been quite a gentleman. She displayed a small cross the general had given her as a token of his appreciation for her hospitality. When the couple had fed their visitor, he thanked them and was again after his quest, but this time he started back toward Panther Mountain.

Following an afternoon's hunt on Panther Mountain, he finally located the lumberman's camp. He rested near the idle steam-operated sawmill. Just before dusk, a half dozen straggly men, each leading a team of horses with a line of logs behind it, filed into the camp and deposited their logs near the mill. The last man in was his brother, Lewis. Finally, he had found him.

The men in the camp welcomed their coworker's brother and fed him a hearty dinner. Chris' run of misfortune continued to wane when the lumberman asked if he could manage a team of horses. Chris had found a new home indeed.

Chris worked with his brother that summer skidding logs and hauling lumber to below Gauley Bridge. There the lumber was placed on flatboats for its trip down the Kanawha River. Chris liked his work. About once a month he would make a trip to Vaughn's and mail a letter to his mother telling his family about his trip down the New River. He always included some of his earnings "to buy a little something for the girls."

When Gauley Ran Blood

Lewis and Chris had occasions for long talks about the war, family, and life in general. Lewis encouraged Chris to find out about the hillbilly girl he had spoken of so frequently. Chris would always come back with an excuse about her being too young or him being too old or her not writing during the war. Lewis wondered if the war had changed his brother so much. He had never seen Chris so indecisive. Maybe a gentle prod would help.

A few days passed and Chris was using a horse with a scoop to build a dam for a millpond to make log handling easier. Lewis, at a distance, motioned with his hand for him to come. Chris secured his horse and walked in Lewis' direction. He could see that Lewis had a bandage around one of his hands.

"What happened to you?" asked Chris.

"I was trying to free a J-hook and the horse spooked. He jumped, and I couldn't get my fingers out in time. It's nothing, really, " said Lewis.

"Well, if you need any help with anything, just let me know," responded Chris.

" Brother, as a matter of fact, I was supposed to make a delivery of some floorboards to a Virgil Hughes south of Summersville. I can't handle the team like this. Could you help me out?" Asked Lewis.

He held his bandaged hand in front of him and moved it up and down as if to indicate its uselessness. Chris felt obliged to help out his younger brother. After getting his wagon loaded, Chris departed. Before he was out of sight of the camp, Lewis had his bandage off and was repeatedly working his hand into a fist and then flexing his fingers.

"Why, it's a miracle. Look at that. My hand is already better," stated Lewis with a sheepish smile on his face.

Chris headed for Cross Lanes and then over the hills to Gad and then to Hughes Ferry. As Chris made his way down the grade that led to the ferry, his hands began to sweat and his mouth became dry. His thoughts again returned to Becky. What would he say to her?

Chris halted his team and set the brake. He started to walk to the house when a handsome young man with dark hair in a leather apron called to him.

When Gauley Ran Blood

"Ain't nobody home," stated the man.

Chris responded, "I'm looking for the Virgil Hughes place. I have a load of flooring."

In the back of Chris' mind he pondered who was this man? Could he be Becky's husband? Chris got a queasy feeling in the pit of his stomach and feared he might throw up.

"The whole clan is up on the farm hepin' with the new house," said the man.

He gave Chris directions to reach the building site. He sent him toward the Joe Branch hollow. The Joe Branch hollow held a broad shallow valley with small rolling mounds and short spurs that shot out from the ridges on its sides. The tall poplar and hemlock forest provided a mystical charm to the place. Like a series of great "S's," the stream wandered up the valley and past fields and laurel covered rock outcrops that once hid cattle and sheep from foraging soldiers during the war.

A wagon trail ran along the north side of the river and made its way up the side of a ridge that topped out on the cliffs at the mouth of the Joe Branch hollow. The trail at this point neared a precipice that overlooked the river and the falls of the Joe Branch below. This was a beautiful view especially in the fall. The river gorge widened at this point and the high white cliffs continued up the Joe Branch hollow. Water from the stream drifted over the rock face and floated in a mist toward the rocks below. It appeared to magically rise as one watched the spray and mist as it fell upon the rocks below.

The cliffs at the falls were vertical but were undercut at the bottom. Not one rock face was within fifty feet of the base of the falls. When you stood near the base of the falls in the laurel, it appeared that it was merely raining hard with not a hint of a waterfall to be seen. This just happened to be one of Becky's favorite bathing spots and who, but Becky, would just happen to be cleaning up after a hard day of helping her brother Virgil build his new home. Her brother, Mathew, had volunteered to watch the ferry while he worked at his blacksmith shop.

Chris guided the team up the river and along the hillside to the edge of the precipice that overlooked the falls of the Joe Branch. The horses slowed as they neared the top of the grade, and

When Gauley Ran Blood

Chris carefully gazed at the edge of the cliff. His eyes followed the edge of the cliff ahead of him and to the right where he saw the waterfall. Through the hemlock and poplar forest he followed the falling water to the woman below. WOMAN! Could it be? Oh, my, it was! It was Becky! Yes, it was Becky!

Poor Chris had been here before, in a matter of speaking, and he quickly thought of what could go wrong? Would the horses bolt off the top of the cliffs, or would they just run and cause him to be thrown from the wagon to a grizzly death below. His ribs still ached from his last encounter with this unfeathered hillbilly. What was this man to do? How would he deal with this situation? Was disaster inevitable?

He had to go with what he knew. He knew he had to talk to Becky again. With reckless abandon, he came too near the edge while securing the team and the wagon wheel nudged a handful of loose stones over the precipice. The stones fell with a muffled clatter on a sloping rock beside Becky. Some of them bounced and danced around her ankles getting her attention. She stepped from the misty falls and froze in place. She held her head at an angle as she intently listened, expecting an intruder. Becky wiped the water from her eyes and face and quickly put on her dress. It was the queerest feeling. She remembered another time she was bathing. It was during the war, at the Big Chute, when she heard a crashing sound. She was possessed by that same fear. Something, or someone, was out there. She crept along the base of the cliffs cautiously peering ahead for danger. She silently prayed for courage.

Chris set the brake and ran back down the road toward the base of the cliffs. He realized it would take him forever if he followed the road back down the gentle slope to where it converged with the base of the cliffs. He had an idea. Chris started climbing down the cliffs. It was only eighty feet or so to the bottom by this route. It would be at least a quarter of a mile if he went by the road and would take an eternity. He made his way over the edge of the cliffs and proceeded to climb down to the bottom. The hand holds and ledges soon disappeared and he was just out there. Not one crack or crevice was below him. No place to put his foot and no place for a hand hold. Again, as when he first saw her, he was in the lurch. He thought he must be crazy.

As he explored the white sandstone rock face below him with his eyes, he saw Becky making her way along the base of the cliffs some fifty feet beneath him. With no regard for danger and the greatest desire to be with this mountain girl, he sprang from the face of the canyon wall flailing his arms wildly. He finally made contact and wrapped his arms around a tall slender poplar tree and completed his descent landing upright directly in front of the young woman.

Becky was startled and flinched. As if heaven had answered her prayer, here before her was the man she had pined for, prayed for and saved herself for. Their eyes met and nothing else in the entire world mattered at that moment. Words were not necessary. She ran to his now open arms and they were finally together.

⋯⋯⋯⋯

Madison and Captain Halstead pulled hard on the towline that drew the ferry to the middle of the Gauley. The flatboat was full. The sober crew spoke not a word. The rest of their lives hinged upon the outcome of this day's event. Captain Riley Ramsey waited with his son Nick's widow, Amanda, to hear the outcome of the day's events. He ran his finger around the "noose," trying to loosen the grip of the collar of his white shirt. The mix of blood that would occur in Gauley today would forever seal the fate of future generations.

They each held on to the ferry rope to steady them in the cool wind that blew across the Gauley. The date was November 29, 1866. All eyes were focused on the couple. Chris was in his Confederate uniform and Becky wore her green dress and bonnet. Madison and Mirriam were joined by two of Becky's brothers, Virgil and Mathew. Even those who stayed ashore focused intently upon the picturesque couple. Virginia Halstead held a handkerchief to her face as another one of her sons escorted her to a better view from the landing. Ginny Dotson followed.

When Gauley Ran Blood

The ferry had brought them together and they thought it was an appropriate place for them to tie their marriage knot. Mirriam had protested but knew the chance of Becky relenting was unlikely, and she was right. Madison liked it. He reveled in showing off his new flatboat with the initials RJH painted across the bow in bold red letters.

Reverend Dountain concluded his message, "May their union be unbreakable. May it be as strong as this ferry rope that binds the north with the south. May it never be broken in this life. Let only the departure of this life unto the next separate this pair. What God hath joined together, let no man put asunder. I now pronounce you man and wife. You may kiss the bride."

It was another day when Gauley ran blood, but it was a good day. Becky let go of the rope and placed her arms around her husband's neck. Chris held her tightly at the waist. Becky picked a small birch sliver from Chris' mouth and flipped it into the water. They both smiled. Their bond was secured as they closed their eyes and their lips met. They embraced until the ferry was jerked back toward the landing. Becky's head whipped backward.

<hr />

"Hold on to the rope. Hold on tightly, " said Anna as she pushed Becky in the swing.

The aged lady stiffly sat in the swing with her hands clasped around the rope. Her granddaughter stood behind her and pushed as she swung in her circular path.

Becky smiled a pleasant and contented smile as she opened her eyes and said, "Don't you fret, honey, I will hold onto it forever."

❖ The End ❖

Epilog

Gauley River

In 1966 the United States Army Corps of Engineers completed the second largest rock-fill type dam east of the Mississippi River. It was constructed on Gauley River a short distance below the mouth of McKees Creek. The Corps' custom of naming dams after nearby post offices was abandoned when they chose to name it Summersville Dam, after the town of Summersville, rather than after the community of Gad which the lake displaced, for quite obvious reasons.

The Gauley River National Recreation Area below the dam is truly a whitewater heaven. It has been rated 2nd most difficult whitewater rafting river in North America and 7th in the world. As the troops during the war fought its raging torrents, thousands of thrill seeking water sport enthusiasts now battle its waves and spiraling vortexes. It still demands a toll from all that pass its shores.

Southern Sympathizers in West Virginia

In 1866 West Virginia voters ratified a constitutional amendment denying citizenship to southern sympathizers.

Chris (C. C.) and Becky Hughes

Following their marriage in 1866 they raised seven children. Becky was a midwife like her mother. C. C. was a farmer, horse trader, and statesman. Their remains rest in the Dotson-Simpson Cemetery near Zoar Church having been relocated by the Federals from the Methodist Episcopal Church South Cemetery because of the construction of the Summersville Dam.

Madison and Mirriam Hughes

Madison operated their ferry until their son Virgil assumed control. Mirriam continued as a midwife and delivered 998 children. Their remains rest at the Gilgal Cemetery at Mt. Nebo, West Virginia.

Epilog

Anna Madalene Hughes

The granddaughter of Chris and Becky married Dennis "Dock" Foster in 1931 and raised a family of ten children. "Mad's" youngest wrote this book. Her faith impacted innumerable lives. Her remains rest in the Zoar Church Cemetery overlooking the site of the battle of Cross Lanes. Remnants of Captain Riley Ramsey's log fort used during the war are often found when individuals are interred at this location.

Hughes Ferry

In 1894 the Nicholas County Court established fixed rates for passage on the ferry across the Gauley River.

4 horses and wagon	$0.70
3 horses and wagon	$0.60
2 horses and wagon	$0.50
1 horse and wagon	$0.25
2 horses spring wagon or carriage	$0.50
1 horse buggy or road cart	$0.25
man and horse	$0.15
lead horses per head	$0.10
cattle per head	$0.05
sheep per head	$0.02
hogs per head	$0.02
footmen	$0.05

The demise of the ferry occurred when an iron truss bridge was built near the ferry across the Gauley in 1902. The final blow by the Federals occurred in 1965 when the ferry site was sacrificed to antiquity with the completion of the Summersville Dam and inundation of the site by the Summersville Lake.

Captain John James Halstead

He married Virginia (Ginny) Dotson a short time after the war and raised seven children. He was a successful merchant, real estate dealer, and statesman. His grandson, John Halstead, was the best friend of "Dock" Foster.

Epilog

Johnny Blizzard

He joined his father at the battle of Carnifex Ferry and served in the Confederacy the remainder of the war. Honorary Colonel John W. Blizzard spent part of this service as a courier for General "Stonewall" Jackson in the Valley Campaign. He passed into eternity as one of the oldest remaining survivors of the war on January 28, 1941, at the age of 98.

Nicholas (Nick) Hance Ramsey

Nick Ramsey was buried beneath a cliff near where he was killed in 1861, a short distance from Carnifex Ferry. A book was compiled and edited by Richard L. McGraw about his illustrious son and only child, William Hance Ramsey, entitled, *The Wit and Wisdom of William Hance Ramsey*. "Billy" Hance had a stone monument erected at his father's gravesite near Mt. Lookout, West Virginia.

Colonel George S. Patton

Chris' beloved leader of the 22nd Virginia Infantry was mortally wounded at the battle of Winchester in 1864. His grandson, General George S. Patton, Jr., was a famous commander in Europe during WWII.

Carnifex Ferry

The site of Camp Gauley and the Patterson farm was made into a beautiful 156-acre West Virginia State Park March 14, 1935. Carnifex Ferry Battlefield State Park contains remnants of roads used during the time of the battle. Numerous hiking trails lead to overlooks of Gauley River and to the ferry site. The park offers many amenities. A reenactment is held annually in the fall.

Patterson House

The house was used as a hospital after receiving fire from both armies during the battle of Carnifex Ferry. It was restored and is now used as a museum of Civil War artifacts at Carnifex Ferry Battlefield State Park.

Epilog

Combatants at the Battle of Carnifex Ferry

In his book, *September Blood,* author Terry Lowery states that combined in the Union and Confederate Armies there were 20 current or future Civil War generals on the field in the Battle of Carnifex Ferry.

General W. E. Jones

Following his notorious raid with General Imboden through western Virginia in 1863, he led his troops to fight in numerous battles in southwest Virginia. "Grumble" Jones was killed in the battle of Piedmont, Virginia on June 5, 1864. Sergeant Issac Prottman Hughes was killed at the same battle only a few hours earlier.

Brigadier General William Rosecrans

As a rising star in the Union military he suffered a humiliating defeat at Chickamauga and was assigned to the western theater of the war. He became a successful businessman and statesman, serving in the United States Congress.

Brigadier General John Floyd

The troubled political appointee never attained prominence as a military leader. Following his victory at the battle of Cross Lanes in 1861, he began a downward spiral until he died in 1863.

Major Rutherford Hayes

After Carnifex Ferry and Hughes Ferry, Major Hayes would later see action at numerous battles in the Shenandoah Valley including Cedar Creek, Virginia, in 1864 where Private Chris Hughes fought with the South. Following the war, Hayes served as a congressman and governor of the State of Ohio. He became the 19th President of the United States. His diary reveals that he never forgot the place he was first under direct enemy gunfire, Hughes Ferry.

Private William McKinley

Following his military exploits in the 23rd Ohio Volunteer Infantry in western Virginia, he would later serve as major with General Sheridan at the battle of Cedar Creek where he encouraged the retreating

Epilog

Union soldiers to turn and defeat the Rebels. He would later serve as governor of the State of Ohio and become the 25th President of the United States. He was assassinated in office.

Colonel John McCauseland

He was the commander of the 36th Virginia Infantry at Carnifex Ferry and many other battles during the war. Prott's leader, who attained the rank of brigadier general, was best known for his burning of Chambersburg, Pennsylvania, the only northern city destroyed during the war. It was destroyed by the order of General Jubal Early in retaliation for Union General David Hunter's destruction of property in the Shenandoah Valley of Virginia to give the North a taste of its own medicine. McCauseland was the next to the last living confederate general when he died in 1927.

Colonel Erastus Tyler

After the humiliating surprise attack and rout by the Confederates at the battle of Cross Lanes in 1861, he compiled a successful military career that included facing the 22nd Virginia Infantry again in several battles in the Shenandoah Valley. He became a Brigadier General less than a year after his defeat at Cross Lanes.

Woodrow Wilson

The young boy Chris met in Staunton, Virginia, in 1864 became the 28th President of the United States. In 1919 he named November 11, Armistice Day, in honor of the treaty that ended WW I the previous year.

General George Custer

He served with General Sheridan in the Shenandoah Valley Campaign. Following the war, the flamboyant general remained in the military and served in the western United States. He was killed and his troops decimated by warriors led by Crazy Horse and Sitting Bull at Little Bighorn, Montana.

Glossary of Civil War Terms

abatis - sharpened and arranged trees or tree limbs pointed at the enemy and used to impede their forward motion

accouterments - soldier's equipment

ague - recurrent chill or fit of shivering normally associated with malaria

arabica - variety name of a type of coffee grown in Arabia

bridle - that part of a horse's tack that fits into the animal's mouth (bit) and holds it in place over its head and is used by the rider to steer via the reins

blouse - shirt or jacket

britches - pants or trousers

brogans - shoes

bushwhacker - soldier or individual engaged in guerrilla warfare; criminal engaged in highway robbery

camp fever - infectious disease transmitted by fleas, lice, or mites, and characterized by severe headache, sustained high fever, depression, delirium, and the eruption of red rashes on the skin

canister fire - cannon projectile of iron balls contained in an iron casement which disintegrated on firing releasing the shot in a wide band

cap - small metal enclosed explosive charge used to ignite powder in a pistol or musket

cap pouch - leather or painted cloth pocket used to store caps; normally worn on belt and used to isolate caps from bullets which contained explosive gunpowder

caisson - two-wheeled, horse drawn vehicle used for storing supplies used for firing a cannon

corndodger - small cornmeal cake fried in grease in skillet

dugout - a canoe made of a hollowed-out log

double-quick step or pace - rapid deployment of infantry troops

eddy - water moving contrary to the direction of the main current, especially in a circular motion; (colloquialism - slower, non-turbulent flowing water)

flying bridge - river crossing technique utilizing a flatboat, towrope and retrieval line; used for rapid movement of troops

Glossary of Civil War Terms

foraging - exploring the countryside for food

hame - one of the two curved wooden or metal pieces of a draft animal's harness which rests upon the collar around the neck of the animal and attaches to the traces

haversack - a pouch with a strap carried over the shoulder used by many soldiers to carry food and other provisions

hawser - rope used for mooring a boat

hoecake - small cornmeal breadcake; originally cooked by slaves on metal garden hoe in open fire

hooligans - boisterous, unruly, uncouth, or rowdy men

girth strap - that part of a horse's harness that fits beneath the animal's stomach and holds the harness in place

gnat smoke - a small campfire

grape or grapeshot - cannon shell which contained small round projectiles resembling large grapes; very deadly in battle

gum or rubber blanket - blankets treated with India rubber or paint; intended purpose was waterproofing

gunnysack- a large sack made from loosely woven, coarse material such as burlap; often with a strap for carrying over the shoulder

hardtack - hard biscuit or bread made with only flour and water; usually refers to a 3 inch square cracker similar to a saltine cracker, but very hard

Jesse Scouts - Union soldiers dressed in Confederate uniforms performing scouting duties in advance of regular units

kepi - a short billed cap worn by soldiers

Lincolnites - soldiers in the Union Army

limber - two-wheeled, horse-drawn vehicle used to tow a field gun or a caisson

long johns - long underwear

minie ball - convenient for loading, expanding bullet invented by Claude Minie and used extensively during Civil War; called ball, but actually bullet shaped and very deadly

pone - baked cornmeal cake used as bread; cooked in oven or dutchoven

rail pen breastworks - temporary fortification constructed of split rails resembling a "pen"

ramps - wild pungent onions similar to green onions that grow in the Appalachian mountains; often eaten in the spring as a type of tonic

rodding - process of using the rod part of a rifle to seat the bullet in the rifle barrel

runs - diarrhea

saltpeter - potassium nitrate; used in the manufacturing of gunpowder; in pioneer days commonly manufactured from bat and rodent urine contaminated soil collected from caves they inhabited

sesech - soldier or individual supporting the secession of the southern states from the Union

shrapnel - metal fragments or shot from an exploding cannon shell

singletree - part of a harness that consists of a wooden bar attached to the traces and used to concentrate the pull of the animal to a wagon or carriage

slouch hat - soft brimmed felt hat

sop - bread or cracker soaked in liquid; sometimes refers to gravy

spider - an iron skillet with short legs used over coals from an open fire

sutlers - merchants that traveled with the army

teamster - one who drives a wagon

traces - that part of a harness that runs alongside the horse or mule and attaches the harness to the singletree

trots - diarrhea

wagoner - one who drives a wagon

Bibliography

Brown, W. G., *History of Nicholas County West Virginia*, Richmond, VA, Dietz Press, 1954.

Cohen, Stan, *A Pictorial Guide to West Virginia Civil War Sites and Related Information: A Pictorial History*. Charleston, WV, Pictorial Histories, 1989.

Cohen, Stan, *The Civil War In West Virginia: A Pictorial History*, Charleston, WV, Pictorial Histories, 1976.

Fletcher, Virginia, *"Time and Tide"; A Francisco Family History*. Fort Lauderdale, FL, Virginia B. Fletcher, 1989.

Hayes, Rutherford, *The Diary and Letters of Rutherford B. Hayes, Nineteenth President of the United States*, edited by Charles Richard Williams, Columbus, OH, Ohio State Archeological and Historical Society, 1922. (Access Internet: http://www.ohiohistory.org/onlinedoc/hayes/, Rutherford B. Hayes Presidential Center)

Leisch, Juanita, *An Introduction to Civil War Civillians*. Gettysburg, PA, Thomas Publications, 1994.

Long, E. B., et. al., *The Civil War Day By Day; An Almanac 1861-1865*. New York, NY, Da Capo Press, Inc., 1971

Lowery, Terry, *September Blood The Battle of Carnifex Ferry* . Charleston, WV, Pictorial Histories, 1985.

Lowery, Terry, *Last Sleep; The Battle of Droop Mountain November 6, 1863*. Charleston, WV, Pictorial Histories, 1996.

Lowery, Terry, *22nd Virginia Infantry, The Virginia Regimental Histories Series*. Lynchburg, VA, H. E. Howard, Inc., 1996.

Lyle, Rev. W.W., *Lights and Shadows of Army Life or, Pen Pictures from the Battlefield, the Camp, and the Hospital.* Cincinnati, OH, R. W. Carroll & Co., 1865. (Access Internet: http://www.umdl.umich.edu/moa/ Making of America Project, University of Michigan)

McKinney, Tim, *The Civil War in Fayette County West Virginia* . Charleston, WV, Pictorial Histories, 1988.

McKinney, Tim, *West Virginia Civil War Almanac, Volume One*. Charleston, WV, Pictorial Histories, 1988.

Bibliography

Perkins, Harry, et. al., *Nicholas County West Virginia History 1985.* Summersville, WV, Nicholas County Historical and Genealogical Society, Inc.,1985.

Phillips, David, *A Soldier's Story; the Double Life of a Confederate Spy.* New York, NY, Metro Books, 1997.

Phillips, David, *Maps of the Civil War; The Roads They Took.* New York, NY, Metro Books, 1998.

Phillips, David, *War Diaries; The 1861 Kanawha ValleyCampaigns.* Leesburg, Va, Gauley Mount Press, 1990.

Quarles, Garland, et. al., *Diaries, Letters, and Recollections of the War Between the States; Volume III*, Winchester, VA, Winchester-Frederick County Historical Society, 1955.

Ramsey, William, *Billy Hance: The Wit and Wisdom of William Hance Ramsey.* (Complied and edited by Richard L. McGraw)

Ramsey, J. C., *Ramsey Family History*, J. C, Ramsey, 1933.

Scott, J. L., *36th Virginia Infantry, The Virginia Regimental Histories Series.* Lynchburg, VA, H. E. Howard, Inc., 1987.

Taylor, James, *The James E. Taylor Sketchbook.* Dayton, OH, Morningside House, Inc., 1989.

Thomas, Dean, *Round Ball to Rimfire; A History of Civil War Small Arms Ammunition; Part One.* Gettysburg, PA, Thomas Publications, 1997.

Time-Life Books, *Illustrated History of the Civil War Series; Arms and Equipment of the Confederacy.* Alexandria, VA, Time-Life Books, 1998.

Time-Life Books, *Illustrated History of the Civil War Series; Arms and Equipment of the Union.* Alexandria, VA, Time-Life Books, 1998.

Time-Life Books, *Illustrated History of the Civil War Series; Illustrated Atlas of the Civil War.* Alexandria, VA, Time-Life Books, 1998.

Wintz, William, *Civil War Memories of Two Rebel Sisters.* Charleston, WV, Pictorial Histories, 1990.

United States War Department, *The Official Military Atlas of the Civil War.* Avenel, NJ, Gramercy Books, 1983.

United States War Department, *The War of the Rebellion: A Compilation of the Official Records of the Union and*

Bibliography

Confederate Armies . Washington, D.C., Government Printing Office, 1880-1901 (CD-ROM version 1.5, Guild Press of Indiana, Inc. Carmel, IN).

Walker, Gary, *The War in Southwest Virginia 1861-65*. Roanoke, VA, A & W Enterprise, 1985.

Walker, Gary, *Hunter's Fiery Raid through Virginia Valleys*. Roanoke, VA, A & W Enterprise, 1989.

Watts, Dabney, et. al., *Civil War Battles in Winchester and Frederick County, Virginia 1861-65*. Winchester, VA, Winchester-Frederick County Historical Society, 1961.

Bell, Carol, "Out of the Past", *The Nicholas Chronicle*, numerous dates.

Berry, Joan, "Carnifix Ferry: Its Place in History", *News Leader*, numerous dates 1995.

Donnelly, Clarence, "The Battle of Carnifex Ferry"(special publication), *The State Sentinel*, April 1950.

Gray, Clyde, "Remembering the Past 100 Years and Then Some". *The West Virginia Hillbilly*, August 25, 1984.

Lowery, Terry, "Generally Speaking . . . Echoes from the Civil War", *The West Virginia Hillbilly*, numerous dates from April 14, 1884 to September 8, 1984.

Taylor, J. A., "Col. Blizzard Died Tuesday", *The State Sentinel*, January 29, 1941.

"Battle of Carnifex Ferry. Our Special Army Correspondence." *The New York Herald*, 22 September 1861 (Access Internet: http:/ /204.170.102.11/accessible/text/civilwar/htm, Oberlin College: Oberlin, OH.)

Electronic Card Indexes, Military Records Section, Library of Virginia (Access Internet , http:/ /198.17.62.51/collections/ .)

Archives Manuscript Collections, numerous diaries, Virginia Military Institute (Access Internet: http:/ /www.vmi.edu/~archives/arcindex.html.)

Special Collections Department, numerous diaries, Virginia Tech Libraries, (Access Internet: http:/ /scholar2.lib.vt.edu/spec/civwar/guidecw.htm .)

On the Banks of Gauley
By Rock Foster

A Frontier Novel based on the lives of real pioneers.

On the Appalachian frontier land was all many of the pioneers possessed. When land barons attempted to seize control there was war on the banks of Gauley. Contending with the constant threat of Indian attack from the frontier and legal wrangling for land ownership from the elite of the eastern cities, placed these children of the wilderness in the western mountains of Virginia in a difficult situation. With their lives on the line and their families' fate at risk these men and women struggled for survival. Common affairs of life became ordeals. One family's story survives to tell their tale of journeying into the endless mountains, Indian conflict and captivity, and toiling for existence in the new land. A must read for everyone!

About the Author

Rock Foster

Named after the numerous rocks that lie in the Gauley River canyon, Rocky Dock Foster hails from Summersville, West Virginia. He was born on Salmons Creek the last of ten children. He was transiently called "Ten" for a week while his parents Dennis "Dock" Herndon Foster and Anna Madalene Hughes Foster decided on a name. His father was a great sports enthusiast, so his name was eventually derived from the "rocks" his father fished from on the Gauley River and his WWII Navy nickname, "Dock".

He is a 1970 graduate of Nicholas County High School and a 1974 graduate of West Virginia University Institute of Technology. Rock is a professional civil and environmental consulting engineer and his wife, the former Joan Elaine Miller, is an educator. They reside in the Laurel Mountains of Pennsylvania, near Champion.

They would love to hear from you.

Rock and Elaine Foster
4401 Route 31
Somerset, PA 15501
E-mail: rock@lhtot.com

Internet
When Gauley Ran Blood homepage:
http://www.lhtot.com/~rock/